Praise for
THE KIDNAPPING CLUB

"A convincing demonstration of the close links between capitalism and the unconscionable trade in human beings." —*Kirkus*

"Lively prose and vivid scenes of New York–street life complement the meticulous research. The result is a revealing look at a little-known chapter in the history of racial injustice."
—*Publishers Weekly*

"This history of eighteen-thirties New York probes the city's entanglement with the slave economy. . . . Jonathan Daniel Wells details how the funding of the cotton trade fueled a nascent Wall Street and admiringly portrays David Ruggles, a Black abolitionist who gave the Kidnapping Club its name and organized to resist it."
—*New Yorker*

"Skillful portrayal of the culture of mid-nineteenth-century America. . . . Highly recommended for those who like history and readers interested in social justice." —*Library Journal*

"Wells conjures the pungent atmosphere of Manhattan in the early nineteenth century. . . . Wells writes, one senses, not to memorialize the missing, but *to reopen their cases*—to make a larger argument about recompense." —*New York Times*

"Wells makes a significant contribution to the literature of American slavery with a powerful book." —*Wall Street Journal*

"Readers familiar with *Twelve Years a Slave*, the film based on Solomon Northup's 1853 slave narrative, might recognize the horror of free Black people forced into Southern enslavement in Wells's harrowing account of men and women abducted by police officers as they walked the crowded streets of Lower Manhattan. . . . Yet one of Wells's greatest contributions is his reminder that there were many Solomon Northups." —*New York Times Book Review*

"*The Kidnapping Club* offers readers a painful account of how many Black people—both free and self-emancipated—were captured, jailed, judged, and shipped south to live and suffer as slaves to support the profitable cotton economy. . . . This thoroughly researched account reminds readers that New York was a pro-slavery city even as the nation was engulfed in the Civil War." —*New York Journal of Books*

"[A] beautifully researched study . . . detailing how white authorities actively and repeatedly subverted Black freedom." —*Journal of Southern History*

"With New York City as its backdrop, *The Kidnapping Club* offers an important and compelling narrative that explores the long struggle for Black freedom and equality. Wells offers a rich and timely account that uncovers a history of racial violence and terror in nineteenth-century Gotham. To no surprise, law enforcement, politicians, and bankers thwarted Black freedom time and time again. But the power and fortitude of Black New Yorkers pressed white citizens to remember and uphold the ideals of a new nation. *The Kidnapping Club* is a must-read for those who want to understand current debates about the intersection of Black lives and structural oppression." —Erica Armstrong Dunbar, author of *Never Caught*

"Wells's *The Kidnapping Club* is a necessary story of black agency and resistance. Bringing to life the competing strains of humanism and oppression that echo our present-day struggles, Wells paints a portrait of New York that reveals the best of American principles in the bodies of black resistors while showing us the economic complexity and complicity of America's greatest city. It is a brilliant history perfectly suited for our times."

—Michael Eric Dyson, author of the New York Times–bestselling *Tears We Cannot Stop* and *What Truth Sounds Like*

"*The Kidnapping Club* maps and specifies both the top-side financial connections between the capitalists of the North and the slavers of the South and the underbelly of police corruption, violence, and kidnapping that knit together. And it manages to combine acute historical analysis with literary drama and a persistent, gentle humanity. You should read it."

—Walter Johnson, author of *The Broken Heart of America*

"Nineteenth-century New York City was a battleground for African Americans, who most whites assumed to be undeserving of freedom. Wells's *The Kidnapping Club* brings to life the struggles in the courts and on the streets between those who sought to send blacks to slavery in the south; those who benefited from southern slavery; and the small group of interracial activists who fought against slavery and would eventually prevail in claiming freedom for all regardless of race. From politicians and jurists to newspaper owners, and from bankers to ministers to common laborers, everyone had a stake in the central question of the moment: the legality and morality of slavery and the status of people of African descent in the nation. Wells's gripping narrative brings to life the real-life impact of these questions on every New Yorker, and how the struggle over racial equality affected every sector of life in antebellum New York City."

—Leslie M. Harris, author of *In the Shadow of Slavery*

THE
KIDNAPPING
CLUB

THE KIDNAPPING CLUB

Wall Street, Slavery, and Resistance on the Eve of the Civil War

JONATHAN DANIEL
WELLS

BOLD TYPE BOOKS
New York

Bold Type Books
30 Irving Place, 10th Floor, New York, NY 10003
www.boldtypebooks.org
@BoldTypeBooks

Printed in the United States of America

First Trade Paperback Edition: February 2023

Originally published in hardcover and ebook in October 2020 by Bold Type Books, an imprint of Perseus Books, LLC, a subsidiary of Hachette Book Group, Inc. Bold Type Books is a co-publishing venture of the Type Media Center and Perseus Books.

The Hachette Speakers Bureau provides a wide range of authors for speaking events. To find out more, go to www.hachettespeakersbureau.com or email HachetteSpeakers@hbgusa.com.

Bold Type Books copies may be purchased in bulk for business, educational, or promotional use. For information, please contact your local bookseller or Hachette Book Group Special Markets Department at special.markets@hbgusa.com.

The publisher is not responsible for websites (or their content) that are not owned by the publisher.

Print book interior design by Jeff Williams.

The Library of Congress has cataloged the hardcover edition as follows:
Names: Wells, Jonathan Daniel, 1969– author.
Title: The Kidnapping Club : Wall Street, Slavery, and Resistance on the Eve of the Civil War / Jonathan Daniel Wells.
Other titles: Wall Street, slavery, and resistance on the eve of the Civil War
Description: First edition. | New York : Bold Type Books, 2020. | Includes bibliographical references and index.
Identifiers: LCCN 2020021980 | ISBN 9781568587523 (hardcover) | ISBN 9781645037118 (e-book)
Subjects: LCSH: Free African Americans—New York (State)—New York—History—19th century. | New York Kidnapping Club (Gang)—History. | Free African Americans—Legal status, laws, etc.—History—19th century. | Kidnapping victims—New York–New York (State)—History—19th century. | Kidnapping victims—United States—History—19th century. | Fugitive slaves—United States—History—19th century. | Fugitive slaves—New York (State)—New York—History—19th century. | Slavery—United States—History—19th century. | Slave trade—United States—History—19th century. | Ruggles, David, 1810–1849.
Classification: LCC F128.44 .W377 2020 | DDC 974.7/100496073009034—dc23
LC record available at https://lccn.loc.gov/2020021980

ISBNs: 9781568587523 (hardcover), 9781645037118 (ebook), 9781645030331 (paperback)

LSC-C

Printing 1, 2022

I told him of the Fugitive Slave Law, and asked him if he did not know that New York was a city of kidnappers.

—HARRIET JACOBS,
Incidents in the Life of a Slave Girl

CONTENTS

Summer 1832

NORFOLK, VIRGINIA

◈═◉═◈

T HE STREETS OF NORFOLK WERE EERILY QUIET, MAKING IT ALL THE
more important that the group of men and women lurking
behind buildings in the city's small business sector remain
absolutely silent. A heavy blanket of humid air and the smell of salt
water hung over the furtive group of enslaved people. The slightest cough or mere whisper could give them all away. If caught,
there would be hell to pay.

Though they had been toiling in hot, steamy cotton fields since
the sun rose, they had only pretended to sleep when the overseer
rang the bell for curfew. Sure, to a person they were physically
tired, but the danger and excitement gave them renewed energy
and they crouched low, creeping through the alleyways of the
port town.

Their likes and dislikes, their loves and hatreds, their personali-
ties and dreams, have been lost to history. But at least we know their
names: Ben, Caleb, Southey, Ann, George Carter, Joe, John Carter,
Southard, James, Charles, Jack Cooley, Severn, Michael, Slack, Isaac,
Ben, and Henry. One night in August they collectively decided to
risk their lives in hopes of escaping slavery and somehow—against

tremendous odds and in defiance of an entire country whose laws demanded they remain enslaved—reach freedom.

They likely didn't know exactly what time it was as they approached the water, but it was probably long after midnight. The midsummer moon may have allowed them to see the outline of the now quiet row of shops—the cabinetmakers, printers, blacksmiths, butchers, shoemakers, clothing stores, and other small wooden storefronts that lined the streets. Every sound, no matter how soft, would have made them halt in mid-step. They heard every bump and scrape, every tick and knock, their ears attuned to any sign of danger. But the prospect of escaping slavery, or making it somehow to a place where they could live without the threat of the whip, where they could work for themselves and start their own families free from control or division by sale in some dehumanizing slave market, generated all of the courage needed.

A few days before, one of them had passed by the bustling wooden docks along Norfolk's coast, near the US Navy port. Ben had seen a thirty-foot whaleboat tied up along shore, a small vessel barely large enough to fit several of his fellow conspirators, along with the scraps of food and small casks of water to keep them alive on the journey. In fact, Ben had escaped with a similar group years before, but had been arrested as a runaway slave and returned to bondage in Virginia. Thanks to a section of the United States Constitution known as the Fugitive Slave Clause, free states in the North were legally required to return escaped slaves like Ben. This time Ben was determined to make his freedom permanent.

The plan was to sail north to New York, carefully skirting the coast within sight of land but out of the view of passing ships and slowly snaking their way in between islands and peninsulas. Just a few months before Ben and his collaborators fled Norfolk, Virginia had passed a law expelling free Black residents from the state. Some of those free African Americans fled Virginia's latest round of repression and ventured to New York, where they hoped a new community might welcome them. Such hopes were not to be realized. New York's city government responded to the influx of these refugees by devising new ways to keep Black Virginians out of New York.[1]

But Ben and his compatriots probably thought that discrimination in New York had to be better than bondage in Norfolk, and so cooperatively they had risked their lives to confiscate the whaleboat and set their sights on Gotham. They executed the plan to perfection, quietly landing on a small island off the southern tip of New Jersey within a few days. The self-emancipated group then cautiously made its way to New York City, no doubt with a combination of fear and excitement.

They likely first noticed the city's loftiest structure, the two-hundred-foot-tall steeple of Trinity Church that dominated the labyrinthine alleyways of Lower Manhattan. No skyscrapers yet lorded over the southern shores of the island, and the Statue of Liberty was still decades away from beckoning immigrants into the harbor, so visitors would have first gazed at the soaring stone spires of Trinity as they coasted into the busy harbor. The largest church in the city, Trinity was known as one of the places where early leaders had worshipped when the federal government sat in New York.[2]

Coming from the Virginia Tidewater, the fugitives would have never seen anything like Trinity or the hurried and crowded streets of New York City. Although the massive wave of Irish immigrants would not come for a few more years, even by the time this tiny band slipped onto shore the city had emerged as an important port to rival Boston, Philadelphia, and Baltimore. The city already boasted major financial institutions, such as the Bank of New York, as well as major corporations, such as the Mutual Insurance Company and the New York and Erie Railroad headquarters, all grouped together within a few doors of each other on Wall Street. About 10 percent of the population was African American in the early 1800s, some sixteen thousand people who had already created rich and vibrant communities in Manhattan and Brooklyn. The city had several churches for people of African descent, a few Catholic churches (which would balloon in number during the next decade as a wave of Irish immigrants arrived), and about a dozen Baptist churches. In the same summer as the Virginia runaways disembarked from the whaleboat, the city was rocked by a deadly cholera outbreak. For good and for ill, New York by the early 1830s was on its way to becoming a modern and major metropolis.

Still, in countless ways, as befuddling as the city would have seemed to Ben and Ann and the other fugitives, New York in the early 1800s was by our modern standards a mere town. Just after the Revolution, only twelve thousand people called the city home. That number would soon grow exponentially, but even by 1830 almost all of the structures in Lower Manhattan, including the wharves that lined the southern tip of the city, had been hastily built of wood and prone to fire and decay. Little central planning went into the rapid growth of the town or its deepwater port, and so alongside the chaotic and haphazard alleys that carved through Manhattan sat residential neighborhoods intermingled with artisan workshops and warehouses, taverns and teahouses, horse barns and hotels. Three ferries but no bridges provided links to the growing town of Brooklyn, and the lack of clean water was a constant source of consternation among city dwellers. Most streets were muddy and unpaved, gaslights were only beginning to be installed on major thoroughfares like Broadway, and omnibuses, horse-drawn carts that crisscrossed the island, remained the main form of public transportation. Central Park, which wiped out the lively Black community known as Seneca Village, was two decades in the future. New York was still heavily and noticeably marked by a Dutch past that had dominated the first two centuries of European settlement in Manhattan. There were seventeen Van Winkles in the city directory in 1832, the same year that Ben and the others slipped out of Norfolk.[3]

Over the next thirty years, until the Civil War broke out in 1861, New York underwent a dramatic transformation, and this book tells the story of how New York became the New York we know today: a major global capital with a diverse and cosmopolitan culture. Between the 1830s and the 1860s, New York built skyscrapers, paved and lit its streets, began connecting via the telegraph to the farthest reaches of the planet, and became a financial titan equaling London. Railroads connected Lower Manhattan to Harlem, while tracks also carried travelers from the wharves near the East River north beyond Central Park. After a horrific fire destroyed much of the city in 1835, the municipality embarked on a physical transformation: new marble and stone edifices were erected, including the now famous imposing columns of the New York Exchange; Croton Reservoir finally brought fresh water to homes and businesses; and the wealthy began moving to the more bucolic areas north of Houston Street. Railcars replaced horse-drawn omnibuses, and city boosters turned newfound wealth into magnificent opera houses, theaters, and museums. Setbacks like major financial panics in the first half of the nineteenth century only temporarily halted the long-term trajectory: New York was becoming an economic and political powerhouse. That often-stirring account of Gotham's rise to greatness, however, hides a much bleaker history about the human costs expended on the path to wealth and power.[4]

The costs were high indeed. Much of the city's growth had been built on the backs of southern slaves who picked cotton for hundreds of thousands of cotton bales every year, a crop that was financed by Wall Street banks and exported to New England and British textile mills via New York brokers, businesses, and financiers. Slave masters depended on New York insurance companies to protect their investments in bondage and embraced the credit extended by the city's banks. As the dependence of Wall Street on slave-grown cotton became ever more apparent through the early 1800s, New York's rise to prominence and prosperity harbored a somber and sinister side, one that rendered the city a dangerous place for vulnerable people, especially African Americans. It sometimes seemed that the entire city, knowing that its richness and supremacy depended on southern slavery, was more interested in reassuring slaveholders than in protecting the basic human rights of its Black residents.

The forces arrayed against the city's Black community were seemingly insurmountable. African Americans were up against a pervasive racism that suffused the city's Democratic Party and its political machine based in Tammany Hall, a police force that violated Black civil rights at every turn, Wall Street financiers who cared far more about increasing trade with the cotton South than they did about the enslaved families picking the crop, and a legal system that at best proved indifferent to the claims of Black folks. New York was a perilous place for Black people despite a small cadre of dedicated activists (like the indomitable David Ruggles) working tirelessly for the abolition of slavery. And perhaps worst of all, the federal government made it easy to ignore the calls for protecting Black civil rights. After all, the recapture and arrest of runaways was enshrined in the nation's founding document, explicitly requiring northern communities to return those with the audacity to flee slavery. Conservative Democrats running the Tammany Hall political machine were more than happy to comply with the law.[5]

The explosion of Irish immigrants escaping the potato famine greatly empowered the Democratic Party. The Irish, too, suffered discrimination and poverty, and politicians played upon their misery. Leading Democrats told the Irish working class that Black people were to blame for their economic and social ills, as African Americans hustled for jobs in the city's businesses and along the docks that welcomed ships from all over the world. In speeches, newspaper editorials, and before rallying audiences, demagogic politicians preyed on Irish workers, claiming that their dreary living conditions in large tenement buildings, where crowded families yearned for natural light and fresh air, or the low wages they brought home, which barely allowed those families to buy enough to eat, had one easily understood cause. Democrats told the white painters, bootmakers, blacksmiths, cartmen, and stevedores that Blacks were to blame for their low wages and unlivable tenement apartments.[6]

At the other end of the economic ladder, support for Democratic policies could also be found in the business community around the Stock Exchange. At the center of New York's beating heart sat the banks, insurance companies, and stores of Lower Manhattan, the making of what would soon fall under the umbrella term "Wall Street." The exchange was still in its infancy in the early 1800s, and Wall Street was known as an open-air market in which virtually anything could be traded, rather than the behemoth that it is today, but the watchword "Wall Street" is convenient shorthand for the nascent business world of antebellum Manhattan. Even before the Civil War, the phrase "Wall Street" stood for the dramatic expansion of banking and credit systems, the vast and lucrative cotton trade with the South, the humming wharves along the southern shores of Manhattan, and the thousands of merchants whose shops sold everything from apples and silk garments to furniture and sewing machines.

New York was the most potent proslavery and pro-South city north of the Mason-Dixon Line, due in large part to the lucrative trade between Manhattan banks and insurance companies and the slaveholders of the cotton South. The city council, the board of aldermen, the mayor, the police department, the legal system, and other city agencies seldom acted without consulting the business community. Whether Wall Street businessmen joined the Democratic Party or the opposition Whig Party, they agreed almost to a man about one thing: the need to protect the cotton trade with slaveholders that had made them incredibly wealthy. It was a system that rendered both sections of the nation heavily dependent on the continuance of slavery and the constitutional government that had made the trade possible. Merely mentioning the abolition of slavery quickly earned the scorn of those on Wall Street and in the Democratic Party who knew exactly where their wealth came from.

In defending the cotton trade with the South, Wall Street and Democratic politicians could count on support in the city's growing newspapers, where journalists and editors jockeyed for public attention by publishing sensational stories of murders, crime, and prostitution alongside current prices for dry goods; a wide range of advertisements; editorials on political and economic matters;

local, national, and foreign news; and even poems and serialized novels. By the 1850s, just before the Civil War broke out, New York boasted dozens of daily and weekly newspapers, aided by the emergence of the penny press.

While Wall Street, the New York Police Department, the conservative press, and the Democratic Party aligned to defend slavery and the constitutional compact with slaveholders, the legal system often proved just as hostile to African Americans in New York. The federal courts made it very difficult to prosecute slave traders who used the Port of New York to build ships designed for the illegal transatlantic slave trade. City police officers collected reward money for returning runaways, essentially serving as a patrol force for southern masters.

While the tribulations of Solomon Northup (made famous by the book and film *Twelve Years a Slave*) are now more widely known, the true extent of the kidnapping of African Americans from free cities like New York is only now coming to light. This book tells the street-level stories of an epic battle over the soul of New York, over whether an increasingly powerful and wealthy metropolis would choose basic human rights over money and trade, generating daily struggles that rocked Gotham in the decades before civil war tore the nation apart.[7]

The allied forces of wealth and power did not go unchallenged. Relentless African American activists like Thomas Van Rensselaer, Charles B. Ray, Samuel Cornish, Philip Bell, and scores of others risked their lives to protect human rights. They formed antislavery organizations, held conventions and rallies, delivered speeches and sermons, and marched in the streets to defend their communities. Radical David Ruggles, whose story will unfold in the following pages, fought back vigorously, leading a large Black public determined to thwart the kidnapping and fugitive recapture of its fellow citizens. Ruggles burned with passion and anger over the mistreatment of his people, those who toiled under southern bondage as well as those struggling against the rigid discrimination and pervasive racism that he experienced firsthand in the North. Several dedicated white abolitionists joined Black New Yorkers to fight against kidnapping, but the movement to eradicate American slavery was small. Ruggles and the tiny abolitionist community in New York were up against a true Goliath, a potent, systemic enemy that believed Black bodies were cheap and expendable. Ruggles labeled this enemy the New York Kidnapping Club.[8]

It was not an organized party or ring, or even a group of men who socialized together, but nonetheless what Ruggles publicly declared the New York Kidnapping Club was a powerful and far-reaching collection of police officers, political authorities, judges, lawyers, and slave traders who terrorized the city's Black residents throughout the early nineteenth century. They cared little whether an individual they arrested was in fact an escaped slave or born free. Alongside them stood the city's business community, cheering on every attempt to return fugitives so that peace with the slave South remained intact. The New York Kidnapping Club was a microcosm of the much broader and more widespread disregard for Black lives that pervaded the city.

At the apex of the New York Kidnapping Club stood two police officers named Tobias Boudinot and Daniel D. Nash. When Virginia's governor realized not only that Ben and his compatriots had absconded from Norfolk, but also had stolen a vessel in the process, he angrily fired off a letter to his counterpart in New York. Governor William Marcy granted Boudinot a wholesale right to arrest anyone he could even remotely accuse of being a runaway. Boudinot and his fellow officers, including the notorious Nash, used the Constitution's Fugitive Slave Clause as a subterfuge to terrorize Black New Yorkers. The New York Kidnapping Club was born. Boudinot wielded the document he received from Marcy for the next two decades, using the paper so often that he eventually had to have it copied and signed at least once more.

Boudinot and Nash were soon joined by leading powerful white men like City Recorder Richard Riker, judges on the federal bench like Samuel R. Betts, and lawyers like Fontaine H. Pettis and the legal firm of Beebe, Dean, and Donohue. All of them knew each other, despite their different stations in life, and Ruggles battled with them so much and so often over Black civil rights that his health began to fail. Ruggles especially tangled closely with Boudinot, Nash, and Riker. In fact, further demonstrating the small-town feel of Lower Manhattan in the early 1830s, Ruggles lived on Lispenard Street, just a few doors down from the home of Chief of Police Jacob Hays. Mere blocks away, on the other side of City Hall, lived Recorder Riker. Boudinot lived a few streets to the west on Warren. Such close proximity meant that the battle for the future of New York would play out in the neighborhoods, parks, and city buildings of Lower Manhattan, where Trinity Church faced down Wall Street businesses and where City Hall stood at the literal and symbolic center of Gotham.[9]

THE SEVENTEEN MEN AND women who risked their lives to flee slavery in the summer of 1832 could not have known the repercussions of their desperate voyage. In a modern, well-worn tale, the flapping wings of a butterfly can be magnified through cause and effect, ultimately affecting global weather patterns. The self-emancipation of Ben and the others would have similarly far-reaching effects, leading quickly to the massive search for their whereabouts, a search that not only helped to create the New York Kidnapping Club, but also rendered freedom highly precarious for Black residents all the way to the Civil War. The forces unleashed by the simple desire to live free, to be able to work and love and raise children away from the violent scourge of southern slavery, would shake the foundations of liberty in New York City and its environs.

The following chapters, then, tell a sordid tale, difficult to read at times, especially when children are involved, but ultimately it is a story about how a booming and prosperous metropolis proved tragically indifferent, complicit even, in the abuse of its Black residents, who toiled every day to resist and fight back. In that important sense the chronicling of antebellum New York is the also the narrative of the young republic itself.

Chapter One

The Battle Engaged

AFRICAN AMERICAN ACTIVIST DAVID RUGGLES FOUND HIMSELF riding the nighttime rails through the hills of western Pennsylvania in 1833 on his way back to Manhattan, the clacking of the metal wheels on the tracks creating a droning sound that would have put him to sleep if not for the adrenaline running through his veins. Returning from an invigorating meeting in Pittsburgh, a gathering of Black and white protesters who had promised to work harder for the end of slavery and segregation in America, Ruggles was filled with optimism. Slavery had plagued the nation since its founding, thought Ruggles, and though northern states had mostly outlawed bondage by the early 1800s, slavery seemed stronger than ever in the southern states. In fact, by writing a Constitution that protected slavery, the Founding Fathers had left future generations a colossal problem.

Thomas Jefferson, Alexander Hamilton, James Madison, and the others who helped found the United States created a Constitution filled with compromises over freedom and slavery. Ruggles and his fellow activists wanted to take the founding idea of liberty and extend it to Black folks. Now, nearly fifty years later, another generation of politicians was dealing with a nation bitterly divided.

White southerners defended the institution with a fierce determination that rendered mere mention of abolition grounds for physical attack. Though the Civil War lay in the distant future, America was riven by the tension between freedom and bondage. That same strain threatened to rip New York City apart, just as it was beginning to emerge as a world commercial and financial capital.

The transplanted New Yorker Ruggles lived at the heart of that tension. In his mind, even worse than white southerners who supported slavery was the complicity of northern whites in maintaining bondage. Most white citizens in the free states like New York, Pennsylvania, and Massachusetts thought slavery had little to do with them. It was a southern problem only, for the southern people to deal with, and without interference from others. The only time northerners had a role to play in slavery was not to end the institution but to make sure that any runaways who fled southern farms and plantations and made their way north were returned to their masters. As northerners knew, the Union would have been stillborn were it not for compromises between the North and South over servitude. Ruggles thought these northern compromisers and conciliators were abettors of southern slavery.[1]

Riding the train that evening, though, Ruggles had reason to believe that the abolition of slavery seemed to be moving ahead, just as train travel had quickened the pace of movement for a hurrying young nation, speeding journeys between cities like New York and Pittsburgh from punishing days over bumpy wagon roads to mere hours. As the train gained momentum on its tracks, Ruggles took his seat, hopeful that the momentum to end slavery was finally gaining steam among the hectic citizens of the Northeast.

Ruggles settled into a train car so dark (for it was now well past midnight) that he could not even see who was sitting across from him. Given the voices nearby, he surmised that his fellow passengers were two women and three other men, and not long into the journey the conversation turned to slavery and abolition. It is not clear who broached the subject, but the irascible Ruggles was certainly not shy to prod acquaintances about their views on holding

The indomitable David Ruggles.
(Negro Almanac Collection, Amistad Research Library, New Orleans, LA)

people in captivity, and given the fact that he was freshly removed from a meeting that had just established a new antislavery society, Ruggles likely worked the topic into the pleasantries as the unlit train left Pittsburgh.[2]

In particular, Ruggles tried to discern what his fellow voyagers thought about the great question rocking the Black community in cities like New York: Should those opposed to bondage work for its immediate and unconditional end, or should they follow the course of moderates and conservatives and recommend colonization? This latter position entailed sending Black Americans back to Africa, an increasingly unpopular position among more radical abolitionists like Ruggles, who not only demanded an immediate end to American slavery, but also insisted that the nation's future lay in a biracial democracy. In fact, Ruggles and other immediatists derided the American Colonization Society, a group that many middle-of-the-road politicians like Abraham Lincoln and his idol Henry Clay supported, as "the Negro Shipping Company," little better than the transatlantic slave trade itself.

In the pitch-black train car, Ruggles clearly wanted to gauge what his fellow travelers thought about colonization. Most of them articulated half-formed thoughts or ventured lukewarm support for the movement. One man on the train, though, loudly and forcefully championed colonization and denounced abolitionists as "Madmen! fanatics! disorganizers! amalgamaters!" Ruggles quickly took umbrage at the man's use of the term "amalgamaters," which was the nineteenth century's byword for interracial sex and marriage.

To incite the man further, Ruggles claimed that he would be proud to take a Black woman to the altar, and in fact that he "would marry a colored lady in preference to a white one." The fellow traveler almost jumped out of his seat, declaring his disgust: "You would! Would you marry a black?" The stunned colonizationist turned to the two women and asked if they would marry a Black man. "I am not prepared to give myself up to any man," one lady replied. Increasingly frustrated, the man admitted that he never really believed that someone would openly advocate race mixing, until that night. Ruggles stepped up his jabbing: "After all, it is a mere matter of taste whether one married a *white* or a *black*." In reply, the man sputtered his disgust and they settled into a quiet truce as the train rolled on, making its way east through the wee hours.

Soon the early morning began to shed its light on the train, and Ruggles again delighted in nettling the colonizationist. "As soon as I thought my complexion would appear to an advantage," Ruggles later recalled, "I raised the curtain." Realizing for the first time that he had been verbally sparring with a man of color, the colonizationist screamed aloud, "Good heavens! a negro! why you are a black man!!" The other four passengers could barely contain their laughter, but the man huffed his dismay that his interlocutor was Black and retreated into silent anger for the rest of the journey. As morning broke, the train stopped for breakfast and Ruggles sat at the same table as his fellow travelers. When the white man approached the table, Ruggles uncharacteristically volunteered to move, but the other men and women insisted that Ruggles remain.

Ruggles reveled in the reaction he roused in the man, whom Ruggles called a "two-legged animal." He seemed to enjoy needling people who thought themselves devoutly religious but who had given little more than a passing thought to the plight of three million people living in slavery in the American South. Ruggles likely realized he had a rare combination of skills: he stood ever ready to take on the clichéd slogans about interracial marriage that racists employed to thwart abolitionism, and he could be combative or polite as the situation required. He was also brave, smart, a good writer, and unashamed to call out the powerful and the wealthy who benefited from the status quo.

For all the frustration of confronting strangers who cared nothing about slavery or Black civil rights, Ruggles sat content on the train knowing that his adopted home in Manhattan awaited. He was born in Connecticut in 1810 when the glow of the American Revolution and its fight for freedom and independence was still very powerful. Ruggles's own parents, who were probably recently freed slaves, were born in the midst of the Revolution, and he grew up hearing stories of the bravery of the fighters for liberty. As historian Graham Russell Gao Hodges points out, from this early, formative exposure to the rhetoric and ideas of the Revolution, Ruggles understood well the importance of freedom and equality, and in turn refused to accept the racism, segregation, and abuse that he saw whites inflict on Blacks in the New York of the 1820s and 1830s.[3]

Ruggles's family was also key to his later embrace of fundamental principles of justice. His father was a blacksmith, a respected artisan craft, and David Ruggles Sr. was likely highly regarded within the mixed-race and mixed-class communities of Norwich. Ruggles's mother Nancy was also widely respected; she was a prominent cook and caterer who was often called upon to provide food and drink for the town's celebrations. While by no means completely free of racism, eastern Connecticut provided Ruggles with an unusually tolerant community in which to grow up.

As the oldest of eight children, Ruggles was expected to earn a living and to make his own way in the world at a young age, and at around sixteen he found work as a seaman along the northeast coast. Ruggles worked on the steamships that plied the coastal towns of Connecticut, Massachusetts, and New York until settling in Manhattan around 1826. Hodges points out that Ruggles befriended and was powerfully influenced by Nathan Johnson, a New Bedford seaman who championed civil rights and the abolition of slavery. From Johnson, Ruggles learned about mobilizing, organizing, and protesting, training that would carry Ruggles into his new life in Manhattan.

Ruggles would eventually set up his home and business on Lispenard Street, where today restless passersby might glance at a plaque that marks the redoubt from which the city's most important Black activist launched his crusade against slavery and racism. Though he did not live as long or render as significant a contribution to the cause as did the much more famous fugitive from slavery, Ruggles would likely have relished the suggestion that he was the Frederick Douglass of antebellum New York City, battling racism, slavery, and discrimination in all of their nefarious forms.

And as far as Ruggles was concerned, "nefarious" was the correct term. Throughout Manhattan and Brooklyn, his Black neighbors were under siege, even as the city busily hatched deals with southern cotton merchants and slave masters to ship bales to textile factories in New England and Britain. New York had been growing wealthy by becoming a conduit for the cotton trade, helping to turn raw materials, now much easier to process thanks to Eli Whitney's cotton gin, into finished curtains, table linens, and fine clothing. A growing number of powerful insurance companies similarly buttressed cotton and slavery by offering policies that would reimburse businessmen and masters for lost cargo or dead slaves. Banks offered millions of dollars in credit so southern plantation owners could purchase land and seeds and farming equipment. All of this wealth and power made Black lives cheap in the minds of white leaders, and Ruggles risked his health every day to combat these powerful forces. Yet even as he rode the rails back home, even as he looked forward to the warm comfort of his own bed, he probably suspected deep down that he was losing the battle for the soul of New York. Black residents were being stolen from the streets, torn from families, kidnapped from the footpaths and docks around the town, all in the name of making New York rich.

Ruggles knew exactly how Wall Street was rising to compete with the most celebrated cities of the world. He knew that in no small way the city's emergence had come at the price of its most exposed citizens. In fact, the Manhattan to which Ruggles returned after attending the antislavery meeting in Pittsburgh in 1833 was mired in crisis. African American children were vanishing into thin air and no one seemed able to stop it.

AT FIRST THE REPORTS of missing children were sporadic, but if city police had bothered to investigate, town leaders might have noticed a dangerous trend. Soon, distraught parents reported many more vanished children, more than one a week as the city's winter turned to spring and summer. Frances Shields, a young girl of twelve with a dark complexion, short hair, and a scar over her right eye, disappeared one morning on her way to school, dressed in a purple and white frock and a straw hat. Eleven-year-old John Dickerson had been sent out on an errand by his parents and went missing from Broadway near the family home. Jane Green, a light-skinned African American girl the same age as John Dickerson, seemed to have been enticed away by a stranger. Rumors swirled that the stranger might have taken Jane to New Orleans, but no one saw her abductor.

The New York Police Department might have been a logical place for Black families to search for missing children. Records from the era show that police departments located in each of the city's wards constantly dealt with lost white children brought in by conscientious strangers, children who were usually quickly claimed by distraught parents. But Black families could not count on such commitment from officers who tended to view their neighborhoods primarily as places to conduct patrols and arrests. A pleading letter from the New York Anti-Slavery Society to the

mayor and the board of aldermen to confront the problem was
ignored and summarily returned to the society.[4]

New York police constables and judges refused to listen, but
desperate mothers and fathers kept up their search. They placed
newspaper ads describing in minute detail their children's clothes
and physical appearance at the time of their disappearance. Relatives scoured neighborhood streets and visited orphanages,
prisons, and poorhouses, hoping that someone might have taken
the children in. As anguished parents were coming to realize,
missing children rarely reappeared. In fact, no one heard from
Frances, John, or Jane ever again. Mothers and fathers wondered
if a dark spirit had snuffed out their children's existence, some
malevolent force come to make real every parent's most hideous
nightmare. But Frances, John, and Jane had likely fallen prey
not to a supernatural force but to a very real and human ring of
kidnappers.

In fact, the corrupt and criminal networks into which these
three young Black New Yorkers fell were dark enough without
resorting to mythical evil. Dubbed the New York Kidnapping Club
by Ruggles and its Black victims, the ring held sway over the city's
African Americans, striking fear in the hearts of even the most courageous protesters.

Children like John, Jane, and Frances were especially easy targets, though by no means the only victims. Kids could be lured
away with the promise of a treat or through the offer of work or
some other form of trickery. Other children, though, were seized
not through deceit but with the active help of New York's police
and judges. Southern slaveholders demanded their aid in fulfill-
ing the North's constitutional responsibility.

In fact, southern slaveholders loudly and publicly demanded
the return of their so-called property by placing thousands of ads
in newspapers, petitioning political leaders for more stringent
protections against absconding, and denouncing white and Black
abolitionists for encouraging enslaved people to emancipate
themselves. Southern communities lacked the police forces of
major cities like New York and Boston, but they relied heavily on

a network of spies and detective agencies as well as slave patrols to catch suspected fugitives. John H. Pope & Co. of Frederick, Maryland, operated a private detective firm with the ability to secure runaways all over the Northeast. In one of its ads, the firm promised "an efficient corps of spies" who "have been very successful in their captures of runaway slaves." All Pope needed was a detailed description of the fugitive and timely notice, "by telegraph if possible." New York marshals like the notorious Isaiah Rynders, a racist law officer known as one of the Democratic Party's most ruthless henchmen, actively aided slave catchers like Pope, Tobias Boudinot, and Daniel D. Nash, the ringleaders of the New York Kidnapping Club.[5]

By the time Ben and his enslaved followers left Norfolk in the dead of night in 1832, Tobias Boudinot was already fast earning a reputation for brawling and indebtedness, despite the fact that he was a member of the New York Police Department. Boudinot, a cigar-smoking, rough-talking brawler, tried to arrest African American John Scott as a runaway by beating him with a fence post and tying his hands and feet with rope. Scott, however, sued Boudinot for assault in the New York Court of Common Pleas. Scott and his heroic attorney, Horace Dresser, a man who would go on to defend many accused runaways, sued Boudinot for $500 in damages in a suit that was later settled.[6]

In part because Boudinot's victims like John Scott fought back through civil actions, Boudinot found himself constantly in debt, further fueling his need for money. Records from the city and state archives show that Boudinot was regularly being taken to civil court for failure to repay debts of amounts from $150 to $1,000. At one point Boudinot's landlord swept into his apartment and confiscated bookshelves, chairs, sofas, and other personal belongings because of Boudinot's failure to pay his rent. Throughout this vicious cycle of debts and assaults, Boudinot remained fixated on using the writ from Governor Marcy to terrorize the Black residents of Lower Manhattan.[7]

Southerners themselves organized political and social associations to facilitate collaboration with men like Boudinot and Pope.

Not long after Ben and the others left Norfolk and reached New York, frustrated white Virginians met to form the Society for the Prevention of the Absconding and Abduction of Slaves. Meeting in the Hall of Delegates of the state capitol, they tried to thwart "the evils" caused by "the loss of their slave property." Just a few years removed from the hysteria caused by Nat Turner's Rebellion, the society wanted not only to recover financial losses, but also to ensure that runaways and free African Americans did not encourage other enslaved people to revolt. The minutes of the society's meetings evince concern on both accounts, with the members especially committed to controlling the movement of Black southerners, free or enslaved. But they also singled out New York as a common destination for runaways, and raised several hundred dollars to investigate and prevent the loss of their slave property to the anonymity of Manhattan. Given the active collaboration between northern and southern officials, a "reverse underground railroad" smoothed the path of African Americans, especially the children who were so easily tricked and manipulated, back to the chains and fields of slavery.[8]

ONE MAJOR REASON THAT New York became the home of a kidnapping gang was the fact that it was growing so rapidly that during a stroll down a street like Broadway, strangers abounded. In fact, New York City would be both familiar and peculiar to modern New Yorkers. Though major street names and landmarks like Wall Street and the Battery remain largely unchanged, and though the basic outlines of land, coast, and waterways have endured, the look and feel of the city have changed dramatically. Before the Civil War, virtually all homes were made of wood, rather than steel and glass. Most streets were unpaved, so dirt and mud were everywhere, and horses provided the main means of transportation. The city would have smelled different than it does today, with wafts of horse manure mixed with the smoke from burning hearths and factories and the stench of an inadequate sanitation system. The loud shouts of the stevedores, bricklayers, lumber merchants, and others working in the city added to the noisy movement of railroads and omnibuses, not to mention the constant whinnying of horses pulling people or goods.

For much of its first two centuries, Manhattan was first an important Dutch colony and then a growing British settlement dependent on the fur trade. Blessed by natural advantages, especially the ease with which transatlantic ships could coast into the deepwater ports around the southern tip of Manhattan, thanks to a harbor that rarely froze even in the middle of winter, and given New York's inland access via the Hudson River, the city competed with both Boston and Philadelphia as a center of the lucrative European trade. Though slavery had thrived throughout the colonial era, the number of bondsmen had steadily declined so that a little more than five hundred enslaved people inhabited New York City by 1820. A few years later the state provided for the gradual abolition of slavery altogether, long after Pennsylvania and Massachusetts had done so. The opening of the Erie Canal sealed the competing states' fates, since goods could be hauled up the Hudson and across the canal, connecting New York to markets in and around the Great Lakes. The city seemed poised to become the country's leading metropolis, a rich and frenzied center for finance and commerce that attracted people from around the world.

Sightseers who found themselves in Lower Manhattan marveled at the city. Tall brick buildings painted red and gray and outlined with darker shades lined the streets, while other blocks would feature grand structures like the Crystal Palace, with its futuristic glass enclosure, which dominated the area now known as Bryant Park. The American Theatre, the Bowery Theatre, the Broadway Theatre, and the Astor Place Opera provided entertainment. The recently constructed round theater called Castle Garden jutted out from the west side of the Battery into the Hudson River. Famous for its central location as a popular watering hole, Fraunces Tavern was often sought out by visitors before setting out to explore the city.[9]

More than one hundred omnibuses, large covered wagons towed by a team of horses, crisscrossed the city. Coaches often charged one dollar for transportation over several blocks, more for longer trips. Railroads began operation by the 1830s, taking locals and tourists the length of Manhattan and throughout Long Island. Heading north on Broadway, visitors could stop at P. T. Barnum's American Museum, with its exterior walls displaying huge, elaborate paintings of animals, or visit Peale's Museum at 252 Broadway to see mummies recently sent from Cairo and other curiosities (such as stuffed animals posed in re-creations of their natural habitats). Visitors could leave the museums and continue on for evening entertainment in the opera houses and theaters that lined Broadway's west side. Past Canal Street stood still more theaters and opera houses, including the Astor Place Opera, as well as beautifully landscaped gardens and the homes of leading writers like James Fenimore Cooper and Edgar Allan Poe, and later, Herman Melville. If Broadway didn't suit your fancy, you could explore the eastern side of Lower Manhattan, with its wharves lined with seafood restaurants and the publishers and booksellers that lined Printers Row. Taverns near the wharves often featured gardens with puppets, music, live animals, and other amusements to entertain guests. The Black Horse Tavern near City Hall Park and the Tontine Coffee House near the East River docks were just two of the important gathering places for New York businessmen.[10]

Wherever tourists decided to go, they were confronted with a dynamic city already known for its fascination with business and finance. Bales of cotton; barrels of rice, salt, or flour; hogsheads of sugar; boxes of tea; and all kinds of other goods were stacked and strewn on the streets and along the wharves, constantly loaded and unloaded into and out of ships and shops.

The cacophonous Wall Street district must have been a startling experience for visiting farmers and other rural folk more accustomed to the bucolic quietude of the countryside. Just after the Revolution, the Bank of New York opened on Pearl Street, and soon was birthed Wall Street's symbolic status as a financial center for world commerce. A strong prejudice against stock trading and financial maneuvering still prevailed; real estate seemed like a much more tangible commodity. As newspaperman James

A coffeehouse in early New York. *(New-York Historical Society)*

Gordon Bennett, a keen observer of Wall Street, sarcastically put it, land was "supposed to be the solid article," but stocks were "mere air bubbles." By the 1800s, Wall Street was also an important physical address and many of the most prominent banks, insurance companies, and businesses jostled for a place near the Stock Exchange. As both a symbol and a place, Wall Street used its power and influence with the city's politicians to shape policy and legislation.[11]

When New York had been a Dutch settlement known as New Amsterdam and then a British colony in the 1600s and 1700s, slavery had been a fundamental part of its economy. In fact, slave auctions were held at a market on Wall Street, and several thousand enslaved people were sold in New York before the Revolution.[12]

Maps from the mid-seventeenth century show that once Native Americans had been pushed out of the area, several blocks of buildings had been laid out on the very tip of southern Manhattan, including the large Fort Amsterdam in the southwestern corner, with farms, forests, pastures, swamps, and wind-powered mills to the north. Much of the area known as Lower Manhattan today

remained rural, including the substantial acreage of the Dutch
West India Company's farm and a large common cow pasture just
south of the Collect Pond. The first enslaved people were forcibly
taken into New York by the Dutch East India Company just a few
years after they had appeared in the Virginia colony of James-
town. In addition to New Amsterdam, the Dutch directed slaves
to colonies in Aruba, Bonaire, and Curaçao. Colonial New York
was a vital part of a vast transatlantic slave system that stretched
from Africa across the Atlantic to the New World and from North
America to Brazil.[13]

Bondage emerged in New York from its infancy, and enslaved
people helped to build the future city from the initial clearing of
the forests and swamplands to the plowing of the first European-
owned farms. In fact, the proportion of enslaved people in New
York was comparable to that of colonial Maryland and Virginia,
and the number of slaves placed the city third in the nation
behind New Orleans and Charleston. By the late 1600s, colonial
New York had become the leading slaving port in all of North
America. Slavery was not some system borrowed from the Old
World, grafted onto New York's economy against the will of its
founding generations. In fact, the stealing of Black labor under
slavery was stitched into the fabric of the city from its very birth.[14]

Enslavement in colonial New Amsterdam was a bit more flexi-
ble and open than later forms of bondage as they would evolve in
the southern United States. Unlike southern slavery in the 1800s,
the Dutch colonial system permitted enslaved men and women to
marry and even to earn small wages. They could testify in court,
petition the government, and own property. By the late 1600s,
several free Black families owned property in the "free negro lots"
northeast of the Dutch settlement along the southern tip of Manhattan. These early settlements were the progenitors of the vibrant
and important Black communities that would later take root in
New York. Under British control in the 1700s, bondage would
emerge even stronger in New York, as the Royal African Company
embarked on a mission to make the town a major North American
entrepôt for slaves. As a result, the colony's slave population grew

even faster than its white populace during the early decades of the 1700s. On the eve of the American Revolution, nearly twenty thousand enslaved people lived in New York. They toiled in the fields on white-owned farms, they served as maids and domestic servants in middle-class and wealthy homes, and they loaded ships along the docks bordering the Hudson and East Rivers.[15]

Despite the ludicrous claims by Europeans that enslaved people were content with bondage, African peoples demonstrated their anger at an unjust system in ways large and small. For some, feigning illness, stealing small provisions, and minor acts of sabotaging their masters' property were ways to even the score. For other slaves, only a rebellion against the whole system would suffice. In 1712, New York burned over the course of several days as enslaved people rose up and killed and wounded more than a dozen whites. The revolt was quickly subdued by militia and colonial arms, but not before scores of buildings had burned to ashes. In the wake of the revolt, New York's white authorities cracked down on Black freedoms, but another massive rebellion erupted in 1741, emblazoning a scar on the city's memory long after New York left behind colonial rule and became an integral part of the new United States.[16]

Popular cries of liberty and independence during the American Revolution led some New Yorkers to question the morality of slavery. In the years leading up to the colonial rebellion against England, American protesters like Thomas Paine compared the colonial predicament to that of enslaved Africans. In their eyes, much like slaves, Americans were subject to domination by the crown, a comparison that was hyperbolic to be sure but nonetheless quite effective in generating feelings among the patriots that they had to rise up and break the chains that bound them to Britain. Parliament and King George mocked these colonial claims and pointed to the hypocrisy of slaveholders like Thomas Jefferson who compared the crown to an overbearing master.

Americans themselves often acknowledged the irony, which helps to explain why the new State of New York would plan for the end of slavery. Even before the Revolution officially ended, the New

York Manumission Society formed to promote the end of bond-age in the city. The organization founded African Free Schools that sought to provide at least a rudimentary education to Black children, both free and enslaved. Like Quakers elsewhere in the Northeast, New York's Quaker community began to take a firmer stance against slavery, and during the Revolution they explicitly prohibited members of their congregations from owning slaves. A growing number of Methodists even welcomed Black members into their faith, though strict policies of segregation continued to sepa-rate Black from white. Protestant Evangelical teachings emphasized the need to save all peoples from damnation, and the leveling rhet-oric of the drive for independence from England meshed well with the Methodist rebellion against high-handed and elitist religiosity.[17]

In the wake of the powerful twin forces of independence and evangelicalism, New York began planning for emancipation. In 1817, the state legislature declared that as of July 4, 1827, any enslaved people remaining in the city would be free, except those born between 1799 and 1827, who would remain enslaved until they reached a certain age. Lest Gotham's lucrative trade with slaveholders be endangered, visitors from the South would be able to have their enslaved people join them in New York for up to nine months. It was gradual emancipation to be sure, and much too gradual for those remaining in bondage, but at least New York and nearby towns like Brooklyn would eventually become free cities.

Though slavery would be abolished by 1827, strict racial seg-regation governed nearly every aspect of the lives of Black New Yorkers. Just a few years after the abolition of servitude, white New Yorker Thomas Rice birthed the infamous character of Jim Crow, performing in blackface at the Bowery Theater on the Lower East Side. Race was a complicated subject for most New Yorkers, as it was for most white Americans. Even if they opposed slavery for religious, moral, or economic reasons, white north-erners did not consider African Americans equal in intellectual capacity to Europeans, and could not imagine a future nation in which Blacks and whites might work and live together in the same communities. Wealthy African Americans, like the millionaire

investor Jeremiah G. Hamilton, were considered extreme outli-
ers, almost accidental exceptions to the rule. The notion of Black
doctors or senators would have been absurd to most whites; the
notion of Americans one day electing a Black president would
have provoked immediate laughter and ridicule.[18]

Neighborhoods of color were surprisingly diffused throughout
Lower Manhattan. Maps from the 1830s show that free African
Americans mostly lived within a several-block radius of the intersection of Canal Street and Broadway. But there were Black families
across at least five wards south of 14th Street. Only later, in the
1850s, as they were pushed out of white communities, would they
concentrate more in the Fifth, Sixth, and Eighth Wards. In Brooklyn, too, Black residents would make their homes throughout the
town but generally stayed within a few blocks of the East River.[19]

Black intellectuals like Theodore S. Wright fought against the
powerful tide of racism and segregation by organizing, delivering
sermons on Sundays, founding newspapers, writing essays, and
giving speeches. In the newspaper *The Colored American*, Wright
lamented that prejudice allowed slavery in the South to prosper
and rendered precarious the rights of free African Americans
in the North. "The prejudice which exists against the colored
man . . . is like the atmosphere, everywhere felt by him," Wright
told a Black audience. "We are all slaves—everywhere we feel the
chain galling us." Of course, Wright's listeners knew exactly the
same feeling. They sympathized with those in southern bondage,
but they remained fully aware that a system that existed far to the
south also shaped white racism in places like New York.[20] Long
before David Ruggles boarded the late-night train on his way back
to New York, his adopted community there had already witnessed
more than two centuries of African slavery. Human bondage had
helped to define the city and its economy since the earliest days of
European settlement, but enslavement by no means fully defined
the people caught within that system. On the contrary, when he
decided to leave Connecticut and make Manhattan his home in
the 1820s, Ruggles joined a thriving Black culture that thrummed
with families and communities despite New York's decades-long

devotion to slavery. Racism and segregation would remain hall-marks of Gotham for decades to come, to be sure, and each new year brought indignities and abuse from whites who could not contemplate a biracial society. Examples of such scorn abounded in the early 1800s, such as the time that the African Burial Ground in Lower Manhattan was covered over by several feet of landfill to make way for the city's first department store, or when the city shut down the African Grove Theatre in 1822 and arrested Black actors for daring to perform against the wishes of white residents. White city leaders even prohibited Black celebrants from joining Fourth of July parades, forcing them to celebrate Emancipation Day on July 5.[21]

New York State placed significant restrictions on Black men's ability to vote, requiring them to own property of at least $250 to cast a ballot, a limitation not placed on whites. In the 1830s, the restriction meant that only about seventy Black men qualified to vote in Manhattan and only about thirty in Brooklyn. Because of the widespread racism and the proslavery views of many of New York's leading politicians, African American voter participation fell far below that of other northern cities like Boston. More than six hundred men of color signed a petition in 1837 to win the vote, and the Political Improvement Association of New York included many of the city's leading Black voices, such as Philip A. Bell and Charles B. Ray. Alas, when the amendment came before the electorate several years later, the proposal to grant the suffrage to Black men garnered little support and failed.[22]

The forces aligned against the New York Black community were powerful indeed. But so, too, were there immensely important triumphs and milestones. They organized parades and marched in celebration of their freedom while also decrying the status of African Americans in the South. They gathered in anger and frustration each time one of their own was arrested for running away from bondage. They celebrated their children's achievements at school graduations. They gathered for family meals in between job demands. They fought and loved one another as all communities have always done. They disagreed about the future of Black people in a racist nation, and they met at conventions to hash out resolutions to battle intolerance and exclusion. Some left the United States, believing that America would never live up to its own Declaration of Independence. Others insisted that they were as much American as they were African, no matter what white folks said, and they were just as adamant about staying in cities like New York to make their case for freedom and equality.

It was not until shoe shiner Andrew Williams bought three lots in 1825 that the prominent Black community that would become Seneca Village was born. Today that area is bounded by 80th Street and Central Park West on the Upper West Side of Manhattan, but before it was destroyed to build Central Park in the 1850s, Seneca Village was one of the most vigorous working-class Black neighborhoods in the country. Until the village was leveled, Seneca Village was a shining example to people of all races and classes that African Americans could create stable and thriving societies of their own. Perhaps that was the reason it was removed and forgotten as the city began to lay the plan for Central Park.[23]

As African American workers competed with the Irish for jobs in domestic service, manufacturing, and manual labor, a nascent Black middle class had begun to form in commercial and professional circles. Thomas Downing opened a famous oyster restaurant near Wall Street, while Dr. James McCune Smith operated a pharmacy at 55 West Broadway, and Edward V. Clarke and B. A. Burgalew tended jewelry and watch shops along Canal Street. Samuel Cornish presided over a Presbyterian church on Prince, while the AME Zion Church on Leonard and Church Streets proved a common meeting place for gatherings. Thomas Jennings ran a secondhand clothing store, while William Hamilton made his living as a carpenter.[24]

African American women often worked in domestic service as maids or cooks while raising families. Work and home demanded a great deal of time and energy, but women of color also contributed mightily to their neighborhoods. They established the Dorcas Society to provide clothing for the poor while also encouraging attendance at the African Free School, which educated Black children barred from white schools. Although leaders like Samuel Cornish helped to oversee the Dorcas Society, women usually met together away from direct male supervision at the home of members like Margaret Francis. In just one year, the group sewed enough clothes to help more than sixty children to attend school. The important newspaper *Freedom's Journal* printed the constitution of the Dorcas Society, which declared it "a great blessing for our children . . . to enjoy the advantages of a good education." Even white newspapers praised the work of the schools and the Dorcas Society.[25]

By the time David Ruggles arrived in Manhattan, some eight hundred children were enrolled in the city's African Free Schools, producing generations of leaders like Charles Lewis Reason and James McCune Smith. The son of Haitian immigrants, Reason became a professor of mathematics but was also active in the city's Black literary societies. At about the age of twenty, he joined the Colored Young Men of New York City to push the call for Black suffrage and thus embarked on a long career of protest and political action on behalf of Black civil rights. Smith's parents had fled bondage in South Carolina and enrolled their son in the African Free School. Smith, a close friend of Frederick Douglass, earned his medical degree at Glasgow University after American colleges refused to accept him, and he returned to New York in 1837 to embark on an illustrious career as one of the city's leading voices.[26]

African American women in Seneca Village and in other Black neighborhoods came together to promote learning, moral uplift, religious teachings, and for their own edification. They gathered for a weekly Ladies Literary Association, led by Henrietta Ray, an early version of a book club in which women read essays and gave speeches, while also delving into political issues like raising money to aid runaways. In fact, the Literary Society was just one of more than a dozen organizations for Black women in the period. Reformers like Maria Stewart often criticized sexism within the Black community even as they angrily denounced enslavement and racial bias. Though born in Connecticut, Stewart moved to New York, where she was already known as a powerful pioneering

orator whose speeches had been published in *The Liberator*. One
of the first Black women to speak to an interracial audience, Stewart delivered fiery lectures on abolitionism and gender equality.
Women like Ray, Stewart, and Henrietta Regulus also helped to
oversee and manage the Colored Orphan Asylum and the Colored
Home for the elderly and indigent. More than twelve hundred
children would pass through the orphanage before the Civil War,
while the four physicians at the Colored Home aided poverty-
stricken African Americans.[27]

African Americans in New York were well aware of the plight of
their enslaved brethren in the South. By the 1830s, nearly three
million southern slaves, toiling in fields from Texas to Virginia,
picked cotton under the threat of the lash. Whipped if daily quo-
tas went unmet, enslaved men and women under the southern
sun bagged cotton that was then deseeded by the revolutionary
cotton gin. Millions of bales passed from the fields to southern
ports like New Orleans, Savannah, and Norfolk, bales destined for
the North or the United Kingdom. The sprawling brick factories
of Lowell, Massachusetts, and Liverpool, England, spun the cotton into clothing, curtains, sails, tablecloths, and dozens of other
finished products offered for sale around the world. When a New
York lady entered a fine linen shop on Broadway, she probably
had little idea of the thousands of miles the product had traveled,
from an Alabama cotton plantation to the wharves of Manhattan,
across the Atlantic to a factory in Liverpool, and then returning
across the ocean to the elegance of Broadway. It was probably not
the most efficient way to produce and sell goods, but New Yorkers
knew that they were dependent on southern cotton and the slave
system that planted, picked, and packaged it.

EVEN WITHIN A METROPOLIS so impersonal and callously indifferent
to the plight of the poor and powerless, where an individual could
melt into the rushing masses, David Ruggles seemed to be everywhere at once. He kept constant vigil, listening for any gossip and
perusing the daily papers for word of Black people in danger of

kidnapping or slave trading. No doubt he missed scores—perhaps hundreds—of fellow New Yorkers who had been taken from the streets of the city to toil on some faraway southern plantation. But he could and did save many others, with a tirelessness and dedication that rankled politicians, policemen, and judges.

This sharply divided and increasingly faceless city proved the perfect hiding place for new kinds of criminals like the members of the New York Kidnapping Club, who could snatch people off the streets and into the darkness of slavery. But the notorious ring did not spring up overnight; it developed over time, encompassing more and more police constables, slave catchers, judges, lawyers, and spies. What had begun in the early 1800s as a prosperous but informal ring had become big business by the late 1830s. How did this ring flaunt the laws of the city, state, and country? In part the answer lies in the intricate network of the New York Kidnapping Club itself, a network aided by a city too busy to notice that Black children were vanishing from its neighborhoods. But the case of one child taken from his school would begin to reveal to Ruggles and other New Yorkers the depths of the problem. The arrest of Henry Scott while he sat at his desk would rock the Black community and scar the city for decades to come.

Chapter Two

The Birth of the Kidnapping Club and the Rebirth of Manhattan

⤙⤙▭ ▭⤚⤚

O N A SATURDAY IN MARCH 1834, SEVEN-YEAR-OLD HENRY SCOTT sat at his desk in the African Free School on Duane Street in Manhattan, practicing his letters as his teacher Mrs. Miller watched. African Free School Number 5 had just opened in 1832 under the direction of African American teacher Jane Parker, and like the other Black schools Number 5 had been absorbed into the public school system. Abruptly the classroom door opened and in walked two men Henry had never seen before. One was a well-dressed southerner, the other a New York sheriff, and they had come for Henry.

Richmond industrialist Richard Haxall had built a fortune in the 1820s and 1830s by serving as the president of railroads and other businesses, including running his family-owned flour and milling operation, and like other southern businessmen he traveled frequently to New York. Haxall's daughter would marry the youngest son of Robert E. Lee, connecting one of the region's most prominent merchant families to one of its leading military families. But the blood and business ties between Wall Street and slavery were too intertwined to untangle. In fact, Haxall's brother made the city his home, and on this March morning he had come to the school for Black children on family business: he claimed that Henry was Haxall family property, and he intended to take Henry back to slavery.[1]

Announcing to the teacher and school superintendent that Haxall and the New York sheriff would be arresting Henry as a runaway, the school immediately erupted in chaos. Henry screamed and cried, while his young classmates shouted, "Kidnappers!" and "Let him alone!" and tripped over each other to run out of the school. Some children ran to their parents, while others chased Haxall and his police escort as they left the school with Henry. Pandemonium and disbelief at the brazen arrest of a schoolchild created enough chaos that Haxall could make off with his prey.[2]

The Black and white abolitionist community in New York sounded the alarm bells and mobilized for the legal battle that everyone knew would now ensue. Haxall and the sheriff dragged Henry before New York City recorder Richard Riker, who sat on the bench in City Hall just blocks from the Duane Street school where Henry had been studying. Black activists like David Ruggles came into all-too-frequent contact with Riker because, as the city recorder, Riker also served as the main judge in the Court of Common Pleas.

Just blocks removed from Ruggles's home on Lispenard Street in the middle of Lower Manhattan, but a world away in terms of wealth and privilege, Riker presided over criminal cases in a stately judicial building. The son of a US congressman and the descendant of a prominent Dutch family, Riker had been a district attorney, a second in a number of duels, a member of the New York State Assembly, and a prominent Democratic lawyer in a long and distinguished career. Bald except for a fringe of hair around his ears, with a pointed nose and small chin, "Dickey" Riker as he was known looked more like a clerk or bookkeeper than a distinguished politician. In his early days, he had fought a duel on the shores of Weehawken, just months before Alexander Hamilton would be killed in a duel with Aaron Burr on the same spot. Shot in the leg during the duel, Riker was taken to his home on Wall

City Recorder Richard Riker.
(Museum of the City of New York, Portrait Archive Collection)

Street where a surgeon gave him only a one-in-ten chance of saving the leg. "I accept the chance cheerfully . . . do what you can, and by the aid of the Almighty and a fine constitution I may yet save both limb and life." Though he walked with a limp for the rest of his life, Riker went on to serve the city and the state in a number of important political and legal roles, from a committee on the completion of the Erie Canal to the position of recorder.[3]

By the time Henry Scott appeared before him, Riker had already been serving as the city's recorder for more than five years. Unfortunately for the city's Black residents, one of the chief responsibilities of the recorder's office was to hear cases of people accused of being runaways from southern slavery. Dragged before Riker at all hours of the day and night, accused runaways found themselves before a judge known to sympathize with the South and slaveholders. In fact, Ruggles had publicly named Riker as a key cog in what Ruggles had branded the New York Kidnapping Club in a newspaper editorial. With little more than the word of a white person, and with little concern as to whether the accused was actually a runaway or had been born free, New York's Black men, women, and children fell prey to kidnapping.

Riker served his southern masters well, always eager to promote the Union by reaffirming New York's willing participation in the return of suspected runaways. He was well aware that the Fugitive Slave Clause of the Constitution required so-called fugitives from service (which could only mean escaped slaves) to be handed over to their owners. Many northern states and cities acquiesced reluctantly to the constitutional compromise over slavery, returning runaways only after every attempt to keep them free had been exhausted. Not so in New York City. Although a dedicated band of Black and white activists, lawyers, and politicians stood ready to join the fight to keep an accused fugitive from being returned, the city's legal and political system was rigged against them.

Riker made his pro-South stance clear toward the end of one cold November day in 1836 when an alleged runaway was brought before him. An agent representing a southern slave owner had claimed a fugitive and appeared before Riker to make his case. The recorder had a message for the southern agent: "Tell your southern citizens that we Northern Judges damn the Abolitionists—we are sworn to abide by the Constitution. Tell your Southern citizens that the great body of the northern people are all right." As Riker knew, the city teamed with pro-South and even proslavery Democrats, many of them Wall Street merchants, Irish laborers, members of Tammany Hall, and others who actively sought ways to entrap Black residents in the web of the kidnapping club. Riker unabashedly positioned himself near the center of the web.[4]

At the courtroom hearing Haxall was joined by several prominent southerners then in the city on business. On the other side sat Black observers, all of whom saw Riker as a notorious friend of white southerners. Some even whispered that Riker himself had owned slaves when it was legal in the city. White abolitionists like Elizur Wright sat watching as well, gathering intelligence for a series of newspaper articles he would write called "The Chronicles of Kidnapping." As Haxall and his pals walked into the courtroom, Wright noticed that Haxall did not even have the decency to look "honest people in the face."[5]

As a sobbing and terrified Henry sat before Riker at the start of the hearing, it became quite clear that Riker intended to live up to his reputation as the friend of southern masters. Richard Haxall claimed that Henry actually belonged to his mother, Clara Haxall, and that he had entered the courtroom to claim Henry on her behalf. New York law required that agents acting on behalf of owners had to present proof that they were an official and documented representative of the slave owner, but Haxall had no such proof. Riker could have released Henry then and there, but instead, unsure about what course to take since he was convinced that Henry was in fact a fugitive, he ordered the young child to jail while Haxall was given time to produce his father's will. In the meantime, Henry's classmates had begun raising money for his legal defense. By gathering pennies from parents and the Black community, the children in the city's public schools helped to release Henry from the clutches of the New York Kidnapping Club, one of the few to escape from the long and powerful reach of Boudinot, Nash, and Riker.[6]

THE SCARS OF HENRY'S arrest remained emblazoned on the city for a long time, especially among the city's Black residents, who remained constantly on alert for kidnappers. Parents warned their children about being tricked by strangers, even those who seemed friendly and kind. They knew that New York City was a dangerous place for Black children.[7]

Even as they watched over their kids, fathers and mothers themselves were always vigilant for the agents of southern masters, well aware that while children could be manipulated and easily overpowered, grown men and women were stolen almost as easily. Professional slave catchers made money—and a lot of it—in pursuit of runaways. Thousands of ads promising rich rewards for runaways dotted newspaper columns across the country, offering fifty dollars or more for recaptures. Armed with detailed descriptions of runaways, slave hunters lurked in New York's dark alleyways and in the crowded taverns, on the lookout for their quarry.

One such agent was a white lawyer named Fontaine H. Pettis, who had moved from his home in Virginia to New York City in 1833 for the sole purpose of recovering fugitive slaves for money. Pettis had been convicted of perjury in Washington, DC, in 1831 and sentenced to five years in prison, but President Andrew Jackson pardoned him. In a strange pamphlet he wrote after the incident, Pettis declared that if "any man shall speak of this unhappy affair . . . either in my presence, or out of it . . . I am *determined* without *form* or *ceremony, sword in hand*, to avenge the injustice thereby done me, with the *crimson blood* of the *prostituted* offended, whether he be *judge* or *juror*, or any other person whom I shall deem worthy of my notice." Clearly, even before he became a member of the New York Kidnapping Club, Pettis was a violent and vile man.[8]

Pettis placed advertisements in Virginia and Washington, DC, newspapers for his services. "Persons in the South," one of his ads read, "who have, or may hereafter have, runaway slaves, suspected to be in either N. York or Philadelphia, may find it to their advantage to send a minutely descriptive communication." A native of Orange County, Virginia, Pettis moved his law practice to New York specifically to represent slaveholders "in the northern cities to arrest and secure runaway slaves." In fact, Pettis noted in his advertisements that the complicity of federal and local officials "renders it easy for the recovery of such property." All slavers had to do was send Pettis $20, and information on the region to which the fugitive might have fled. At the end of his ads, the lawyer noted that "New York City is estimated to contain 5,000 runaway slaves." He was only guessing at the number, since no one really knew how many runaways had escaped to the North, but Pettis obviously believed that such claims would induce slave masters to recover their lost "property."[9]

By abducting New York's African Americans, not just children but women and men of all ages, the New York Kidnapping Club, with the help of attorneys like Pettis, could with remarkable speed place victims on ships docked at the many wharves that lined Manhattan. Kidnappers then transported their victims through New York harbor and into the southern and foreign markets to be sold as slaves, or they could then collect the substantial finders' fees that appeared in the fugitive slave ads in newspapers. It was almost too easy, especially when kidnapping rings knew that they had little to fear from white politicians, judges, and constables. The problem was not so much complacency as complicity, as John Lockley learned one day during the same month that little Henry Scott was taken from his classroom.

Lockley lived with his wife and their twelve-year-old son in Lower Manhattan. One evening in March around midnight, Lockley received a knock on the door. Such an intrusion is often the harbinger of bad news, but for Black New Yorkers a knock on the door in the middle of the night could be deadly. One prominent northern Black man reputedly kept a powder keg underneath his front porch, ready to explode if a slave catcher arrived in the dark. When Lockley went to answer, he knew that the lives of his family hung in the balance.[10]

Lockley's worst fears were realized when at the door appeared a North Carolina plantation owner and a police officer who intended to take the family to southern slavery. Lockley was claimed by Dr. Rufus Haywood, who had earned his medical degree at the University of Pennsylvania and whose family owned a sprawling plantation in the Tar Heel State. Just like Henry Scott, John Lockley and his family were brought before Recorder Riker the next day.

Before Riker, Haywood declared that Lockley's real name was Joe Branch, and Haywood relied on two New York lawyers, Thomas Lawrence Wells and B. D. Silliman, to make the case. Often the New York Bar could be counted on to defend the interests of slaveholders. Wells and Silliman asked for a delay in the trial so that Haywood could travel back to North Carolina and return with several witnesses who could vouch for his claim. Remarkably, Riker allowed Haywood the time while Lockley and his family sat in jail. New York's Black community, realizing that the legal and political system was so powerfully arrayed against them, was always ready to offer testimony that they had known the accused in the free states long before they supposedly had run away. Such testimony was a legal tactic that African Americans across the North employed in dozens of fugitive slave cases. If a white southerner was allowed to enter a Black community and with the help of local police arrest a runaway without so much as a legitimate trial, then Black activists would combat a rotten system by claiming that they had seen or had worked with the accused fugitive for years and even decades if need be.

Haywood, however, held a trump card: he could prove that Lockley had in fact been enslaved in North Carolina. The proof came in the form of an embarrassing fact about plantation life in the South: when white slave owners raped enslaved women, children of mixed heritage could provide an awkward demonstration of white power. Rufus Haywood's father, the rich and powerful Sherwood Haywood, had a Black brother, who was not permitted to take the family name. Rather, the family decided to allow this brother to run a small plantation of his own in Edgecombe County to the east of Raleigh and to live as a free man. This brother was John Lockley's father, meaning that when Rufus Haywood stepped into the New York City courtroom to claim Lockley, he was in fact attempting to take his own cousin back to slavery. Using this intimate family story to his advantage, Haywood convinced Riker that Lockley was in fact an enslaved man named Joe Branch, who had run away from Raleigh in December 1832. Lockley was sent back to bondage and later sold even deeper into southern slavery.[11]

From the perspective of political and legal officials like Riker, federal and state law could be maddeningly vague when it came to accused fugitives. By the 1830s New York City was approaching a quarter of a million residents, about fifteen thousand of whom were Black. It is impossible to tell precisely how many of those had been born free, or how many had once been enslaved in New York but had been freed by the state's gradual emancipation laws, or how many had escaped southern slavery to find a precarious freedom in the city. We do know that tens of thousands of runaways, perhaps as many as five thousand a year, managed to escape bondage to settle in cities like Philadelphia, Boston, or New York, while others crossed the border into Canada or Mexico. Both neighboring countries had already outlawed slavery long before the "Land of the Free" ended bondage after the Civil War. Enslaved people heard about such far-off places from southern whites or from other slaves who had knowledge of places where slavery was made illegal.

Running away from slavery entailed tremendous risks, and the fact that so many thousands endeavored to flee the South belies any claims—in the nineteenth century or today—by those who label slavery a benign institution. Fugitives, especially those close to port cities like New Orleans, Charleston, or Norfolk, tried stowing away on ships bound for free states. Some gathered enough money to bribe ship captains to let them hide on board. Others hopped on trains in disguise; couples tried to escape by having one pose as the slave of the spouse. They paid forgers to falsify travel documents or legal papers testifying to their free status. They walked across farms, through fields and forests, traversing county and state borders at night to avoid the slave patrols that prowled the back roads. Black southerners repeatedly laid their lives on the line to reach freedom.

Because of the constant flow of runaways, southern slave owners demanded that their enslaved property be returned. After all, the cost of a slave could run more than $1,500, equivalent to about $40,000 today. So white southerners had every incentive to locate self-emancipated men and women, and they had every intention of making sure federal law required northern communities to help in returning them.

No matter how much Black abolitionists like Ruggles protested this system, federal law was clearly on the side of southern slavery. Recorder Riker might have been feared and despised by the city's Black residents, but even if he was disposed to favor the accused, he claimed with clear justification that the Constitution required him to return runaways. Without such cooperation, Riker thought, the Union would be doomed and the Constitution would lie in tatters. The great republican experiment would be over.

In the opinion of Riker and other Democrats in New York and on Wall Street, there were larger issues to consider aside from the liberty of individual fugitives from slavery. Even if some African Americans, people who were accused of being runaways but who were in fact born free, ended up being sent to southern slavery, the sacrifice would mean that New York was upholding its end of the constitutional bargain. Governors of slave states repeatedly wrote to their counterparts in the free states, requesting help in capturing runaways, and northern politicians responded with a mix of indignation and obligation. Even Democratic governors of states like New York, those who most ardently backed the Constitution's requirement to return "fugitives from service," had to be careful not to appear too weak when it came to southern requests. Northern citizens demanded that their leaders protect their own state laws against slavery, and if free-state leaders bent over backward to give in to slaveholders' requests, what point was there to pass emancipation laws declaring free soil? Was slavery a national law that essentially rendered bondage legal everywhere, or were states allowed to keep bondage out of their own borders?

Even New York governor William Marcy, the same leader who had granted Tobias Boudinot the blanket slave-hunting writ in 1832, struggled with requests from southern governors. In 1835, Alabama governor John Gayle wrote to Marcy, seeking the rendition of Robert Williams, accused of sending abolitionist pamphlets through the mail to southern communities in an attempt to incite slaves to rebel against their masters. Gayle appealed to Marcy on the basis of the Constitution's clause requiring the return of those who fled to free states to escape justice. Gayle was really reaching here, because he admitted that Williams was not in Alabama at the time of the alleged crime of distributing incendiary material, and therefore could not legitimately claim that Williams had absconded. Marcy rightly argued that if Alabama could pass laws that New York was bound to enforce, such a move would be "undoubtedly enlarging the rights of the states in one respect, but it is a serious diminution of their sovereignty in another." So Marcy declined to grant Gayle's request.

Lest he be misunderstood, however, Marcy reaffirmed to his fellow Democratic governor that northern states were constitutionally bound to return fugitive slaves. Marcy and his New York citizens were not abolitionists, he assured Gayle, and the "mad course of this fanaticism," the movement to abolish slavery, would not endure. "You may rely," Marcy told Gayle, "that the people of New York generally entertain the most friendly sentiments toward their brethren of the South." Marcy continued, in a passage that he no doubt hoped would be printed in the Alabama newspapers, that "they know your rights and will respect them. They know their duties to you and will fulfill them." Though he could not arrest Williams and send him to Alabama, Marcy wanted Alabama's slaveholders to know that New Yorkers acknowledged their obligation to return runaway slaves.[12]

If any northern judge doubted the seriousness of the sectional compromise over runaway slaves, he had only to pick up a southern newspaper, for they were filled with angry editorials and letters denouncing the ease with which their erstwhile slaves had found freedom and protection in the northern states. Southerners like Virginia senator John Y. Mason or New Orleans editor James D. B. De Bow charged northern citizens with ignoring the law, and they tallied estimates of the cost of runaways to the tune of millions of dollars. If northern judges refused to uphold the Constitution, white southern political leaders claimed, then civil war would be the natural result.

The US Constitution could only have been forged with a series of compromises at its heart: bargains between small and large states, between populous and sparsely populated states, between free and slave states. In fact, it is not an exaggeration to argue that the Constitution in fact protected and defended slavery, and radical abolitionists like Boston's William Lloyd Garrison said as much. Agreeing with this view, African American activist H. Ford Douglas declared, "I hold, sir, that the Constitution of the United

States is pro-slavery, considered so by those who framed it, and construed to that end ever since its adoption."[13]

From the view of Ruggles and the city's abolitionists, New York leaders like Riker were nonchalantly allowing Boudinot and Nash to send possibly free people into bondage. Throughout the heyday of the New York Kidnapping Club in the 1830s, residents could even be whisked away without the benefit of a jury trial, which Ruggles and his allies maintained was a violation of due process. Riker and pro-South leaders in New York, though, saw the jury trial as an inconvenient obstacle. When the Black community marshaled witnesses to testify to the free status of the accused, Riker dismissed their truthfulness, and he clearly also resented the drawn-out process that a jury trial entailed. Riker preferred a quick hearing and an easy transfer of the accused into the hands of the southern claimant.

The Lockley case presented Riker with a chance to get rid of the jury trial hurdle. To help make his case that Lockley was in fact a runaway, Haywood relied on his attorney, Thomas Wells. Haywood could have chosen from any number of city lawyers who would eagerly have taken the case, for numerous firms boasted of expertise in the return of slave property. Wells was a prominent city Democrat, a leading member of the political juggernaut known as Tammany Hall, and known throughout the city as a pro-South litigator. Wells argued that, in fact, jury trials in fugitive cases were unconstitutional because they placed a barrier between a slaveholder and his slave property.

African Americans and their white allies were incensed. How could the city allow a supposed fugitive to be taken into slavery without so much as a trial? How could Black families defend themselves without testimony and witnesses to bolster their cases? "Freedom" was severely circumscribed if you could not vote or hold office, or if you lacked the right to a jury trial, or if at any moment a southerner might claim you as a slave.

Riker allowed Wells to appeal the case to the New York Supreme Court, another body that would prove sympathetic to the claims of southern slave masters. Justice Josiah Hoffman wrote the opinion for the supreme court, an opinion that proved every bit as favorable to the South as Riker, Wells, and others had hoped. The court declared that the requirement of a jury trial violated the US Constitution because "the legal rights of the Southern Slaveholder are so clearly defined, as at once to mark him, who in any way impede their exercise, as a violator of the public space." New York's judges and politicians, Hoffman wrote in his opinion, had "as little right to meddle with any legal property at the South, as a South Carolinian has to set himself up as judge and jury in the validity or our remote deeds from the Indians."

Riker and Wells could not have written a more proslavery decision themselves. Lockley was sent to the South and Hoffman even added a final insult to Black New Yorkers at the end of his decision by calling opposition to slavery a "delirious fanaticism." The developing metropolis, now beginning to sprawl beyond Houston Street and into the farmland north of Lower Manhattan, had once again faced a choice, and had decided to continue to ransom Black lives in order to facilitate its financial rise. Every accused runaway returned to a southern master cemented the economic relationship between cotton growers and Manhattan brokers. And that is exactly how the powerful and wealthy in both sections understood their relationship. Protection and defense of slavery meant protection and defense of the cotton trade.[14]

Just how determined Riker and other southern sympathizers in New York were to accommodate the wishes of slave masters became abundantly clear in a third case that shook the Black community. Like the stories of Henry Scott and John Lockley, the sordid tale of Stephen Downing combines dismaying complicity on the part of city officials to return an accused runaway to bondage. Virginia planter William Taylor claimed that Downing had in fact been an enslaved man in Northampton County, Virginia, named Levi Ames, the property of Margaret Lyons, and when she married Taylor, Ames (along with the rest of Lyons's "property") passed into the hands of her husband. Sometime in May or June 1832, Taylor claimed, Ames took advantage of a chance to escape along with several other enslaved people and settled down in a small house up an alley near Walnut Street in New York, and took the name of Downing.[15]

Just months after quietly settling down in the city, Downing was discovered by Taylor and arrested by New York sheriff's officers. Downing was jailed in Bridewell Prison, and meanwhile the months rolled by as attorneys on both sides tried to convince Riker and other judges that Downing was a free man or a runaway slave. After considerable legal wrangling, Riker elected to pass the decision on to the state supreme court. While everyone—especially Downing—waited for the supreme court to reconvene from its summer hiatus, Riker promised that he would reserve interfering further. Riker reneged on his word. He surreptitiously sent a missive to the justices outlining his views of the case and likely offering the justices a reason to return Downing to Virginia.[16]

By the fall of 1833, Downing had sat in prison for nearly eighteen months while judges and lawyers bandied his case about, and Taylor, who claimed Downing as his property, had grown increasingly impatient. One night, with the apparent approval of Bridewell's prison guards, Downing was taken from his cell, quietly moved out to the prison's back alley, placed into a carriage, and forcibly taken to Robert Murray's Wharf on the East River. A few decades prior, President-elect George Washington had landed at the wharf to take the oath of office. Now the crew of a Norfolk packet docked at the wharf waited eagerly for Downing to arrive so they could whisk him away back to bondage. Before the city's Black community could rally or respond, Downing was quickly aboard and pushed off into the Atlantic, bound for Taylor's Virginia plantation. It was open season on the city's Black community, and thanks to Riker, Boudinot, Wells, and their friends in the courts and within the police force, grown men like Lockley and Downing were as vulnerable as children like Henry Scott.[17]

As WOEFUL AS ARE the tales of Scott, Lockley, and Downing, New York seemed to be distracted by its own growth to care very much, and that was as much true for its native citizens as it was for accused fugitives. The city had a long way to go to address its disintegrating poorer neighborhoods. Unsanitary sewage systems, which basically required dumping animal and human waste into local waterways and even streets, where pigs and dogs foraged in the gutters, led to repeated cholera outbreaks. Rancid smells filtered into the coal-choked air, creating breathing difficulties for young children. Rains washed the streets but unhealthy conditions soon returned. In fact, the whole city suffered from a lack of reliable fresh water until the early 1840s, when the Croton Aqueduct finally brought a consistent flow of clean water to the city. But at least the wealthy could afford to have water for drinking and bathing shipped into their mansions from the countryside. New York's lowly denizens had to make do with water drawn from local ponds and reservoirs. The city did often provide funds for poor and orphaned African Americans, and merged the Colored Home with the city almshouse in 1842 to provide better care for elderly and indigent Black residents. As hard as simply obtaining the basic necessities of life had been, the city itself would soon suffer an unprecedented disaster.[18]

Although Manhattan's wealthy homes were bedecked with marble columns and stone fireplaces, those expensive additions hid the facts that the skeletons of most buildings were made of timber and fire was a constant danger. In fact, the world's great cities had fallen victim to fire ever since civilization began: Jerusalem in 587 BC, Rome in AD 64, Hangzhou in 1137, London in 1666. Urban dwellers faced a number of health and sanitation concerns, but inhabitants within city walls feared fire above all. Virtually every home, each stick of furniture, every church and public building were made from wood. Even great public buildings like the Merchants' Exchange on Wall Street hid wooden supports behind their stony faces. Though a blaze could erupt at any time, winter was the most dangerous season, when wood burned constantly for heating or cooking, and when merely a tipped candle could ignite a raging inferno in the parched, frigid air.

Like most cities, New York made sure that city constables on patrol kept a watchful eye for the first signs of fire. If caught early, fires could be contained; New York had a number of fire companies trained and on guard day and night, ready to put their horse-drawn wagons into action. New York watchmen like William Hayes walked their beats every evening, always on the lookout for criminal activity, suspicious characters, or signs of a developing fire.

On December 16, 1835, Hayes stepped through the financial district, turning left onto Wall Street. The night was unusually cold; a chilly wind blew hard and fast from the northwest. Wharves and harbors around the tip of Manhattan stood motionless, iced over by a string of daily temperatures below freezing. The air was dry, sapped of moisture by the constant chill. Now long after dinner, most New Yorkers had settled into the warmth of bed. A quick glance at his watch fob would have showed that it was 9 o'clock.

It was the worst possible time for Hayes to smell smoke.

As he sought the smoke's source, Hayes likely turned onto the intersection where Pearl Street met Wall Street, and the scene probably haunted him into old age. Several buildings had already caught fire. He yelled for help and several nearby constables joined him in sounding the alarm.

Within several minutes of the first alarm, Engine Company 1 appeared, followed quickly by more firefighters and even the city's aldermen, town leaders who were expected to be on the scene of major disasters. Despite the valiant efforts to subdue the flames, more than forty buildings in Lower Manhattan were leveled by 10 o'clock by a rampant blaze fed by potent winds.

Getting enough water to fight the inferno proved the hardest task. Fire hydrants froze; any water that made it through the hoses also quickly turned rock-hard. Firefighters tried pouring brandy into their boots and onto the hoses in futile attempts to keep them from icing. With the East River thick with frozen water, craftsmen and other volunteers tried to cut holes in the ice, only to see the water solidify in the lines. Meanwhile, ash rained down on the streets as building after building succumbed to the unquenchable fire. Looters made off with warehouse boxes and luxury items from downtown stores. Merchants ran to their establishments to save whatever they could.

By the early hours of December 17, the major edifices of Wall Street, including the Merchants' Exchange, were swallowed by fire. Ships anchored in the harbors became engulfed, and city leaders debated their next moves in haste, finally deciding to blow up buildings bordering the fire in a desperate attempt to deprive the flames of fuel. James Hamilton, son of the financial Founding Father who was almost single-handedly responsible for creating the capitalist economy thriving on Wall Street, lit the fuse, but the attempt failed. By daylight, the streets of Manhattan lay smoldering, felled by a fire that had finally exhausted itself. New Yorker Charles Graham wrote, "It is exceptionally cold here & we shall soon have great distress, for want of fuel" that had been burned in the conflagration.[19]

The devastation was unprecedented and brought the city to its knees. Business basically halted, and even the Chamber of Commerce could not meet because of the destruction of the Merchants'

An illustration of the destruction caused by the 1835 fire. *(Library of Congress)*

Exchange and the mass confusion among shops owners and restaurateurs. The city's First Ward, which had seen massive growth over recent decades, was laid waste and the wharves and docks along the East River were severely damaged. It was hard for people to comprehend the magnitude of the wreckage. Wall Street insurance companies could not settle claims because their paper records had been destroyed, and bankers begged Congress to help. David Lyon wrote to his congressman asking for loans from Washington to deal with the losses, reporting that on Wall Street "all is consternation and distress." John W. Richardson noted solemnly that the fire "will injure our prosperity as a city for ten years."[20]

Like most of those working and living in Lower Manhattan, David Ruggles and other Black leaders in New York were devastated by the fire. They gathered "a respectable meeting of colored citizens" like Samuel Cornish and Thomas Jennings to draft a series of resolutions expressing condolences to the merchants and bankers near Wall Street. "We do deeply sympathize," one of the resolutions read, "with the mercantile part of our community," and as a result the Black community would refrain from celebrating the New Year. Signed by the foremost African American men of the city, including Ruggles, Cornish, William P. Johnson, Thomas Downing, Charles B. Ray, and Peter Williams, the resolutions reached white readers on Wall Street through publication in the New York papers.[21]

Ironically, African Americans would help to save one of the businesses that would ultimately work the hardest against their interests. Oyster restaurateur Thomas Downing, together with other volunteers, raced to a building that held the printing press and offices of the *Journal of Commerce*. Seeing the flames reach the structure, Downing and his men found casks of vinegar that they used to douse the fire, saving the newspaper's offices. Editor Gerard Hallock claimed that Downing had prevented at least a million dollars of property destruction and he praised the men for their heroism. Unfortunately, the journal would prove a stalwart defender of the cotton trade and the Constitution's Fugitive Slave Clause.[22]

THE NEW YEAR WAS one of the most morose that New Yorkers would face before the Civil War. In the *Journal of Commerce*, editor Gerard Hallock spoke for Wall Street when he declared solemnly that "the New Year opens upon our citizens with an air of sadness on account of the heavy calamity which has recently befallen them— and the congratulations of the day will, in too many cases, have to be mingled with condolence." Hallock had been reared in Massachusetts and had edited the *Boston Telegraph* before landing in Manhattan. He became editor of Wall Street's leading business newspaper in the late 1820s. For the next three decades, Hallock used the *Journal* to promote the interests of Wall Street merchants and bankers, which meant discounting the rights of African Americans to live peaceably in Manhattan. Hallock and the *Journal* promoted the Union, the constitutional compromise over slavery, and the lucrative trade between North and South that permitted Wall Street to emerge as a global economic powerhouse.

That powerhouse had absorbed a sharp blow. Much of the business community in Lower Manhattan lay in smoldering ruins, and Hallock tried to lift up the despondent Wall Street community. "The loss, however, great as it is, and in some instances nearly overwhelming, will soon be retrieved by the elastic energy of our merchants. In the place of unsightly ruins, will rise stores and warehouses equal to those which have been destroyed." Though it was hard to envision for the despondent citizens of Lower Manhattan, even the most ardent optimists could not predict how quickly the area would be rebuilt. Out of the ashes would emerge the modern banking capital of the world, a Wall Street gleaming with sparkle and glamour to rival the most vaunted structures of the classical civilizations of Greece and Rome.[23]

Lower Manhattan would be rebuilt, and it would happen much faster than some on Wall Street had feared in the fire's immediate aftermath. Rather than taking years to rebuild, grand structures began emerging in mere months. Just a few months after the fire, Judge Samuel R. Betts, who would later figure prominently in cases involving the slave trade, beamed to the city's mayor that Gotham would soon regain its "prosperity and influence." By the summer,

work crews could be seen up and down Lower Manhattan, especially in the most heavily damaged areas around Pearl Street and
Wall Street. Tradesmen found work in the city's reconstruction,
and the docks off Water Street would soon welcome back ships
from around the globe. By the end of 1836, one year after the fire,
the US Post Office would be humming again and handling well
over one million pieces of mail each year.[24]

The rebuilding of Manhattan on a grander and richer scale
would have dramatic implications for the social and economic
life of the city. After the 1835 Great Fire, real estate prices rose
quickly and dramatically; former mayor Philip Hone complained
that "everything in New York is at an exorbitant price . . . rents
have risen 50 per cent for the next year." One reason for the
escalation in prices was the changing pattern of residential neighborhoods. The commercial district was reconstructed but without
the wealthy homes that had grown up near the wharves on streets
along the Battery.[25]

Wealthy New Yorkers instead relocated to the northern edges
of the city, particularly along Lower Fifth Avenue above Prince
and Houston Streets. And the new homes were far more opu-
lent, as rich merchants and financiers replaced their solemn
Federal-era homes with impressive and elaborate copies of European mansions. New streets in the northern reaches were clean
and orderly, far removed from the dirty and close quarters of the
streets to the south and of neighborhoods like Five Points. In
fact, no obstacles could keep the wealthy from eating up more
land for their homes and gardens. One New Yorker complained,
"Overturn, overturn, overturn is the maxim of New York. . . .
The very bones of our ancestors are not permitted to lie quiet a
quarter of a century, and one generation of men seem studious
to remove all relics of those which preceded them." Cemeteries,
older homes, long-held family farms, Black neighborhoods: all
were fair game as cotton shipping magnates looked for land to
accommodate their grand designs.[26]

The crowded city haphazardly spread out into a network of
streets, a labyrinth from which the kidnapped were being taken

and to which they might never return. In the colonial era the town was small enough to conduct trade in person, and people knew their neighbors. But by the 1830s, New York had become a far different city, one too hectic and crowded to notice anyone out of place. So many ships moved in and out of the wharves around lower Manhattan and Brooklyn that customs officials couldn't possibly keep track of them all. Small ships, fast schooners with bright white sails, steam-powered boats with paddlewheels, mail boats, cargo ships, and many other kinds of vessels came and went through the harbor. So many travelers and businessmen from around the world arrived in the city that a constant influx of strangers appeared and disappeared. People of color could be free or enslaved, or somewhere in between, unlike the southern cities where Blacks were just assumed to be slaves. It was hard to know who belonged and who didn't.

The city also seemed to grow more callous as it grew more impersonal and anonymous. Voices in Black and white communities had begun to question slavery as a national antislavery movement took root in the 1830s. William Lloyd Garrison had founded the abolitionist newspaper *The Liberator* in Boston in 1831, but New Yorkers of both races subscribed to the paper and even contributed news and letters. The national Anti-Slavery Society had been born to thwart colonizationists and to provide a forum for opposing bondage, and newspapers like *The Emancipator* and the *National Anti-Slavery Standard* were sent through the mail to the Northeast and Midwest. Soon the great Frederick Douglass would be traveling around the free states to relay to rapt audiences his biography and to denounce slavery and racism.

Yet Black and white New Yorkers who agreed with Garrison and Douglass that the immediate end of slavery was the best and only course to rid the nation of its original sin remained a tiny minority. Wealthy merchant brothers Lewis and Arthur Tappan proved that not all the rich and powerful were blind to the suffering of African Americans, while white lawyer Horace Dresser would contribute his talents to represent accused runaway slaves in court. The vast majority of white residents, though, gave little

thought to the plight of enslaved or impoverished free Blacks, or, worse, believed that subjugation of people of color was designed by God and should remain unquestioned by men. As white New Yorker William Lee wrote to the mayor, "Our abolitionists are a set of vile fanatics [who] are getting outrageously insolent—some of them ought to be hanged." Lee's sentiments likely reflected the views of many white citizens.[27]

There were other abolitionists to be sure, both Black and white, and the small number of antislavery activists in Gotham worked every bit as hard as Ruggles to fight against racism and kidnapping. But Ruggles seemed to be a magnet for the ire of Wall Street's defenders of slavery. He generated anger and hatred among the white community in Lower Manhattan, which could not tolerate such insubordination and troublemaking as Ruggles seemed to generate each week. Ruggles was not the only Black abolitionist in New York, but he was definitely the most vocal and visible one. That made him a prime target for the conservative forces of Wall Street, the police, and the Democratic leaders of Tammany Hall.

New York Divided

T HE GREAT FIRE FOREVER CHANGED NEW YORK CITY, BUT NOT IN
the way that contemporary observers feared. Given the
expanse of the decimated blocks in Lower Manhattan,
it had first seemed that the city would take years to rebuild, but
the rebound was fast and dramatic. New and shining tall marble
facades replaced colonial-era timber structures, and planners
widened streets and improved drainage. The docks were sturdily
reconstructed to an extent that would have been impossible without the clearing power of the conflagration.

New York in the decades before the Civil War was a city of
massive contradictions. On the one hand, vast wealth was fast
constructing one of the world's most stunning financial capitals.
Based on earlier models of exchanges like the Dutch East India
Company's trading in the early 1600s and Frankfurt's even earlier
stock exchange, a handful of New York businessmen had begun to
trade shares under a buttonwood tree in 1792. From those humble beginnings, the New York Stock Exchange emerged.

As the trading in securities like bonds and company shares was
taking root, the city's banking industry began to unfold, based in
part on large and profitable banks that had been founded in rival

Philadelphia. Shipping magnates earning profits from international trade required savings and loans, and southern slaveholders required hefty lines of credit to fund the long stretches between the sowing of seeds, the harvesting of crops, and the selling of those crops in global markets. Unable to meet these long-distance clients in person, and unfamiliar with the creditworthiness of plantation owners and merchants in the Deep South, banks sent teams of observers to travel throughout the South to determine who was trustworthy and who was a credit risk. Ironically, the forerunner of modern credit rating agencies like Moody's was founded by Lewis Tappan, brother of Arthur, a leading antislavery advocate. Lewis Tappan helped to form R. G. Dun and Company, which rated large and small southern businesses to maximize the profits of lending institutions in New York. While earning high rates from private customers, the Bank of New York also made money by extending large loans to the US government in times of crisis like the War of 1812.

Insurance companies similarly profited from slavery, modeling themselves after eighteenth-century Dutch insurance institutions that had helped to protect the slave trade. In fact, American insurance companies helped to underwrite slavery by taking on slaves as collateral as well as by insuring ships destined for the illegal transatlantic slave trade. The profits of banks, insurance companies, and the Stock Exchange helped make Wall Street synonymous with high rates of return.

As the city's financial sector blossomed, so too did new and enterprising commercial endeavors. Newly rich businessmen like Irish-born A. T. Stewart, who opened a massive department store that made him one of the wealthiest men in the world, joined forces with other Wall Street millionaires like Moses Taylor, who controlled the City Bank of New York (the forerunner of today's Citibank), to form a potent political federation in city and national politics. Taylor in fact would become one of Gotham's leading conservatives by constantly reminding his fellow New Yorkers that their multiroom mansions, sprawling gardens, and armies of domestic servants were made possible by the cotton

trade. As one prominent woman wrote to a female correspondent in Massachusetts: "Talk of Boston, indeed! Why it would be a poor provincial town in the Empire State! . . . If you want anything beautiful or magnificent, send to New York. . . . I bought a famous new rainbow shawl, and thought I should be quite in order to wait upon you up and down Broadway, with my ample new silk, and my French gloves."[1]

In the midst of such unprecedented prosperity, New York also contained shocking poverty and misery. Five Points was still sinking into an unhealthy and violent morass, overcrowded and dirty tenements grew into multistory traps for poor laborers, and African American communities suffered from criminalization and over-policing.

The city itself ached under the tensions created by conflicts between ethnic, political, and religious groups. On one side stood the pro-Union and pro-South Democrats under the firm grip of Tammany Hall, a political machine that relied on the distribution of government jobs and a kind of immigrant hall that could help newly arrived Irish workers to find apprenticeships and jobs in all manner of industries, from boot and shoe making to printmaking and painting. With help from the large influx of Irish immigrants, the Democrats controlled the police and dominated City Hall. On the other side were nativists and Whig Party leaders who prized the emerging commercial and financial spirit of New York but who also valued old money and Anglo-Saxon Protestantism. Distrustful of the Irish and their allegiance with the Democrats, these WASPish New Yorkers wanted progress without the Catholic immigrant underclass.

Those tensions played out in New Yorkers' views toward slavery, too. New Yorkers had neither the will nor the power to fight a system that had been part of America since its founding, and had only a generation ago been outlawed in the North. Even those who counted themselves as liberal on matters like slavery and race harbored deep-seated beliefs about the inferiority of African Americans. New York minister Richard Cary Morse wrote to his son at Yale, "The diamond and a piece of charcoal, brilliant as

one is at the expense of the other, have a common basis which is carbon; so the ignorant slave and the profound philosopher may have the common basis of a Christian character." It seemed ludicrous to the vast majority of northerners and New Yorkers that the entire American experiment in democracy would be jeopardized by the antislavery rantings of a small group of radicals who thought ending slavery was worth endangering the ties between North and South.[2]

A civil war might have seemed like a real possibility to New Yorkers in the 1830s, for the city witnessed racial tensions that erupted in violent anti-Black riots in the summer of 1834. Tensions had simmered between whites and Blacks for decades, with occasional flare-ups that rose above the usual interactions. African Americans in New York were concentrated in the most poverty-stricken areas of Lower Manhattan, as well as small but important neighborhoods like Weeksville across the East River in Brooklyn. But even while Black businesses, churches, schools, and neighborhoods harbored emerging working and middle classes, the growing presence of Gotham's Black society raised fears within the white community, particularly among the city's rapidly growing Irish working class.

White working-class fears, which were stoked by the quickly growing number of daily newspapers in the penny press, really amounted to increasing unease with sexuality, work, and crime. Whenever whites wanted to denounce Black people or racial equality, they always marched out the bogeyman of interracial sex. Antebellum New York was no stranger to this canard. In every partisan city election, the Democrats printed handbills and delivered speeches against their political opponents accusing them of favoring racial mixing. Of course, their political enemies (in the 1830s the competition was the Whig Party, and then, when that party collapsed in the early 1850s, the Republican Party formed to oppose the Democrats) favored no such thing. But American history has shown that politicians can often succeed when using the myth of Black sexual predation as a political rallying cry, and

after years of making such unfounded claims, New York's Tammany Hall helped to create the noxious atmosphere that would coalesce into anti-Black riots.

Closely tied to the repeated cries of amalgamation was the anxiety produced over the competition for jobs, which Tammany Hall, led by ruffians like the infamous rabble-rouser Isaiah Rynders, relentlessly reminded the city's Irishmen meant conflict with Black workers. The infamous potato famine would soon strike and dramatically escalate the number of immigrants coming to the shores of America, most of them moving into northeastern cities like New York. Numbering only a few thousand each year in the 1820s, nearly two million Irish came to the United States from the 1830s through the 1850s, and they transformed the political life of urban areas, though they were often scorned for their Catholicism and willingness to work for low wages. They were a restless and frustrated minority, and the city depended on Democratic leaders like Rynders to quell uprisings.[3]

In fact, tensions across the Atlantic between Irish Protestants and Catholics erupted in their adopted homeland when a riot between the two faiths broke out in Greenwich Village. Due to discrimination, Irish immigrants were forced into some of the worst jobs in the city. Laborers swept streets, cleaned chimneys, and worked in construction and a host of other jobs that native-born whites would rather not have endured. White skilled workers began to form unions and engage in city politics, further marginalizing the unskilled white laborers. Tammany Hall and Democratic politicians ensured that these immigrants saw Black workers as direct competition. Anti-Black newspapers like James Watson Webb's *New York Courier and Enquirer* inflamed resentment and discord, playing on white fears of "amalgamation" and the struggle to find work.[4]

These intense ethnic and racial strains erupted in the summer of 1834 when New York's Black community gathered at the Chatham Street Chapel to mark an important date on their calendar: on July 4, 1827, the state had ended slavery. On that same evening in 1834 white performers of the Sacred Music Society

also thought that they had booked the chapel for the night. What should have been a minor misunderstanding erupted into four days of rioting because of the anti-Black racism that had so consumed the city over the previous years. Marauding mobs made up chiefly of young Irish working-class men set fire to Black businesses and homes, as well as the homes of whites like Arthur and Lewis Tappan who were sympathetic to abolitionism. One Black man's barbershop on Bayard Street was completely destroyed, and Black minister Peter Williams saw his home and Episcopalian church burned to the ground, but dozens of others across Lower Manhattan were razed as well. Men like Stephen Lane, a twenty-four-year-old mason who lived on Ridge Street a few blocks from the East River, and Abraham Levy, a seventeen-year-old clerk who lived on Water Street, were typical of the white rioters, who terrorized the city's African Americans for days.[5]

Despite the fact that African Americans had far more to fear from whites than the reverse, white political leaders and police officers repeatedly stoked rumors of Black violence and crime. Whites such as George Coles wrote to the mayor's office about noise and fighting outside his door. "We are very much annoyed and afflicted every day of our lives," Coles complained, "by a number of boys who cluster together on the pavement at our front door." The boys were pitching cents, brawling, and using profanity "as is not fit to be heard."[6]

The anti-Black riots in the summer of 1834 rocked New York and led individual citizens to question where they stood on crucial issues like slavery, racism, and the growing rift between the northern states, which had all provided for emancipation by the 1830s, and the southern states, which seemed increasingly beholden to slavery as the years went by. Though white southerners were well aware that abolition (if not racial equality) was becoming the norm in Western civilization, they rejected the notion of joining that trend, particularly after the hysteria caused by Nat Turner's Rebellion in 1831. If white southerners were as committed as ever to protecting and defending bondage, how would that intransigence shape the relationship between North and South? New

Yorkers began asking themselves and each other what the future of the nation might be with a country so badly divided.

The answers, not surprisingly, were deeply contested, endlessly complicated, and created nuances and shading that reflected individual senses of right and wrong. Even Riker, who happily played the villain when accused runaways appeared in his court-room, thought that the 1834 race riots boded ill for democracy. "No man—no friend of liberty and law, could, under any circum-stances, countenance" the mob's destruction of property. Like Riker, conservative newspaper editor James Watson Webb opposed abolitionism and decried the influence of the Black community within the city, but Webb's suspicion of mob behavior meant that he also could not countenance the wanton attacks on Black peo-ple's homes and businesses.[7]

Other New Yorkers blamed the abolitionists themselves for asserting the rights of African Americans, and, in a clear case of "blaming the victims," openly called for Black and white anti-slavery activists to stop inciting the white working-class community. Webb's paper often referred to Black New Yorkers in a derogatory manner, like the article on crime that called one eleven-year-old boy an "ugly little negro." But Webb saved his most vitriolic racism for the editorial section, using the power of the press to declare slavery the natural state for people of color and denouncing Black and white abolitionism, the promoters of "amalgamation and an equality of social and political rights." Discord and civil war would be the natural consequence of "inflaming the men, and more especially the women, with hate and abhorrence of a large portion of their countrymen and brothers of the South, as brutes, thieves, and man-stealers." "They care not," Webb ranted, "if the soil of this country resembles a volcano smoking with gore, or if its rivers run red with the blood of hundreds of thousands of sacrifices at the shrine of fanaticism." In fact, Webb argued in a summary of the conservative New York perspective on emanci-pation, the evidence that racial equality would be a disaster could already be seen in the British West Indies, where schemes to turn former slaves into apprentices had failed: "Everybody knows the

natives of Africa and their descendants are a lazy race. Nothing but want, which is every man's master, will make them work; and when the cravings of nature are satisfied, like other animals, they go to sleep." Webb spoke for the conservative Wall Street assumptions about the need to preserve social, political, and economic order. Abolitionism promised disunion, civil conflict, racial mixing, and the radical disruption of the highly profitable trade between North and South.[8]

Like Webb, Sidney Morse edited a prominent New York newspaper and sought to lay the blame for the summer riots at the feet of abolitionists. The brother of the famous telegraph inventor Samuel F. B. Morse, Sidney Morse ran the *New-York Observer* and shortly after the 1834 riots penned an editorial denouncing abolitionist Elizur Wright for refusing to abide by the constitutional compromise over fugitive slaves. Returning runaways was "the price of the Union," Morse reminded Wright and his newspaper audience. In fact, Morse specifically blamed Wright's series of newspaper articles titled "The Chronicles of Kidnapping," in which Wright had highlighted the stories of Henry Scott, John Lockley, and Stephen Downing in the first half of 1834. Morse argued that the summer riots were directly attributable to Black and white abolitionists like Ruggles and Wright and their verbal attacks on Riker, Boudinot, and the kidnapping club. Why call Riker and Boudinot "cut-throats," "villains," and "murderers"? Such assaults could only incite trouble. "Would it have been surprising if some of the more ignorant multitude, suffering their passions to take the place of their reason, should have assembled in mobs and proceeded to actual violence? It is by such epithets, which the Abolitionists have been incessantly using in their publications for a year or two past, that they have exasperated the public mind, and brought on the late lamentable riots."[9]

Wright rose to the challenge and defended himself and Ruggles against Morse's attacks. In what would later be termed the "higher law" argument that justice and morality superseded the Constitution's compromise over the return of runaways, Wright

maintained that he would continue to call out Boudinot and other members of the New York Kidnapping Club. With God and Christian faith on his side, Wright declared, he would continue to speak out against the kidnapping of free Blacks as well as the return of runaways. "It was enough for me," Wright responded to Morse, "to know that in the City of New York men, women and children had been arrested and thrown into miserable dungeons, for no offense—but merely because they were claimed as PROPERTY." Wright reminded Morse and other conservatives that neither the Constitution nor Wall Street's business ties with southern cotton would trump the immorality of slavery and kidnapping.[10]

IN FACT, THE KIDNAPPINGS, if anything, became even more numerous in the wake of the riots. Children continued to be tricked into leaving the safety of their homes and communities, falling into the hands of kidnappers. Fifteen-year-old Joseph Long lived with his mother, Margaret, at the corner of Hammersley and Varick Streets on the west side of Lower Manhattan. As Margaret stated in her desperate attempt to recover her son, Joseph was light in complexion, had a large mole on his right cheek, and a burn scar on his right ear. Joseph had been enticed away by a stranger to Philadelphia and then taken to Richmond. While in Virginia's capital, the stranger booked a room at the Eagle Hotel and told everyone that Joseph was his servant. Alas, the man sold Joseph to a slave trader and he was never heard from again.[11]

Dismayed as he was by Long's kidnapping, Ruggles suddenly faced his own personal crisis. One September afternoon, as a hint of fall could be felt in the air, Ruggles walked to his office on Lispenard in Lower Manhattan only to see the storefront on fire. It was not the first time anti-Black and anti-abolitionist white criminals had sought to quiet the New York activist; back in 1826 another of his offices had burned at the hands of a mob. This time, though, the arson was accompanied by a large placard that was posted throughout the city:

TAKE NOTICE!

There is an incendiary depot at the corner of Broadway and Lispenard street, where the notorious Garrison's incendiary Liberator is received and distributed through the city by David Ruggles, a black amalgamator, who lately married a white wife! Let him be Lynched!

[signed] *A Voice from the South*

Ruggles denounced "the spirit of outrage, robbery, and assassination" that put him in danger, and noted that he had never been married. He had in fact become an agent for Garrison's *The Liberator*, selling subscriptions and individual copies through the small reading room he opened for the Black community. But for proslavery New Yorkers—as in the American South itself—the protections offered by the free speech and free press provisions of the First Amendment did not apply to abolitionism, and they not only set Ruggles's workplace on fire but protested outside the partially burned office on September 10, 12, and 14. Ruggles offered a fifty-dollar reward for information on the arsonist or the protesting mob, but found no one willing to identify the perpetrators.[12]

At the same time that Ruggles was being harassed, white New York abolitionist Arthur Tappan was the target of an assassination threat. The city's abolitionist press was indignant at the intimidation, announcing that fantastic sums of money "have been offered for his person in the southern states, that swift vessels are prepared in our waters to carry him off, and that southerners (the 'chivalrous south') are nightly convened in our city to mature their plans for seizing his person and conveying him beyond the reach of our laws." Despite his stature as a leading merchant, Tappan was the chief bogeyman for proslavery and anti-Black protesters within the city. In fact, he had been one of the main targets of the anti-abolition mob in 1834. Now it appeared a substantial bounty

Isaac Hopper,
David Ruggles, and Barney
Corse. *(The David Ruggles
Center for History and
Education)*

had been placed on his head. So much for the right of free speech
and assembly.[13]

Tappan and Ruggles seemed to be paired as the leading voices
of abolitionism in the eyes of pro-South New Yorkers. As if light-
ing his home ablaze was not sufficient, Ruggles continued to be a
target, but he refused to back down even though his very life was
in peril.

Not long after the threats to Ruggles and Tappan, a man
named Hill came to New York from Philadelphia and knocked at
the door of a Black couple, the Browns. Hill announced that he
was a long-lost uncle of Mrs. Brown and quickly convinced her of
the fact. She introduced the supposed uncle to her husband, who
"bid the stranger a hearty welcome to enjoy all the comforts which
his humble station in life could afford him." One evening the man
asked Mrs. Brown if she would accompany him on a walk, and,
fearing he might get lost, she obliged. On the walk, another man

grabbed Mrs. Brown with the so-called uncle's help. Black neighbors, concerned about Mrs. Brown, confronted Hill and accused him of betraying their race for financial gain. As they gathered around Hill, none other than the New York Kidnapping Club's Tobias Boudinot appeared to protect Hill. Within mere hours, Mrs. Brown was arrested as a runaway slave, brought before a judge, and swiftly placed into the custody of her claimant. Ruggles was distraught: "What an outrage—what a blow!" he wrote to the New York papers.[14]

Ruggles had helped to organize meetings and speeches in churches, he had fought against the New York Kidnapping Club in the newspapers, and he had suffered direct attacks on his office and home by anti-Black mobs. Now it was time to rally the Black community to maintain vigilance in their communities and to sound the alarm whenever kidnappers and slave catchers appeared. Ruggles expected he could count on a score of African American leaders to join the crusade.

Alas, much to Ruggles's chagrin, there were divisions within the Black community that rendered a united front more difficult than he had hoped. Middle-class embarrassment at the behavior of lower-class members of their community led to patronizing and demeaning attitudes. Members of the Black elite like Samuel Cornish and James McCune Smith, discomfited by what they considered rowdiness or ill-mannered behavior, desperately wanted working-class African Americans to avoid dance halls, street gambling, and drunkenness, lest they appear undisciplined in the eyes of whites. Guided by what historians have called "respectability" politics, middle- and upper-class African Americans hoped that by presenting good behavior and moral character, whites would be less likely to stereotype their race. Class tensions within the Black community often flared in the decades before the Civil War, adding to the stresses of white racism on Black families and communities. In fact, white abolitionist leaders like Arthur Tappan often condescendingly told the city's Black population to be content with their roles as domestic servants and wagged their fingers at the rampant prostitution in Five Points.[15]

Given such disapproval even from abolitionists like Tappan, many wondered if racial equality in America was a realistic possibility, and they explored the potential of leaving the United States behind altogether and emigrating to Haiti or to Liberia in West Africa. A gut-wrenching and emotional debate had emerged in the Black community by the 1800s over whether to stay and fight for Black civil rights in America or to start anew in a place where they would be able to shape their own destiny free of racism and slavery.

The split among Black ministers, editors, and intellectuals about whether to stay and fight in America or whether to leave proved to be an intensely personal question but one with significant implications for the civil rights movement. The disagreements over emigration actually broke friendships and collaborations. Samuel Cornish and John Brown Russwurm founded the important newspaper the *Freedom's Journal* in New York, the first journal dedicated to Black readers, in the late 1820s just after David Ruggles moved to Gotham. It is hard to overestimate the significance of the paper to the city's Black community; for the first time, they could read a paper dedicated to publishing news of direct and personal interest. The city's other newspapers, though there were many, mostly appealed to white audiences and only occasionally printed articles for Black readers.

Not long after starting the *Freedom's Journal*, though, Cornish and Russwurm realized that they entertained different views on colonization. The American Colonization Society had been established by wealthy and powerful whites who could not dream of a biracial America, and over the 1700s and 1800s the society sent thousands of people to Liberia. Cornish remained firm that Black New Yorkers needed to remain in America and fight for an end to discrimination, and he believed that one day people of color might be able to achieve equal citizenship with whites. Russwurm, on the other hand, doubted whether people like him could ever achieve equality in a nation so dedicated to white superiority.

Russwurm ultimately decided to leave New York and moved to Liberia, where he thought freedom and equality far more likely.

"The mere name of color," Russwurm argued in the paper before he emigrated, "blocks up every avenue . . . from which it is impossible to rise, unless he can change the Ethiopian hue of his complexion." Others would follow Russwurm to Africa, but the majority of Black New Yorkers stayed. Despite the germ of truth in Russwurm's arguments about the seemingly impossible task of changing white minds about racial equality, the notion of leaving America for Africa or the Caribbean was tantamount to surrender in the minds of African American leaders like Ruggles and Cornish. In fact, over the next decade or so, support for colonization would abate noticeably in the abolitionist movement, though it remained a topic of debate among Black intellectuals. The fight for Black lives and the end of slavery and discrimination would not be given up just as it was beginning. Cornish and other Black leaders trusted that by continuing to persuade white New Yorkers of their abilities and of the basic unfairness of racism, whites would eventually see the merits of their cause.[16] Still, Cornish left the paper, and the *Freedom's Journal* only lasted a few more years.

IN AN ATTEMPT TO reassert the need to remain and fight, Ruggles helped to found a new and unprecedented organization: the New York Committee of Vigilance. Financed through fundraisers and donations, and composed of both Black and white activists, the committee resolved to coordinate a number of tasks that up to this point had been arranged haphazardly: members of the committee would provide shelter and aid to self-emancipated former slaves; they would organize a legal defense for all cases of Black residents who were accused of being fugitives; they would gather outside City Hall, Riker's courtroom, and Bridewell jail whenever a person of color was arrested on suspicion of being a runaway; and they would spread the word throughout the community when they ascertained that a slave catcher had entered the city.

Many in New York's Black community, including Ruggles and Thomas Van Rensselaer, took leadership posts in the Vigilance Committee. James W. Higgins owned a large grocery store at

131 Washington Street and was an active member of the American Anti-Slavery Society, while George R. Barker was a broker with an office at 60½ Wall Street. Theodore Sedgwick Wright was born free in Rhode Island, became the first person of color to graduate from the Princeton Theological Seminary, and was in his late thirties when the committee formed. He had become a leading voice against racism and slavery from his post as pastor of the First Presbyterian Church on the corner of Frankfort and William, just a block or so east of City Hall. White attorney Horace Dresser, who defended many accused runaways before Recorder Riker and other judges, also spoke before the committee at its founding.[17]

Beginning in late 1835, the New York Committee of Vigilance helped hundreds of people of all ages. Some, as the committee suspected, were no doubt escaped slaves making their way north through the Underground Railroad, and committee members hid the runaways in their homes and provided them food and water before sending them farther north. Others were just as obviously victims of outright kidnapping, the prey of Boudinot and Nash. As secretary of the committee, Ruggles led a publicity campaign,

African American leader Theodore S. Wright. *(Beinecke Rare Book & Manuscript Library, Yale University)*

announcing to the kidnapping gang and to the city's growing Black population that the Vigilance Committee would watch out for illegal slave trading in the city's harbor and would keep a watchful eye on Boudinot, Nash, and the New York police. African Americans in other cities across the North would form their own vigilance committees. A loose network of these vigilance committees corresponded with one another, keeping fellow Black activists in Philadelphia, Boston, Detroit, and other cities in the free states abreast of kidnapping cases in their midst.[18]

Even as they battled mighty forces like the police, Wall Street, and the courts, activists still had to contend with the daily indignities of being Black in New York. Public transportation systems were segregated across the Northeast, and New Yorkers going to work, or dinner, or church were likely to face a string of insults from the time they stepped out their front doors. Frustration grew and sometimes burst into the open. One cold day in January, Ruggles booked a ticket to travel from New York to Newark, a journey of only a little more than ten miles but one that required travel by ferry as well as stagecoach. When Ruggles began to board the coach, the white driver told him that it was "against my rules to allow colored men to ride inside." Ruggles had met with such racism before, never taking the slight lightly, and he argued successfully that he should be permitted to ride inside with the other passengers. Ruggles considered himself a respectable businessman, having opened a grocery store on Cortlandt Street just a short walk north of Wall Street. He had become a member of the First Colored Presbyterian Church, a leading institution that also included important members of the Black community like Cornish. Ruggles believed he had more than earned the right to remain inside the coach with the other passengers.

During the short trip, though, the driver and his passengers stewed. Suddenly the driver stopped the coach and rushed into the cabin "with the ferocity of a tiger, and with his hands like claws tore both clothes, buttons and skin," as Ruggles later recalled. The other passengers aided in the assault by throwing Ruggles out of the coach and into the muddy street. He recalled painfully that the

whites had "trampled on my feelings" and that they were "robbing me of my rights, my liberty, my all." Ruggles was not the first to be so egregiously attacked on a public conveyance, and he would certainly not be the last, but such assaults cut him profoundly.[19]

Because such abuse could befall African Americans at any moment, many armed themselves with some form of defense as they went about their routine activities. At any moment Boudinot or Nash or some other officer could seize a new victim, and self-defense might become necessary. Ruggles often stated flatly that he would kill any man who might try to drag him into slavery, and he encouraged others to resist by any means necessary, even if it meant killing a potential abductor or if it might result in one's own death. The case of Martin Parmer, though, demonstrates that self-defense could still be overcome by the potent force of official authority.

Parmer had begun life as an enslaved man named Francis Smith in Williamsburg, Virginia, but he was hired out to work as a domestic servant in a boardinghouse used by the members of the Virginia General Assembly in Richmond. Hiring out was a common practice in the American South; slave owners could loan or hire out excess labor for a contracted period. Through the Underground Railroad, Smith had slipped into New York and changed his name to Parmer. He knew that at any moment he might be approached by slave catchers, and he always carried a dirk, a long thin knife useful for personal combat, up his right sleeve in case a slave hunter attacked.

That day arrived around the same time that New York was inflamed by the anti-Black riots in the summer of 1834, when Parmer made a crucial mistake. He wrote a letter to his mother, who was still enslaved in Williamsburg, encouraging her to try to escape and providing clues on how to make her way to New York. Parmer's key mistake, though, was including his home address on the letter. His owner intercepted the missive and knew exactly where Parmer could be found.

Parmer caught word that his former enslaver from Williamsburg had enlisted the help of Boudinot, police constable Charles

Riddell, and the New York Kidnapping Club to find him. He quickly decided to leave the city, booking passage on a ferry to New Haven, Connecticut. Parmer waited on board no doubt keeping one eye on the departure time and another on the ticket booth, hoping that the steamboat would push off from the dock before his pursuers chased him down.

Alas, someone had tipped off Boudinot that Parmer had fled, and the officer arrived at the dock minutes before the boat was to push away. As Boudinot tried to grab Parmer from behind, he dropped the dirk from his right sleeve and into his right hand. Seeing the long knife emerge, Constable Riddell took out his nightstick to strike Parmer's dirk, but the blow missed Parmer and hit Boudinot's wrist instead. As Boudinot reeled from the blow, Parmer stabbed his dirk an inch deep in Boudinot's thigh, jumped off the steamboat, and ran onto Fulton Street near the docks along the East River.

As Parmer desperately hurled himself into the street, Boudinot and Riddell slyly shouted to white dockworkers to "Stop the Murderer!" The dockworkers obliged and, thinking that they were helping to apprehend a serious criminal, tackled Parmer, who managed to wriggle free until he met another angry crowd on Wall Street that waylaid him. While catching his breath, Parmer tried to stave off Constable Riddell by throwing stones, but he was finally nabbed and put in prison. White abolitionist Elizur Wright visited Parmer in prison just an hour after he had been captured, and Wright noted that the fugitive's "tears were mingling freely with the blood that trickled down from the barbarous cuts." After a few days passed, Parmer had the misfortune of appearing before Recorder Riker in a hearing to determine whether he was to be returned to bondage.[20]

Parmer's "owner" admitted at the hearing that he did not really know Parmer, as he had inherited the enslaved man from his father-in-law. But Parmer was well known in and around Richmond. When the Virginia Assembly adjourned, Parmer was no longer needed at the boardinghouse, and he was permitted to hire out his own time. He ran a small fruit shop near the Richmond

Post Office and so came into contact with many white Virginians around the capital. Riker allowed Virginians to testify that Parmer was in fact Francis Smith who had run the fruit shop, but the Black community provided its own witnesses who testified that they had known Parmer long before he was said to be a Virginia slave. Ever eager to provide as much leeway to southern slave owners as possible, Riker also postponed any decision while Parmer's owner was gathering further documentation. In the meantime, Parmer was lodged back in prison.[21]

There in prison, in the summer of 1834, sat no fewer than eleven men of color, all captured by the New York Kidnapping Club. In fact, five of them were arrested in just a few days: William Miller, James Carter, William Carter, William Scott, and Peter Martin joined Parmer and several others in Bridewell, and they all had suffered at the hands of the notorious gang. The two Carters were likely two of the men who had originally fled Norfolk in the summer of 1832. But others were probably born free. Peter Martin, for example, had been living in New York for four years, working at a store at 57 Water Street owned by the merchants Forestall & Berthoud. Martin was trusted to open the store, and one morning he was met at the front door by police officers who demanded he accompany them. When Martin refused, they grabbed him, struck him in the face, and tried to carry him off. At the store, Martin was used to carrying a knife with him to open bags, and he managed to use the weapon to cut Deputy Sheriff Westervelt. As he ran, a lying Westervelt yelled out to bystanders, "Thief! Thief! He has stolen a thousand dollars." As with Parmer, the white onlookers were only too happy to oblige, and with their help Martin was imprisoned. Parmer and Martin and their fellow prisoners were more than likely sent to slavery in the South by a court system that cared little whether they had been born free or enslaved.[22]

Even as Boudinot recovered from the stab wound in his leg, he continued to track down more victims. His increasingly desperate financial condition, probably caused by another wave of substantial debts he could not repay, drove him to collect more and more

rewards for capturing runaways. The frequent appearance of advertisements for runaway slaves in newspapers from Baltimore and other southern cities provided ample clues.

Not long after hunting down Parmer, Boudinot and Nash found an ad in a Maryland paper that promised another lucrative reward. A prominent Baltimore landowner named Dewitt Kent placed the ad, hoping to catch a man named Henry William Webster who had run away two years ago. Around 10:30 at night, Webster and his wife received a knock on their door at 62 Cedar Street, just two blocks from Wall Street, and before Webster could stop them, five or six men led by Nash and Boudinot rushed in and gagged and handcuffed the twenty-four-year-old Webster. Webster's wife was so shocked that she was hardly able to yell out, and she and her friends spent all of the following day at City Hall in an effort to determine what had happened to her husband. Eventually she learned the horrible truth: Boudinot and Nash had taken Webster before the city recorder, and within minutes he was sent to Baltimore. The New York Kidnapping Club ringleaders likely split the handsome $250 reward among themselves and their collaborators.[23]

BY THE EARLY 1830s, a sharply divided New York had fractured along the jagged lines of race and class. Riker, Boudinot, Nash, and Pettis had demonstrated how easy it was to abduct Black people, whether they were escapees from servitude or not, and to collect the financial rewards. The complicity of Wall Street financiers and their allies in the newspaper press created a culture that was far more interested in the price of cotton than who had picked the bales in the first place. African Americans knew that they could become victims of the gang at any time, but they were determined to fight back. On their side sat Ruggles and other Black and white activists who risked their lives to fight kidnapping and runaway recaptures.

The city was coming to terms with its increasing diversity, on the way to becoming the ethnically and racially complicated metrop-

olis that is modern New York. But this was not a positive story of a melting pot or a tale about the celebration of difference. Like the nation itself, Gotham was being torn apart by passionate battles over race and slavery.

The profits garnered by Boudinot and Nash paled in comparison to the amount of money that could be made in a newly emerging and equally evil business that was beginning to take over the city. While the kidnapping club plied the alleyways of Lower Manhattan, an illegal transatlantic slave trade was using New York's waterways to build ships that would kidnap thousands of women, men, and children from West Africa and sell them to slave traders in Cuba and other areas of the Caribbean. With little to fear from New York customs officers, port officials, or maritime judges, the transatlantic slave trade soon made Manhattan one of the key points in a triangular business in Black bodies across the Atlantic Ocean, turning kidnapped African peoples into enslaved commodities that would grow cotton, rice, and sugar and generate even more wealth for New York and Caribbean merchants and shippers.

Chapter Four

New York,
a Port in the Slave Trade

⊶⫷⊘⫸⊷

N EW YORK GOVERNOR WILLIAM MARCY, IN HIS MID-FIFTIES AND
heavyset with thin lips, piercing eyes, and bushy eyebrows,
was a Democrat and strong ally of President Andrew
Jackson, who had already served a stint in the US Senate. Like
many New York Democrats and businessmen near Wall Street,
Marcy cared little what happened to the city's African Americans,
for the more they cracked down on Black freedom, it seemed, the
more prosperous the metropolis became. As if by some wicked
mathematical formula, the freedom and physical safety of African
Americans were in greater jeopardy than at any moment since slavery had been outlawed in the Empire State back in 1827. And yet,
or perhaps because of that fact, business on Wall Street boomed.
Ornate granite buildings rose up from the blocks of Lower Manhattan seemingly as quickly and easily as the cotton plants rose
from southern soil. As the *Journal of Commerce* put it, "So rapid
has been the progress of the State of New York, in her career of
prosperity, and so far has she outstripped her sister sovereigns in
the race of wealth and physical improvement, that it is habitual to

a numerous portion of her citizens to believe that no change of circumstances can arrest this onward march," that nothing could stand in the way of "this very pleasant dream in which we have so long been indulging."[1]

As Governor Marcy knew, there was one obstacle that could in fact wake New York from its "pleasant dream," and it was closely tied to the city's trade with the South. In his State of the State Address in 1836, Marcy devoted much of his time heaping scorn on an antislavery movement that threatened to gain power and influence, lest the radicals employ that power to sever "the bonds of amity and concord which unite us to the people of the South." Abolitionists like Ruggles, Tappan, and their allies were "seditious, incendiary and wicked," Marcy reminded New Yorkers, and, even worse, their activities placed the Union in serious peril.

In fact, so worried was Marcy that white southerners might take offense at New York antislavery protests, he almost seemed to direct his message to southern slaveholders and Manhattan merchants in equal measure. "In our commercial metropolis," Marcy declared, "the abolitionists have established one of their principal magazines, from which they have sent their missiles of annoyance into the slave-holding states." The governor worried that such insults might cause southerners "to suspend business intercourse with our citizens," and in fact, some slaveholders had threatened to do just that. If you undermined the Constitution and its Fugitive Slave Clause, Marcy warned, then you undercut the very foundation on which New York's prosperity was erected.[2]

The question for activists like Ruggles was how far Wall Street merchants and financiers and their political allies were willing to go in protecting trade with the South. With the city's Black population approaching twenty thousand and with their neighborhoods spreading out beyond Lower Manhattan into Brooklyn and north into the Bronx, African Americans were clearly there to stay. For many of them the answer to the question of how far the city would go to protect its special relationship with slave owners was all too obvious. Demonstrations of white supremacy were all around. For example, Brooklyn activist and intellectual William J. Wilson took

the ferry to visit Manhattan one day and reported to Frederick Douglass what he had seen. At a store selling busts of famous men, Wilson asked the Italian shopkeeper if he carried busts of Black leaders like Toussaint L'Ouverture, but the man replied, "They no sell." Only busts of white leaders like Washington and Franklin were worth selling in New York. Busts of Black leaders only sold in the West Indies, the owner told Wilson.

Shaken by the larger meaning of this encounter, Wilson wrote to Douglass that "what we find all around us" are white models. It is no wonder, Wilson remarked, that "we depreciate, we despise, we almost hate ourselves." Even upper-class and well-educated people of color "scoff at black skins and woolly heads, since every model set before us for admiration has pallid face and flaxen head." In fact, the ashen busts of white leaders reminded Wilson "that a black girl would as soon fondle an imp as a black doll— such is the force of this species of education upon her." While not advocating racial separatism, Wilson nonetheless was coming to believe that perhaps Black children should be educated by Black teachers only, at least initially. "We must begin to tell our own story, write our own lecture, paint our own picture, chisel our own bust," he told Douglass.[3]

Simple outings to go shopping or eat dinner were often traumatic, demeaning, and dangerous. Pioneering Black writer William Wells Brown, who had escaped bondage to forge an international career based in part on his novel *Clotel*, recalled a visit to New York City just after he had disembarked from a trip to Britain and other countries in Europe where he had seldom felt the sting of racism and segregation. In search of a restaurant, Brown was twice denied a seat for dinner. One manager told him, "We don't accommodate n——s." Insulted, Brown went across the street and stood under a lamppost, trying to come to terms with a virulent racism that he had almost forgotten while in Europe. Then, Brown recalled, he thought about the Declaration of Independence while staring at multiple church steeples whose spires rose above the buildings and "resolved that I would have my dinner in the City of New York."

Armed with boldness and determination, he eyed a vacant seat at a table and turned over the top plate. Brown was so frustrated and weary, he recounted, that "I . . . struck my knife in something . . . and did not know what it was, until I got it on my plate, when I found it was a big pickle." Brown's Black audience laughed at his story, no doubt completely understanding his agitation. "At any rate," Brown continued, "I went to work at it" and then finished a large meal. When he went to pay, the manager took Brown's dollar but remarked, "You have got the greatest impudence of any n— I have seen for a great while." The proprietor added that he wanted to toss Brown out but didn't want to disturb the white patrons. "Well," Brown replied at the suggestion he would have been yanked up from the table, "if you had, you would have taken the tablecloth, dishes and all with me." Brown added that next time he came in for dinner he had better be treated quietly and respectfully.[4]

David Ruggles, like all Black New Yorkers, would have found Brown's story familiar. Each case of kidnapping or illegal slave trading, each case of police officers arresting Black residents on meager charges, seemed to strike another blow to Ruggles's hopes for a biracial democracy. Optimism and determination were hard to muster when children disappeared from Manhattan's alleyways, when slave catchers and their northern allies prowled the city for anyone they could arrest as a runaway, when kidnapping gangs could operate with little fear of reprisal in the light of day. It seemed to Ruggles and his fellow abolitionists that New York was willing to venture very far indeed in sacrificing the security of African Americans on the altar of affluence.

Even Ruggles and his fellow radicals were soon shocked to learn how commonly the city ignored the fact that slave ships destined for Africa used their city as a major port. Along the East River between Manhattan and Brooklyn, in front of the Battery at the southernmost tip of Lower Manhattan, and continuing along the docks and wharves of the Hudson, the chaos of the waterfront made the shores of New York a perfect place to hide ships engaged in the illegal transatlantic slave trade.

By THE EARLY EIGHTEENTH century, the city had become one of the busiest ports in the world, a focal point for shipping and trade of all kinds of commodities among the Americas, Europe, and Africa. By the 1830s and 1840s, five thousand ships a year docked at New York. Although ships were supposed to register with customs officers who noted the cargo and registry of each vessel, the reality was more difficult, because so many crafts found their way into the harbors. Packet ships were especially common, and New York's port witnessed the constant comings and goings of packet ships traveling the Atlantic.[5]

The Atlantic slave trade had begun almost as soon as Europeans began exploring the African continent in the fifteenth century. In the middle of the 1400s, businessmen from Lisbon began what would become a lucrative trade in captured African people that quickly rendered Portugal, despite its relatively small size, one of the world's leading traders in slaves. By the early 1800s, Portuguese slave traders were transporting hundreds of thousands of kidnapped Africans and selling them into slavery in South America, particularly the Portuguese colony of Brazil.

Brazilian and Portuguese traders penetrated the interior of African places like Angola, offering goods like rum, weapons, and gunpowder in exchange for slaves. Despite the long and often dangerous voyages back and forth across the Atlantic, the ocean was less a barrier between Brazil and Africa and more like a highly efficient highway. Just as enslaved people and goods of all kinds transferred back and forth across the sea, so too did African, Portuguese, and Brazilian cultures influence one another, a broader cultural exchange built by each voyage, each personal interaction between people from different continents.[6]

During the four centuries of the trade, from around 1500 to about 1900, captives mostly came from West Central Africa, the Bight of Biafra, and the Gold Coast. But virtually all people throughout the continent were vulnerable, and the slave trade ensnared those from Senegambia in the northwestern region to Madagascar off the southeastern coast. Following the northeast and southeast trade winds, and the westerlies that circulated back

to Africa, slavers could cross the ocean in a matter of weeks. About two-thirds of the captives were men, and about 20 percent were children. On some voyages, such as the Middle Passage between the Bight of Biafra and the Caribbean, mortality rates averaged 30 percent, so on a ship with six hundred captives almost two hundred would perish from disease.

It is vital to remember that within the deep, dark, and dank cargo holds of these slave ships as many as 650 men, women, and children sat in claustrophobic and disease-ridden shipborne dungeons for weeks after they were forcibly taken from their villages and homes in Africa. In dusty ledgers preserved in archives, we can sometimes make out their names and ages in the spidery handwriting of captains and slave traders, but we know precious little of the enslaved as individuals, parents who dreamed of happy lives for their children, children who aspired to be village leaders and one day parents themselves.[7]

The United States had also participated actively in this transatlantic slave trade until it was outlawed by the federal government in 1808. After January 1 of that year, Congress stipulated that no more people would be imported from Africa as slaves. The reality, however, was much different, and an illegal slave trade brought thousands of Africans to the United States for decades after 1808. No one knows exactly how many were forcibly taken in this later stage of the Middle Passage, but the practice continued up to the American Civil War, mostly because the US federal government refused to commit enough resources to fighting the trade. British navy ships took the lead in patrolling the waters around West Africa, particularly around what is today Ghana, and brave British captains and their crew thwarted many ships outfitted as slavers. Despite complaints from Black Americans like Ruggles, who tried to call attention to the ubiquity of the illegal slave trade in New York, the US government remained aloof, and off the western coast of Africa a massive business based on the buying and selling of human beings continued with abandon.[8]

Despite some protests from even conservative New Yorkers that the use of the city's harbor as a key port in the slave trade

was embarrassing, there was simply too much money to be made from too many different business sectors to curtail the illegal trade. The US Customs House, charged with collecting duties on imported goods, was the country's most important, accumulating some three-quarters of the nation's importing tax revenue. But it was manned by poorly paid officers susceptible to bribery and political manipulation. The reason to seek a job as a customs officer was not the regular pay, but the extra side money one could earn by looking the other way while illicit goods flooded in. Like its control over the New York Police Department, the Democratic Tammany Hall political machine doled out favors by giving customs office jobs to Irish immigrants and political operatives. With the Customs House situated at 26 Wall Street, Tammany Hall's political hacks had easy access to the inner workings of the office.

A slew of other businesses depended heavily on the revenue generated by the use of the Port of New York in the slave trade. Ordinary ships had to be converted into slavers. Compartments belowdecks needed to be outfitted with grids of iron bars that would allow air to pass through the hold but at the same time keep men and women and children separated and under control. Large casks of water had to be filled and loaded, along with food and medicine. Iron chains and shackles, along with other supplies required for the weeks-long voyage down to Cuba and then across the Atlantic to Africa, meant that slave ships required thousands of dollars' worth of goods even before they set sail. Ship chandlers supplied slavers with all of these goods, including the iron and lumber it would take to transform an ordinary vessel into one suited for the transatlantic trade. More than a dozen ship chandlers operated in Manhattan alone, competing for the remunerative business of slavers and choosing not to notice when goods ordered were clearly intended for slaving.

What if a ship sank or was destroyed? New York's insurance companies provided valuable support for slavers even though they knew the practice was illegal. The progenitors of modern companies like Aetna and the New York Life Insurance Company were used to making money off of bondage, for they had long provided

A typical port scene in the nineteenth century. *(Beinecke Rare Book & Manuscript Library, Yale University)*

insurance for southern slave masters by indemnifying the value of enslaved people in case of death. New York insurance companies placed advertisements in all of the major southern newspapers, promising good rates and quick payments should a plague wipe out a large number of slaves on a given farm or plantation. Until they stopped the practice in 1848, the New York Life Insurance Company earned substantial profits from slavery, but other businesses stepped in to fill the void.[9]

Given the costliness of undertaking a slaving voyage, investors often joined the racket, hoping to turn a few hundred dollars into many thousands. New York lawyers John Weeks and Benjamin Wenberg funded many such voyages, but there were plenty of others to be found. The money was simply too easy and the returns too large. On the coast of West Africa, slave ship captains also kept an eye out for African slave traders who had developed elaborate warning and notification systems that advertised their businesses. Once purchased, enslaved people were loaded onto slavers by

the hundreds, of all ages and sexes, families as well as individuals, human beings kidnapped from their homes and villages to be sold as property in the plantations of the New World.[10]

Most of the ships docked in Cuba with the enslaved sold to the vast sugar plantations that grew cane to satisfy the sweet tooth of Americans and Europeans. Sprawling estates, some with thousands of bondsmen, employed brutal force to the clearing, burning, and harvesting of sugar. Like the ship chandlers, insurance companies, investors, captains, and customs officers far to the north in New York, plantation owners and managers stood to make vast sums of money by squeezing profits from Black bodies and the Caribbean lands they farmed.

Slave-trading ship captains, many of whom hailed from New England port towns, regularly sailed in and out of the congested piers of Manhattan. Nathaniel Gordon Sr., a native of Portland, Maine, made a long and prosperous career in buying and selling African peoples beginning in the 1820s, and by the 1830s he was running a regular business in Black bodies among the West African coast, Havana, and New York City. Gordon oversaw

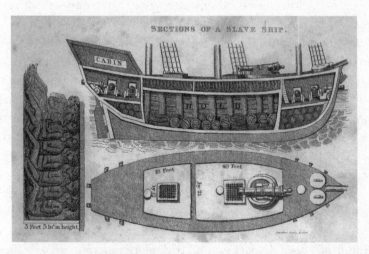

Illustration of the storage area of a slave ship, where untold multitudes of African captives perished. *(From Robert Walsh's* Notices of Brazil in 1828 and 1829, *Brown University Library)*

the conversion of legitimate commercial ships into vessels outfitted for the slave trade, and he remained one step ahead of law enforcement.

Slave ship captains were often quite public about their illegal activities, confident in the knowledge that even if arrested for piracy, they were unlikely to be charged and even less liable to be convicted. In fact, Nathaniel Gordon Sr. maintained a prominent legitimate business as a produce merchant, selling butter, cheese, pork, and beef from his store on Front Street. Though Gordon himself always evaded prosecution, his namesake son would ultimately be the only person executed for slave trading. As we will see much later, Nathaniel Gordon Jr. learned the dastardly business from his father and spent much of the 1850s engaged in slave trading in and out of the Port of New York, until he was caught, tried, and hanged at the beginning of the Civil War.[11]

Every month, it seemed, brought reports of another ship engaged in slaving. During the first week of February 1836, customs officers George Davis and Joseph Hopkins boarded a brig called *St. Nicholas*, which had recently entered New York from Cuba. Davis and Hopkins had no doubt already seen a great many suspicious vessels. Almost immediately the customs officers realized that the ship bore all the hallmarks of having been outfitted for the trade. Several large tanks of water six feet wide were stored in the hold, and only a slaver with hundreds of people on board would have required that much water. In addition, the ship still had gratings belowdecks. Just as telling was the discovery of twenty-five large chests filled with muskets and five hundred kegs of gunpowder, presumably in case a rebellion on board needed to be quelled. This was no merchant ship but a brig clearly outfitted for trading in human beings.[12]

Hopkins and his boss in the customs office notified District Attorney William Price, a prominent New York lawyer born during the American Revolution to Loyalist parents. Price himself was a friend of President Jackson, an ardent Democrat, and a leader of the city's Tammany Hall. A few years into the future, William Price would be accused of embezzlement as the DA and would

flee to England to escape prosecution; unable to pay his debts, he would shoot and kill himself in 1846. But here in 1836, when made aware that a slaver had entered the Port of New York, Price charged Captain Ange Calsamilia and his international crew (including men from France, Colombia, and Italy) with violating American laws against importing enslaved people from Africa. Despite his loyalty to the Democratic Party and the belief in the importance of appeasing southerners, Price thought that the buying and selling of human beings should not exist, especially in a free city. Unfortunately for Price, he had to argue the case before Judge Samuel Rossiter Betts of the Southern District of New York (SDNY), a federal district court that presided over many cases of maritime slave trading.

David Ruggles and his fellow abolitionists considered Betts and his colleagues in the SDNY facilitators of the worst machinations of the New York Kidnapping Club. Born in Massachusetts, Betts moved to New York and had quickly risen through the ranks of the Democratic Party. He became a judge advocate during the War of 1812, a US congressman, a district attorney in Orange County, and then a judge on the Second Judicial Court. President John Quincy Adams appointed Betts to the US District Court for the Southern District, and from this vantage point over the next forty years Betts inflicted a great deal of damage to the cause of human rights. In fact, the Southern District of New York became—in the eyes of activists like Ruggles—synonymous with the interests of southern slaveholders.

Despite the ominous presence of Betts on the bench, Price did his best to prosecute the captain and crew of the *St. Nicholas* and the trial was covered widely in the New York papers. During the trial it quickly became clear that the biggest obstacles in the captain's defense would be the talkative habits of his own crew. John Batiste and Andreas Gehioini, two of the seamen, rented a room in a hotel while the ship lay in the Screw Docks near South and Wall Streets. The crewmen had what turned out to be a bad habit of chatting up a druggist who had a store next to the hotel, and Dr. Thomas Ritter took careful note of what the two divulged.[13]

The doctor asked if the *St. Nicholas* was a slaver, and Gehioini replied, "Yes, we are going after the n——." They were expecting to take on about five hundred chattel in Africa and make their way to slave markets in Puerto Rico, where they would be sold for an average of eight hundred dollars each. Despite the mounting evidence presented by Price and the prosecution, the defendants' attorney David Ogden admitted that the *St. Nicholas* "was bound for the coast of Africa, but contended that she was merely going on a trading voyage." Price wasn't buying it, but Betts seemed to want explicit admissions from Captain Calsamilia and the rest of the crew to match the clear evidence against Batiste and Gehioini. Betts kept those two in jail but allowed the captain and the rest of the crew out on bail.[14]

Not surprisingly Captain Calsamilia and his crew proved flight risks, and when a grand jury handed down a bill of indictment, District Attorney Price was shocked and angered to learn that the *St. Nicholas* had set sail hours before. Price tried to charter a steamboat to run after the slaver, but the steamship did not have enough fuel, so he chartered a pilot boat to chase Calsamilia down. Alas, the *St. Nicholas* had too much of a head start and escaped. Once again, a slaving captain had slipped through Price's fingers, as Nathaniel Gordon had done so often. However, because the condemned ship was secured by bonds, Price was determined to proceed with the trial in hopes of inflicting financial pain on the ship's investors.[15]

Betts's charge to the jury, though, ensured that the slaver and its investors would emerge relatively unscathed. Even Gehioini and Batiste, the two remaining seamen in jail, would be acquitted. It is true, Betts told the jury, that Gehioini admitted to working on slavers, but such statements were merely "good evidence against himself" and could not "implicate any other person, and therefore it would be unsafe to take the admission of Andrew as proof that the vessel was a slaver." This was utter nonsense, but Betts continued in his charge to absolve the ship and its crew. There was evidence, Betts maintained, that the *St. Nicholas* "could be employed in the slave trade. But could she not be employed

for another purpose?" The answer, as Betts knew, was likely no. Customs officials and other captains who had examined the ship knew that it was a slaver. But thanks to Betts's demand for even more evidence, the jury acquitted the captain and all of the crew, including Gehioini and Batiste, who would reemerge in another New York slave-trading case by the end of the year.

Ruggles and the abolitionist community were beside themselves, and this time, at least, even the conservative New York press was dismayed by the outcome. Gerard Hallock, editor of the *Journal of Commerce*, refused to impugn Judge Betts, instead electing to blame the inadequacy of the law. Hallock admitted that Betts's charge to the jury was "essentially a plea in behalf of the prisoners," but Betts somehow was not to blame. Instead the law had to be strengthened, and fast. "Every month's delay," Hallock worried, "may seal the doom of a thousand now happy beings, whose liberty is as dear to them as ours is to us. Surely it cannot be the intention of congress, after declaring slave-trading PIRACY, to permit it to be carried on under our very eyes!" The paper fretted that the outcome of the *St. Nicholas* trial would "encourage all persons disposed to dabble in this nefarious traffic." That assumption would prove all too correct over the next few years.[16]

Readers of Wall Street newspapers might be forgiven, though, if they thought they were reading mixed messages. Wall Street businessmen, bankers, and insurers knew that southerners were monitoring their city through the press, including local southern papers that eagerly took antislavery news from the telegraph wires and reprinted it for southern consumption. Every act of protest by Ruggles and his fellow abolitionists was an insult to slavery that might cause slaveholders to stop sending the cotton bales on which the city's wealth depended. Readers of the *Journal of Commerce* were reminded that with the telegraph and the explosive growth of national newspapers, northerners and southerners knew exactly what each section was up to. In fact, the same day that Governor Marcy delivered his State of the State diatribe against abolitionists and the threat they posed to northern trade with the South,

the *Journal of Commerce* printed several resolutions that had been adopted by the North Carolina legislature. As that state's politicians warned northerners, "North Carolina alone has the right to legislate over the Slaves in her territory," and any interference "will be regarded as an invasion of our just rights." If Wall Street businessmen had any doubts about whether North-South trade could be imperiled by abolitionism, Hallock made sure they were aware.[17]

Even as the *Journal of Commerce* denounced transatlantic slave trading, the paper also angrily attacked abolitionism and any movement that might endanger the city's exploding prosperity. New York's working class, those who labored in factories and in shipping as well as artisans and craftsmen, were beginning to unionize in the 1830s, and Hallock left his readers no doubt about how he felt about such conspiracies.

A week or two after the *St. Nicholas* was charged with engaging in the slave trade, a group of workmen ("miscreants" Hallock called them) protesting for better wages stormed the docks in Lower Manhattan. Armed with portions of pipe, they organized a work stoppage until Constable Jacob Hays appeared with a strong show of police officers to quell the disturbance. One reader wholeheartedly agreed with Hallock that "the Trades Unions are the souls of two evils, viz. ambition and idleness." The "outrage" demonstrated to the city's business leaders that they were facing the menaces of unionism, abolitionism, and other "isms" that could harm or even retard New York's recovery from the Great Fire of 1835. Anything that threatened the meteoric rise of Wall Street's power was to be opposed with determination and severity.

So EVEN AS SOME protested the use of Manhattan as a slaving port, the practice continued. On a cold night in early December 1836, a small ship called the *Brilliante* slowly snaked its way into the Port of New York. With considerable confidence, the *Brilliante*'s captain, Portuguese slave trader Joas Evangeliste de Souza, slid into New York harbor. The *Brilliante*, in common with other brigs,

sported two square-rigged masts and a crew of around a dozen men. The ship was fast and maneuverable, perfect for the quick escapes one might need with the British navy patrol in pursuit. Also aboard were Antonio, Demingo, Jose, Joas, and Pedro, five enslaved men stolen from Africa to become the property of Rio de Janeiro's mayor.

By the time the *Brilliante* sailed into Lower Manhattan's wharves, David Ruggles was even more vigilant than usual, for he had heard that a number of slavers had come into the harbor over the past few months. Ruggles found out that the *Brilliante* was anchored at the foot of Market Street on the East River. Like a veteran reporter, Ruggles walked to the dock and starting chatting up one of the white crew members, slowly gaining the trust of his interlocutor, and during the conversation the sailor revealed to Ruggles that the brig had long been engaged in slaving and that in fact the mayor of Rio de Janeiro owned more than twenty such ships.

Armed with this information, Ruggles marched to District Attorney Price's office in the new City Hall. The *Brilliante* and its slave cargo had already been in New York for a week. Days passed without Price taking any action, and a frustrated Ruggles sought help from the deputy marshal, Sylvanus Rapalje, already known in the city as an enemy of the Black community. Ruggles wanted to enlist anyone who would listen, but an annoyed Rapalje replied to Ruggles, "I have not time to attend to it now." Ruggles returned Monday and Tuesday and was abruptly told to leave.[18]

Only when the *New York Sun* newspaper ran an article on the slaver did Deputy Marshal Rapalje and District Attorney Price take any action. They took de Souza into custody and jailed the five enslaved men in the debtors' prison while the case came before the US District Court. Ruggles knew the judges on this court were friends of Riker and more than likely to find de Souza not guilty.

Betts did not disappoint and with another judge concluded that the five Africans were simply members of the crew who helped man the ship at sea. His only business, de Souza told the court,

was to trade in coffee, sugar, and wine, and the judges bought the argument. On December 16, 1836, they ordered de Souza and his five "crewmen" to be set free. But many days later Ruggles found that the men were still in the debtors' prison, and he questioned prison warden A. B. Fountain as to the reasons for their continued confinement. The embarrassed Fountain admitted he was holding the five men not because of some legal requirement but because de Souza was not ready to leave the city and asked that they be detained. So the prison in City Hall Park was being used to hold chattel at the request of a slave ship captain!

This was more than Ruggles and his fellow antislavery activists could bear, and they petitioned Judge Michael Ulshoeffer, another pro-South justice, who lived at 52 Lispenard just a block away from Ruggles. Again the city's legal system made clear that the constitutional compact over slavery, not to mention New York's cotton trade with southern slaveholders, would hold sway. Ulshoeffer ruled that under state law de Souza could take his slaves into the city for up to nine months without penalty. "This country," Ulshoeffer reportedly stated at the hearing, is "not like England . . . [we do] not interfere with the laws of other countries." In fact, Judge Ulshoeffer admitted openly that if he "was travelling from the South with his slaves, and suspected they meant to leave him, he should avail himself of the convenience of shutting them up in the prisons of the city of New York." De Souza was allowed to leave the Port of New York with little more than the slight nuisance of having been delayed about two weeks.[19]

Shortly, the fury over the *Brilliante* was superseded by the case of yet another slaver. Though more than sixty-five hundred miles separated Manhattan from Benguela on the coast of Central West Africa, the two port towns were linked through countless legal and illegal transactions, including the brutal transatlantic slave trade. Ships that docked in New York hailed from hundreds of locations along the western coast of Africa, the eastern coast of South America, and island stops in between like St. Helena and Cuba. Despite the dangers of shipwrecks and the perils of British navy

patrols, slave traders like Captain Caleb Miller decided the potential profits were worthwhile. Miller imported people captured off the coast of Africa and brought them to the Port of New York on the *America* and found harbor in a dock in the Pine Street wharves.

Captain Miller, a native of New Bedford, appointed as his first mate John Batiste, who had been born in Italy. The second mate, William Muffhauser, oversaw an international crew of seamen from Denmark as well as Americans like George Kennedy and Samuel Whipping. The cook, Francis Heskine, was African American. The brig *America* was a fast ship that carried two hundred tons of dry goods, flour, bread, and hundreds of other items. These daily foodstuffs, so vital to life, were going to be sold and traded along with the lives of Africans.[20]

With the men and goods loaded aboard, the *America* sailed for seven weeks to reach a town on the West African coast. For European traders, the western coast was a complicated and patchwork system of local tribal controls, various authorities who exacted payments and taxes, and European colonizers who demanded bribes. Pirates, gamblers, prostitutes, day laborers, food vendors, merchants, stevedores, short-term seamen called "Cabendy Men," and a hundred other professions mingled and jostled uneasily in the busy port towns. These same towns became the embarkation points for more than 12 million African people who were kidnapped and captured from their homelands and enslaved.

Over the next few months, the *America* crisscrossed back and forth between African ports like Benguela, Loanda, Novo Donda, and the mid-Atlantic island of St. Helena. This volcanic outcropping played a central role as a stopover between Africa and the New World, and later as a camp for thousands of African refugees freed by the British navy. But not all members of the crew were complicit. Twenty-five-year-old Charles Potter did not approve of the ship's mission and he testified in court that the *America* had spent much of the past few months moving from port to port along the western coast of Africa. They moved quickly, Potter said, because African seaports charged $10 per day just to anchor

along the coast. But Captain Miller knew the coast and its slave trade well.

Potter testified that at the African port of Novo Donda, Captain Miller brought a dozen enslaved children and young women on board. The young Africans lined up single file to board, watched by two men "who were armed with clubs that would very quickly kill a man." The hold was stuffed with dry goods so Potter stretched a sail on the ship's deck for the children and young women to sleep on. Potter himself chose to sleep on deck, but that was only to avoid the roaches and mosquitos that filled the cabins below. Miller sold and traded some of them, then picked up twenty more at Old Benguela. Potter stated in court that Captain Miller took them to another dockage in Loango where the captain oversaw their conveyance in launches by Portuguese traders, and that there were other American slave traders active on the coast at the same time. By the time the *America* sailed the Benguela Current and then the South Equatorial Current to shift northward and westward, Captain Miller had spent months trading ivory and slaves between landings.

Captain Miller did not sell all of the enslaved peoples he had purchased in Africa. Deep in the hold of *America* were two girls around the age of ten: Columbia and Joggy. They had both been stolen from Africa, and someone—perhaps Ruggles, since he kept an ear out for slave traders who plied New York's waters—learned of the African girls and alerted the authorities. When Miller was confronted by local abolitionists in New York, he claimed that he had rescued Joggy and Columbia for humanitarian reasons and that he intended to employ them as paid domestic servants for his family. To the pleasant surprise of abolitionists, the police arrested Captain Miller, and he was put on trial for slave trading. Under the law, the punishment if found guilty was death.

The trial drew national attention and preoccupied Manhattan during the summer of 1835. In addition to Potter's testimony, many other witnesses were called, but most denied knowing anything about slave trading. The ship's owner, William W. Swaine of

New Bedford, swore that he gave Captain Miller "no instructions whatever from the owners to engage in any way in the slave trade." The defense counsel called a number of New York merchants, sailors, and financiers to vouch for the integrity and character of Miller and his first mate, Batiste. Then Judge Thompson delivered his lengthy charge to the jury.[21]

Right away the judge seemed to side with the defense. Judge Thompson began by telling the jurors that "our abhorrence and detestation of the slave trade must not influence our oaths." But he also suggested that the jury could not simply take Miller's word that he had transported the girls for humanitarian reasons—to rescue them from the wilds of the African coast—for such a claim "is calculated to throw a veil over the slave trade and ought not to be indulged in." Just as deftly, though, Thompson drew a sharp distinction between the testimony about transporting slaves, for which there appeared to be plenty of evidence, and the indictment for *selling* them. As Judge Thompson put it: "There is certainly strong evidence to show that he [Miller] was aiding and assisting, but the indictment does not charge him with doing so: It charges him with transporting them to sell as slaves himself." Thompson concluded his charge by reminding the jury that many business-men had testified to Miller's "uncommonly good character." The girls were soon sent to work as domestic servants.[22]

Ruggles was hardly amazed that the jury took only a few min-utes to find Miller not guilty. He had seen it all before, too many times to count. The entire political and legal system seemed con-structed to cheapen Black lives, even in a city as cosmopolitan and wealthy as Gotham. It was becoming increasingly difficult to remain optimistic about the goodwill of white citizens and leaders.

The years were taking a physical toll on Ruggles, too. Now nearing thirty, his eyes prematurely continued to fail, rendering his attempts to read the daily papers increasingly troublesome. He was stressed and anxious nearly all the time. Boudinot and Nash were constantly on his heels. But whatever the personal costs, he knew he could not surrender to the New York Kidnapping Club.

He had to match their energy; he had to remain as vigilant in protecting Black souls as the police were in cheapening them. Too many Black lives hung in the balance. And for Ruggles, battling the police had become as natural as breathing. He would need that strength as white New Yorkers continued to use their police force to control and criminalize and imprison their Black citizens.

Policing and Criminalizing the Black Community

⋆⇥⇒ ⇐⇤⋆

ANGER FOR AFRICAN AMERICANS CAME FROM ALL DIRECTIONS, including from the officers of the New York Police Department. By modern standards, the early NYPD was primitive and woefully understaffed. In the early 1800s, the night watchmen, like the vigilant official who sounded the alarm after the 1835 conflagration, were the main enforcers of law and order. The daytime police remained inadequate to deal with the robberies, violence, prostitution, gambling, and other crimes of a city approaching three hundred thousand people in the 1830s. Only sixteen constables, elected by citizens of each ward, along with about sixty marshals appointed by the mayor, patrolled the disordered and dangerous city. The New York Kidnapping Club took full advantage of the small force, as well as the power that Boudinot as constable and Nash as city marshal held. According to city law, only constables and marshals had the power to arrest under a magistrate's orders. Armed with warrants issued by City Recorder Riker, Nash and Boudinot could terrorize Gotham's Black residents, who came to fear the police presence in their neighborhoods.[1]

Part of the fear emanated from the fact that Boudinot and Nash did not wear uniforms or carry any kind of badge signifying their authority. The familiar dark blue uniforms of the NYPD were not instituted until much later, so African Americans harassed or arrested by the police could not even be sure that they were being accosted by legal authorities. Equally problematic was the fact that neither Nash nor Boudinot earned a regular salary on which he could depend; the two men's ability to support themselves and their families came from fees set by state law, which virtually required officials to arrest as many people as possible. Not that they needed any push to over-police the Black community, but patrollers like Nash and Boudinot had every incentive to use their blanket writ to arrest as many accused fugitive slaves as they possibly could. In fact, their financial well-being depended on it.[2]

Then, as now, newspaper accounts of court proceedings almost always noted when the accused was "Black" or "colored." The press was therefore complicit in the perception, aided by the prominence of policing in poor and Black communities, that New York's Black community committed crimes at a much higher rate than their proportion of the population would suggest.[3]

That community chafed under constant police surveillance and harassment. Every street inhabited by people of color was heavily policed; the Sixth Ward, which included Five Points, recorded more arrests than virtually any other area of New York. The same was true for urban areas throughout the North; Black residents were arrested, convicted, and imprisoned at disproportionate rates in Boston, Philadelphia, Chicago, and other major cities. But New York City was singularly and virulently opposed to racial equality, a sentiment reflected in white concerns about Black crime. The mayor of New York City announced to the board of aldermen that he would "cheerfully assume" the construction of new prisons, including one for women.[4]

Even as they counted record profits, enriching men like John Jacob Astor to levels of wealth that would make European monarchs jealous, New Yorkers struggled to deal with the two worlds that emerged from the rapid prosperity of the early nineteenth

century. Wealthy merchants gathered in local taverns amid cobbled streets, well-kept storefronts, and impressive homes in Lower Manhattan, while just to the north, along the neighborhood streets and alleyways of Five Points, stood another New York, one marked by stunning poverty, open prostitution, and violent crime.

Five Points had gained international infamy, a place so poverty-stricken and dilapidated that visitors came just to witness the worst of the human condition. Unlike the spacious mansions in Lower Manhattan, the teetering and rotting three-story homes in Five Points sheltered many families, including large numbers of African Americans as well as increasing numbers of immigrants fleeing the potato famine in Ireland. Cramped rooms, some with no running water and only candlelight to illuminate the crooked hallways, created dangerous conditions, and fire often swept through the poorly maintained tenements, killing and displacing families every year. As journalist and poet Walt Whitman memorably described New York:

> Here are people of all classes and stages of rank—from all countries on the globe—engaged in all the varieties of avocations—of every grade, of every hue of ignorance and learning, morality and vice, wealth and want, fashion and coarseness, breeding and brutality, elevation and degradation, impudence and modesty.[5]

Perhaps the focal point of destitution in 1830s New York was the Old Brewery, a huge Five Points building housing immigrant families in dark, claustrophobic, and overpopulated rooms. The "rookery," or slum tenement, was home to nearly a thousand people of all ages and became internationally notorious for its lawbreaking and dirty streets. When it was eventually demolished, workers found human bones within the walls and basement. Celebrity novelist Charles Dickens, determined to see Five Points himself, remarked that "debauchery has made the very houses prematurely old. See how the rotten beams are tumbling down, and how the patched and broken windows seem to scowl dimly,

like eyes that have been hurt in drunken frays. Many of those pigs live here. Do they ever wonder why their masters walk upright in lieu of going on all-fours? and why they talk instead of grunting?" As Dickens could see, New York encompassed extremes in the human condition, from the unimaginable wealth of the Astors to the hungry faces of the Irish.[6]

The crime and massive inequality Dickens witnessed lay not just in Five Points but in other areas of Lower Manhattan, and the city's police could barely keep up. There were more than forty-five hundred places where New Yorkers could buy liquor, making public drunkenness a constant concern, and more than twenty-five thousand arrests were made each year. Nearly fifty thousand people were jailed in a given year. Frustrated officers dealt with intoxicated and disorderly residents, while burglaries were compounded by the fact that shopkeepers often forgot to lock their doors. Most arrests occurred in neighborhoods populated by African Americans and working-class Irish like the Fourth, Eighth, and Seventeenth Wards.[7]

The New York Police Department patrolled these crowded thoroughfares, but its members were not that far removed from the people they policed. The truth was that policing was poorly paid, demanding, and dangerous. One night watchman complained to New York's mayor that his pay was so low he would soon be forced to send at least some of his children to the poorhouse. "The pay we get," he pleaded to the mayor, "and the manner we do duty will soon turn an old man to clay and leave his children no money to bury him." Low pay was compounded by meager resources, shabby offices, and long hours. Officers often earned their jobs through political favors and received little training.[8]

Policing was hard work, and the small salaries did little to boost morale. Captains repeatedly complained about officer absenteeism, while the officers themselves often complained of fatigue and overwork. And they were under constant supervision. One man, Officer James Scott, was handed a lengthy suspension for "conduct unbecoming of a policeman" simply for saying that "he did not care a damn" for his captain.[9]

Logbooks that officers religiously kept show that the vast majority of those charged with crimes were listed as "laborers," many of whom could only sign their names with an "X." Within just one week in the Twentieth Ward in the area now known as Hell's Kitchen, several women were arrested for prostitution and drunkenness. Eliza Bailey, a twenty-eight-year-old housekeeper; Mary Ann Virginia from Ireland, thirty-two and also a housekeeper; and Rosanna Dunn, married and thirty from Ireland, were all arrested for disorderly conduct. Two other Irish women, Mary Bagget and Anne Martin, both around twenty years old, were arrested twice in one week for prostitution, while Mary Moore was jailed for stealing a pillow.[10]

By all accounts, as neighborhoods became increasingly overcrowded and poverty-stricken, crime rates rose dramatically in the 1830s and 1840s. The density of people living in Lower Manhattan nearly doubled between 1820 and 1850, leading to a rapid rise in arrests. According to one scholar's estimate, by the eve of the Civil War in 1860, about 10 percent of the city's population had a criminal record. This early form of mass incarceration meant that the city had to expend vast sums on its prisons, such as the infamous Tombs and Bridewell, which became a filthy, overcrowded, and dangerous reflection of places like Five Points.[11]

By the mid-nineteenth century, the Tombs and its overcrowded cells with hundreds of inmates were notorious throughout the world. As a municipal jail built in the late 1830s, the Tombs was designed to replace Bridewell Prison, which had incarcerated people beginning in the late colonial era. Unfortunately, the Tombs was built in the swampy and unsanitary Five Points area, and generations of prisoners complained about leaking ceilings, foul odors, and sewage seeping through the floors. The Tombs complex, known formally as the Halls of Justice and House of Detention, included city courts and the police headquarters.

As if mimicking Dante's circles of hell, the Tombs divided its levels according to the nature of its inmates' crimes. The top level harbored petty thieves and small-time criminals, while in the story below lived convicted burglars of more substantial property. The

THE OLD BRIDEWELL.
Which formerly stood in the Park, between the City Hall and Broadway

Bridewell Prison and the Tombs. *(Colored lithograph by H. R. Robinson, Wellcome Collection)*

second floor housed those guilty of higher crimes like murder and robbery with assault, while the bottom level incarcerated the most egregious criminals, those ruled insane, and those destined for the gallows. The cells were a uniform eight feet by six feet, and each housed a single inmate. While the original intent of early nineteenth-century prison reform was to provide a place for the solitary self-reflection of the guilty, incarceration in packed and filthy conditions had become less a path to rehabilitation and more of a way to punish. Many victims of the New York Kidnapping Club found themselves in either Bridewell or the Tombs, and if they weren't careful, Ruggles and his Black abolitionist allies on the New York Vigilance Committee would soon join them.[12]

RUGGLES PAID DEARLY FOR his activism in the *Brilliante* slave-trading case that had so occupied the attention of New York in 1837. The affair had exhausted him physically and emotionally and soon would jeopardize his liberty. Just a few days after Christmas,

between one and two o'clock in the morning, Ruggles heard a commotion outside his door that was soon followed by a careful knocking. He stepped gingerly out of bed and listened at the door. From what he could discern from the voices, there were several men outside. "Is Mr. Ruggles in? We wish to see you," one of the men prompted, to which the activist asked, "Who are you?" "A friend—David open the door." When Ruggles continued to press for more information, his worst fears were confirmed: it was Daniel D. Nash, a local marshal and one of the most notorious members of the New York Kidnapping Club. Like his buddy and accomplice Tobias Boudinot, Nash appears frequently in the court records of the 1830s, sued for debt repayments or for rash actions as the arm of the law. Nash tried to trick Ruggles into believing that he approached his home on Lispenard Street on private business. Of course, Ruggles would not be fooled. "This is rather an unseasonable hour, Mr. Nash, to settle private business; call in the morning at 8 o'clock." "Open this door or I will force it open," Nash declared. When Ruggles continued to stonewall, Nash and his fellow officers dashed off to see the chief of the city's police, Jacob Hays.[13]

Nash and the kidnapping club knew that High Constable Jacob Hays was no friend of New York's Black community. By the 1830s, he had already served for three decades as the head of police, and no city official represented the police force more definitively than Hays, who was known to chase down criminals himself and to insert himself into the middle of riots. Born into an important Jewish family that had immigrated from the Netherlands, Jacob Hays's father had served under General George Washington during the French and Indian War.

Appointed as the first and only "High Constable" by the mayor in 1802, Jacob Hays remained at the head of the city police until his death in 1849. The white conservative community in New York loved Hays, and they promulgated a legend that had Hays single-handedly apprehending criminals with some kind of gift of intuition. Though he stood just five feet, seven inches, Hays was burly and confident. Hays was said to be able almost

supernaturally to "discover 'undivulged crime.'" "When a store has been robbed," the adoring public exclaimed, Hays could "march directly to the house where the goods are concealed, and say, 'these are they.'" Similarly, "when a gentleman's pocket has been picked," Hays might be able to approach "a crowd of unsavory miscreants" and, with "unerring judgment, lay his hand upon one and exclaim 'you're wanted!'" It was clear that the city's business leaders and middle class cared little if Hays and his police force crossed the lines of appropriate behavior, as long as they caught criminals. As the *New York Mirror* marveled, "How is it that he is gifted with that strange principle of ubiquity that makes him 'here, and there, and everywhere' at the same moment? No matter how, so long as the public reap the benefit." Parents warned their children to be good, lest Constable Hays found out about their misbehavior.[14]

Throughout the first half of the nineteenth century Hays was a popular and visible presence in the city. According to one story, Hays sat in Riker's court on a particularly warm day, and though he was present to secure peace and order, he drifted asleep. Soon Hays started snoring loudly, prompting a police officer to whisper in Hays's ear that "someone is snoring and disturbing the court." At once Hays stood up and, using his booming voice, declared: "Silence! There must be no snoring in court!" Hays then turned to Riker and said, "You can go on now without interruption." That story, however, belies the tenacity with which he pursued criminality. Hays had successfully prosecuted robbers of the New York City Bank who had stolen more than two hundred thousand dollars and followed the perpetrators all the way to Philadelphia, where they had buried much of the stolen cash under a tree in Independence Square. Hays seemed to be in many places at once, and he was feared by the city's criminals, but he also helped to enable the infamous deeds of Nash, Boudinot, and the other members of the New York Kidnapping Club.[15]

Armed with a warrant from Hays, Nash returned to Ruggles's front door in the middle of the night with his posse, which included Joseph Michaels, one of the crewmates on the *Brilliante*

A poster alerting citizens of a "seditious" lecture on abolitionism.
(Library of Congress)

hungry to punish Ruggles for his interference. According to Ruggles, under Michaels's hat a small handwritten note lay hidden, which he later learned was authorization in the hand of High Constable Hays to seize Ruggles as a slave. Luckily, though, when Nash left Lispenard Street to see Hays, Ruggles had slipped out a back door. Thwarted, Nash declared that "had I caught the fellow out the door, we would have fixed him." Michaels, the Portuguese slave ship crewman, agreed: "Yes, if he would not go, I would soon have put an end to his existence; he would never interfere with Brazilians again." For the moment, Ruggles had escaped.[16]

Ruggles was not one to remain in hiding, however, and the next day he went at noon to City Hall to see Nash himself. As soon as Ruggles entered the imposing Greco-Roman building, Boudinot pounced on Ruggles and dragged him to the police office. Ruggles protested the rough treatment and demanded to know why he was being arrested. Boudinot grabbed Ruggles, jammed him against one of the marble pillars of City Hall, and muttered, "I was after you last night."[17]

Before the city magistrate, Ruggles was charged with foment-
ing a riot on the *Brilliante* on Christmas Eve, which the activist
denied, stating unequivocally that he had only visited the ship
during the day. "If he did not do it," Nash said of Ruggles, "some
of the Blacks did, and he is the ring-leader among them." In less
than twenty minutes, Boudinot had Ruggles on the way to Belle-
vue Prison. Ruggles was convinced that the ultimate goal of the
kidnapping club was to sell him into southern slavery, a suspicion
strengthened by the knowledge that the infamous slave catcher
Edward R. Waddy, a sheriff in Northampton County, Virginia, had
been lurking in New York and was preparing to take kidnapping
victims to Savannah.[18]

Ruggles was charged with resisting arrest, but he was eventually released; rather than causing him to back down, the arrest
only fortified his will further. He was already beginning to lose
his sight gradually because of an unknown medical condition,
but even after his latest encounter with the New York Kidnapping
Club he remained steadfast. "[I] take fresh courage," Ruggles
wrote to the New York newspapers, "in warning my endangered
brethren against a gang of kidnappers, which continues to infest
our city and the country, to kidnap men, women and children,
and carry them to the South; while Boudinot holds a warrant, by
which he says he has been sending colored people to the South
for the last three years, and with which he boasts he can send any
black to the South."[19]

The city's conservatives relished the possibility that the radical
troublemaker might be chastened by the arrest and imprisonment.
In the view of the *Morning Courier* and its editor, the abolitionists'
interference in the *Brilliante* case was "one of hundreds of impudent and insolent attempts on the part of the blacks to violate the
laws and interfere with the authority of the magistrates." It really
wasn't their fault entirely, the paper condescendingly claimed,
since white abolitionists like Arthur Tappan "have instilled into
them a conviction that they are an injured and oppressed race."
Yet Ruggles did not intend to give his conservative critics the sat-
isfaction of retreating from his now-famous vigilance. Just a few

months after his arrest, Ruggles sounded the alarm again when officers arrested George Jones.[20]

At noon on a Saturday, officers approached Jones at 21 Broadway, a boardinghouse for many of the city's small merchants and shopkeepers. The policemen claimed that Jones was wanted for assault and battery, and Jones knew that he had committed no such offense. But Jones's employers suggested he go willingly with the officers and that they would help straighten the matter out. Within an hour or two of being taken to Bridewell, it became clear that Jones had been arrested for being a runaway slave. Police in pursuit of fugitive slaves often initially accused Black New Yorkers of minor crimes so that they would not put up a fight. Boudinot, Nash, and other officers knew that accused runaways would risk their lives to avoid capture, so they lied and claimed a lesser crime had prompted the arrest. By two o'clock Jones was brought before Recorder Riker, who quickly proclaimed Jones a slave. As Ruggles put it, "In less than three hours after his arrest, he was bound in chains, dragged through the streets, like a beast in shambles!" Presumably Jones was sold into southern slavery.[21]

Ruggles had had enough. He fired off letters to New York newspapers, reminding the Black community that "we are all liable; your wives and children are at the mercy of merciless kidnappers." To the city's white residents, he had a warning: "Self-defense is the first law of nature . . . come what will, anything is better than slavery." Ruggles was beginning to lose patience with any peaceful approach to ending the abuse and asserted that when faced with abduction, Black people would use violence to resist when necessary.[22]

Riker must have been feeling the pressure, because in the case of Abraham Gosley, which exploded onto the front pages of New York papers in September 1836, the recorder seemed more troubled than usual when it came to sending a man into slavery. Sometime in late August, Francis Collier had discovered that one of his absconded men had fled a Maryland plantation and settled in New York, and with the help of slave hunters he claimed Abraham was really Jesse Collier. Nearly all of the fugitive slave trials focused on the identity of the accused, and the Gosley case was no

different. Was Abraham Gosley in fact Jesse Collier? Or was this a case of mistaken identity? Before photographs were used by common people for identification, before fingerprinting or other ways to ascertain one's uniqueness, the task was much harder. Instead, Riker and other judges had to rely on paper documentation and witness testimony.[23]

In Gosley's case, Black witnesses Sarah Mendes and Catherine Peel, who lived together in a boardinghouse at 149 Suffolk Street, testified that they had lived in the same house with Gosley since July 1834, two years before the slave owner Collier claimed Abraham had run away. Mendes, a washerwoman whose husband drove a stone cart, agreed with Peel that Gosley had been living and working in the city long before he was supposed to have escaped from Maryland. Peel was questioned vigorously by Collier's lawyers, but she held her ground. She knew her dates were correct, Peel told the court, because she was sick two winters ago and Gosley had helped Peel's daughter bring in wood. She would never forget that winter, because her sixteen-month-old baby died and was buried in Chase's Burial Ground. "I am telling the truth," Peel testified, "and am not mistaken." Two men of color, James Moore and William Thomas, also testified that they had known Gosley in New York since at least August 1834. During the testimony of one Black witness, a white Marylander stood up and yelled, "It is a damned lie!"[24]

Collier collected his own witnesses, like Edmund Weatherby, who testified that he lived near the Collier farm and had known Jesse Collier for six years. Collier's lawyer asked Weatherby on the stand whether Jesse was present in the courtroom, and he dramatically turned and pointed to Gosley. Some of the white witnesses from Maryland became rowdy and "behaved with the greatest insolence during the trial." Southern whites had read in their own newspapers about runaways being declared free, and the Marylanders had arrived in New York with the idea that in Gotham Black rights would supersede those of whites. Riker, usually a stickler for decorum in his courtroom, did not dress the men down, much to the surprise of other observers in the courtroom. It seemed to

Black attendees of the trial that Riker was bending over backward to appease the white southerners.[25]

With the all-too-common problem of conflicting Black and white witnesses, Riker turned to the available paper documentation. African Americans not under slavery carried "free papers," official written documents that indicated their status as free people. These papers contained specific physical descriptions of the bearer, including details about height, skin tone, scars, and other minute details. In the midst of the trial, Gosley's attorney produced free papers that described "a man of color named Abraham Gosley . . . being the son of a free woman of color" in Somerset County, Maryland. He was "five feet three inches in height, and of dark chestnut complexion; he has a scar on the right hand between the thumb and wrist and one on the outer part of his left thigh." As Riker could see, the accused runaway sitting in his court did in fact have the same scars and the same skin tone as the free papers indicated. There was one major problem, though: the man claiming to be Gosley was at least five-six, three inches taller than the Gosley portrayed in the free papers.

Could Gosley have grown three inches in the last year or two? According to the free papers, he was already twenty-four, past the usual age for significant growth in stature. Dr. Stephen Browne was called to the court to shed light on the possibility. He had examined Gosley and confirmed that the scars listed in the document were also on Gosley's body, but it was not unheard of for runaways to use knives to make their bodies conform to those listed on free papers. Dr. Browne did recall a case in the medical journals of a woman who moved from Virginia to New York City and had in fact grown three inches, but it seemed unlikely that a man in his mid-twenties could have grown that much.[26]

Riker was leaning toward declaring Abraham Gosley to be Jesse Collier and therefore a slave. He told Gosley and the Black witnesses not to worry too much, though. If he was wrong, then the judges in Maryland "would no doubt do him justice, and set him at liberty; for they were fully as tenacious of the liberty of colored people as any Judge here could be." There was absolutely

no evidence to support this stunning claim, and the Black community was flabbergasted. As Gosley was handcuffed in court to be taken back to Bridewell, several Black men created a commotion, surrounded the officers, and yelled threats at the police. John Bowman, Thomas Nichols, and George W. Jennings were charged with trying to obstruct justice by freeing Gosley.[27]

Ruggles was again incensed and accused Riker of being the ringleader of the New York Kidnapping Club. Riker was used to being the subject of Ruggles's ire, but by the fall of 1836, after he had been at the center of a number of New York fugitive slave cases, Riker let the criticism boil over.

One of the tasks of the recorder in the Court of Sessions was to oversee cases involving petty theft, disorderly conduct, counterfeiting, domestic assault, and other ordinary crimes. On a typical day at the end of October, Riker oversaw the usual march of cases through his court, including many allegedly committed by people of color. Given the criticism heaped on Riker by Ruggles and other Black leaders, the recorder was beginning to crack, and he erupted in court with an ad hoc diatribe that revealed his true feelings. After several Black New Yorkers appeared in court, Riker remarked (in comments paraphrased and reprinted in newspapers throughout the city) that it "was an ill omen of what might be expected as the consequence of immediate abolition of slavery in the United States." The recorder complained that "no sessions ever passed without a considerable number of them being convicted of crimes against the peace and prosperity of our fellow citizens. . . . What must be expected if two millions of slaves were at once let loose upon society?" Riker didn't stop there, declaring that the end of slavery "would be such a scene of anarchy, confusion and bloodshed." The judge then gave a wink to his friends on Wall Street, reminding the courtroom that abolitionism would "annihilate our commerce, and rend asunder that Union which our forefathers cemented with their blood." Riker ended by denouncing abolitionists from England and other nations who came to America to stir up trouble.[28]

Infuriated by Riker's comments, African American leaders responded with public letters printed in the New York papers. In the *New York Evening Post,* a writer signed "Immediatist," possibly Ruggles, accused Riker of spreading "darkness" and of sowing "the seeds of distrust in the community." Thomas Van Rensselaer, a former enslaved man in New York who had escaped and founded a restaurant in the city called Temperance House, hit back harder: "I think you have done the colored people of this city a great injustice." The New York activist specifically addressed Riker's claim that Blacks were prone to crime, pointing out that many of them were poor and disadvantaged. When a Black man accused a white man of a crime like assault, Van Rensselaer argued, courts distrusted Black testimony and "the white man goes unpunished." White citizens always received the benefit of the doubt and could escape prosecution for crimes for which Blacks were imprisoned. Van Rensselaer even admitted that "while we have not improved our own condition as much as we could wish, I can . . . show you many hundreds of families, that are living as comfortable and happy as any white families in the middle walks of life." As for the efforts of foreign activists to promote abolitionism in America, Van Rensselaer stated flatly that "we are like the Greeks, or the Poles, or any other oppressed people in this respect, and feel very grateful to any nation or individual that sympathizes with us."[29]

IN LIGHT OF RIKER'S racist comments, the sorry outcomes of the slave ship cases, the demoralizing Gosley/Collier trial, and other attacks on their civil rights, New York's African Americans entered the final months of 1836 angry and frustrated. After four children vanished in just four weeks in November, Ruggles declared publicly that "our city is infested with kidnappers." Eleven-year-old John Dickerson was sent on an errand to deliver a note and was never heard from again. John Robinson Welch, a mixed-race child of about eight, disappeared from his home on Mulberry Street at the end of February. Thomas Bryan and Thomas Oliver had been

taken into slavery in Vicksburg, Mississippi, and New Orleans, respectively. The New York Kidnapping Club was as busy as ever.[30]

Ruggles and his Black neighbors were determined to be not merely victims but to fight back. Gathered at Phoenix Hall toward the end of 1836, the Black community was desperate to identify "further measures in the relation to the continual practice of kidnapping." Many of the city's leading Black activists stood at the front of the hall, which was housed in a school for Black children on Chapel Street. Founded by leading African Americans just a couple of years prior by the Phoenix Society, the school and its hall were devoted to instruction in "morals, literature, and the mechanic arts." Thomas Van Rensselaer and John J. Washington called the meeting to order. Not surprisingly, Ruggles—who seemed to be everywhere in New York working for racial justice—also led the meeting. The audience quieted down, took their seats, and listened solemnly to one case of kidnapping after another.[31]

Yet what power did they have to stop the abduction of their children, mothers, and fathers? They could gather outside of courtrooms and Bridewell Prison to protest, and many times over the past few years their frustration and anger had spilled into the streets. Black New Yorkers had even tested the strategy of overtaking courtrooms to wrestle victims from the clutches of Riker and the New York Kidnapping Club, a strategy that would be used more and more in the coming years. Without the ability to vote or hold political office, without the chance to accumulate wealth in the face of segregation and racism in the workplace, what else could they do? Despite the overwhelming odds against them, Gotham's people of color constantly resisted, individually and collectively.

Like many such meetings of exasperated Black New Yorkers, those gathered at Phoenix Hall acknowledged their reliance on the basic goodness of white New Yorkers and a faith in their ability to see injustice around them. Whether that faith was justified or not, only time would tell. But for now, the belief that shedding light on kidnapping and other forms of abuse would affect the sense of justice among white New Yorkers prevailed. Black New Yorkers sought to make whites aware of the fact that "the

barbarous practice of kidnapping continually menaces, endangers, and invades the peace, safety and liberty of every colored citizen." Just as terrifying, "Captains of Merchants' vessels, Slaveholders, Slavetraders, and their kidnapping agents have sold into slavery citizens of the State of New York." The resolutions, in fact, singled out Recorder Riker for his role in the New York Kidnapping Club, scorning his eagerness to ignore Black witness testimony and believe the claims of white slave owners.[32]

As much as they tried to be optimistic about white intentions, the men and women of the Black community heard one story that night that stood out above the other tales of cruelty: the dark and now forgotten saga of Hester Jane Carr, who had been arrested and taken into bondage to be sold as a slave in Petersburg, Virginia. Carr's story is one of the nation's gloomiest in the long and sordid history of American slavery. Much like Solomon Northup, who wrote *Twelve Years a Slave*, Carr was kidnapped even though she was a free woman. Unlike Northup's experience, though, Carr's did not have a happy ending.

Born sometime around 1815 in Accomack County, Virginia, on the southern tip of the Delmarva Peninsula, Carr came from a free family. Her father, Jacob Walton, was a farmer and hired hand who built the family home himself, while her mother, Anna Carr, kept house. Like almost all free Black southerners, the family lived a precarious existence, and Virginia politicians periodically threatened to expel free African Americans like Walton and Carr. Perhaps because of fears over her safety, young Hester lived for a time with her aunt, also a free Black woman, with a home a few miles away. The family's welfare became even more fragile when Jacob left to find work in New York City but died from smallpox not long after his arrival. Hester and her mother tried to carve out a meager life in farming, but when Anna also passed away, Hester decided to follow in her father's footsteps to see if she could find less racial discrimination and greater economic opportunity in Manhattan.

Hester found work quickly. In the home of Dr. James Cockcroft, she became a domestic servant to help with household

chores like cooking and cleaning. Sitting on a prominent block at 24 Forsyth Street, the house was just a block away from the home of Sojourner Truth and a short but safe distance away from Five Points. Working in the home of a prominent surgeon, Hester likely felt like she had landed quite well. However, if a better job offer might appear, she promised herself that she would remain open to the possibility.

That chance came a year later when Hester met a stranger named Nancy Haws, who was in New York on vacation with her paramour, Timothy Collins. Haws told Hester that she needed a personal maid back home in Columbus, Georgia, and she enticed Hester with the promise of a much improved salary. Hester left the Cockcroft family and unwisely trusted Haws to take her safely all the way to Georgia. They boarded a ship called the *Golden Hunter* and ventured south along the Atlantic coast.

The ship first landed in Virginia, likely somewhere around Norfolk, and then Hester and Haws traveled inland. Telling Carr that they were now in slave territory, Haws convinced Hester to pretend to be a slave so as not to run afoul of the many laws against free Blacks. When one slave trader in Petersburg asked if she was a slave, she sealed her own fate: she answered yes, thinking she was duping an official and that she would soon be on the way to Columbus. Nancy Haws quickly sold Hester for $750 to the slave-trading firm of Beasley and Wood and ran off with the money.

Richard Beasley and William Wood had founded their business to buy enslaved people in Virginia and sell them in the still largely undeveloped lands in Mississippi and Louisiana. In the decades before the Civil War, many slave-trading firms chose the same path: they would buy slaves in the older South Atlantic states, where the soil had been depleted by two centuries of farming, transport the newly purchased people by boat or over land, and sell them for a profit in the bustling new areas of settlement in the Gulf States. Once the southern lands along the Gulf of Mexico had been largely cleared of Native Americans, a cruel and dark part of the nation's history symbolized by the Trail of Tears, more than one million enslaved people would be forcibly moved from older

states like Virginia and the Carolinas to Alabama, Arkansas, Texas, and the more recently admitted states of the Union. Now in the hands of Beasley and Wood, Hester feared with good reason that she would never be free again. The devastated and dumbfounded Hester Carr found herself on the auction block in the same state in which she had been born free nineteen years before.

Hester protested and called for help, so the slave trader had her lodged in the Petersburg jail. Some white Virginians, including a lawyer named William C. Parker, who had served in the unenviable role of counsel for the defense in Nat Turner's trial a few years prior, believed that African Americans deserved to be heard. Parker visited Hester Carr in jail, listened to her sad account, and promised to help.

Parker first wrote to James Cockcroft to corroborate Hester's statement of having been abducted in New York. Cockcroft confirmed that Hester had worked for his family and that she had been lured away rather suddenly. To make sure Parker and Cockcroft were discussing the same woman, the New York surgeon offered a detailed description of Hester. She was about five feet, two inches tall, with closely cropped hair, a stout build, and a dark complexion. Hester also apparently stuttered, which she tried to conceal "by speaking very fast." Parker also secured an affidavit from Hester's cousin Mary Crippen, who lived in Brooklyn. It became quite obvious that Hester Carr had been kidnapped.[33]

In Virginia, though, the testimony of African Americans was only admissible with the corroboration of two or three people, and Parker could count Dr. Cockcroft as the only white witness. The case was heard in the court of Petersburg, and the proceedings of *Hester Jane Carr vs. Richard R. Beasley* attracted notice as far away as London. Unfortunately, the first decision handed down declared Carr a slave, and Beasley and Wood prepared to sell her southward. But Parker asked the court to reconsider and the case dragged on for months. Before a final decision could be rendered, Hester Carr died in prison. She was only twenty-one years old.[34]

Ruggles had seen so many cases like Carr's that he hardly knew how to respond. White jurists, police officers, and lawyers

were quick to uphold the rights of slaveholders and slave traders, "but when the rights and interests of the colored man are
concerned—ah! Now the public functionary is clothed with infalli-
bility, to question or censure his doings and decisions is little short
of blasphemy—the community are well-nigh horror struck at such
astonishing rudeness, and it becomes you most reverently to lay
your hand upon your mouth and be still!" Those who knew Ruggles knew it was not in his character to shut up and remain inert.[35]

No matter how vehemently Black activists protested against
such abuse, the members of the New York Kidnapping Club were
as powerful and prolific as they had ever been, as they had demonstrated all too clearly in the cases of Abraham Gosley and Hester
Carr. Boudinot, Nash, Riker, the New York police, Wall Street and
its Democratic Party allies, Judge Betts, and indeed the whole of
the city's political and legal apparatus seemed powerfully arrayed
against the growing but struggling Black community.

Just as important, New York authorities were helping to buttress
slavery in the South, since runaways returned to plantations to be
made an example. Riker and Boudinot may have cared little about
the lives of individual accused fugitives, but normal practice was to
make a public lesson out of those who had absconded. Runaways
embarrassed masters who liked to claim that they treated their
"property" so well that there was no need to abscond, and chasing
after fugitives cost time and money. So when enslaved people like
Jones were returned to bondage, they were often publicly whipped
and shamed, displays of vengeance that warned other people from
fleeing bondage. With every over-policed neighborhood turning
Black residents into criminals and fugitives, New York's political
and municipal leaders were bolstering American slavery.

Chapter Six

Economic Panic

W HEN THE NEW YEAR'S CELEBRATIONS ENDED ON JANUARY 1, 1837, Wall Street merchants and financiers had every reason to be proud of the previous year's accomplishments and every reason to be optimistic about their prosperity enduring. Just twelve months before, one newspaper had lamented, "the city was in a few short hours reduced to a heap of ashes and waste." The Great Fire of 1835 had destroyed much of Lower Manhattan, including the wooden wharves and the ships secured to them, and inland across block after block of wooden-framed commercial buildings. But in its place—in just one year—Wall Street had become a world-renowned district that connected the South to markets in Liverpool and Manchester and across the rest of the globe. In the wake of the fire, the newspaper marveled, "has arisen stately rows of buildings, forming a spectacle more imposing than can be seen in the commercial section of any city in the world." Nearly five hundred stores had opened up in the area, and the impressive elevation of the Stock Exchange demonstrated stability and audacity, while the "teeming commerce" on which the city's affluence was built seemed as sturdy and unwavering as the fluted columns guarding the exchange.[1]

With this miraculous recovery from the Great Fire in mind, Governor William Marcy again delivered his State of the State speech, and he wasted no time in berating his favorite target. In just the second paragraph of his address, the Democrat crowed that the abolitionism he had warned New Yorkers about in the previous year's message was on the run. During the last State of the State speech, Marcy had devoted considerable space to the "crimes" of the antislavery movement, particularly the hazards of angering the white South. A year later, Marcy now told his fellow New Yorkers that public patience with the agitators had waned, and with it any chance that abolitionists could influence the direction of northern politics. Thankfully, Marcy maintained, the ability of men like Ruggles and Arthur Tappan "to disturb the friendly relations among members of our Federal Union" had come to an end. Abolitionists were mere dying embers, momentarily burning but destined to fade, like the final gasps of the Great Fire itself. With the fire's waste cleared away, and with the equally inflammatory activism of the abolitionists extinguished, the path to New York's fortune seemed clear.[2]

On both counts Governor Marcy's optimism proved chimerical. New York's antislavery movement was not waning, as the city's political and legal authorities had hoped. In fact, thanks to the indefatigable Ruggles and his allies, the battles against police abuse, the struggles against the New York Kidnapping Club, the valiant attempts to end the use of the city's harbor as a way station for the transatlantic slave trade, would be engaged anew. Neither would the confidence in the city's enduring commercial success last long. Less than a month after Marcy's address, New York would be thrown into chaos as a result of an unprecedented economic panic that would hit the Atlantic economy like a tsunami.

The economic crisis seemed to come from nowhere. The past few years had seen rising prices for cotton, in turn raising the prices of slaves, and the economy seemed to be overheating. The economies of England and the United States were intertwined in complicated ways that promoted Atlantic affluence but also rendered the two countries mutually dependent and vulnerable.

North America and Western Europe had suffered economic depressions before, most notably in 1819, but this latest round of tightening credit, business bankruptcies, and moribund trade had exploded with a suddenness and severity that shocked everyone. In late 1836, the Bank of England raised interest rates, and by January 1837 American banks had followed suit. President Andrew Jackson's "Specie Circular" further tightened lending by requiring all western land purchases to be conducted in gold or silver rather than paper money. Land prices plummeted, and the price of cotton dropped more than 25 percent by the spring. Almost immediately the economy ground to a halt in what became known as the Panic of 1837, something of a misnomer since not until the early 1840s would it recover.[3]

Southern planters and merchants across the Black Belt experienced extreme financial hardship, unable to garner credit to fund shipments and unable to attract high enough profits for the bales already in transit. New Orleans merchants were wiped out seemingly overnight. Shops in Charleston and St. Louis selling fine French linens or fancy furniture made in England closed permanently. Newer plantations in the southwestern states of Alabama and Mississippi, where Native Americans were being killed and displaced to make room for white settlers hungry for new cotton land, went under. Cotton prices dropped precipitously, and many southern farmers defaulted on loans provided by New York banks, which lost nearly one hundred million dollars in the crisis. Such financial desperation made slave owners, whether they owned just a few bondsmen or hundreds, eager to recover losses caused by runaways. After all, a single male hand in his twenties could bring over $1,000 in this period. Planters set their sights on recovering these losses, which only enflamed the already dire crisis of kidnappings and slave renditions led by the likes of Boudinot and the New York Kidnapping Club.[4]

In New York, newspapers began reporting on the crisis just days after Governor Marcy's sanguine address. In mid-January one paper reported that the Alms House, the city's chief support for the poor, "was thronged with male and female applicants to

the number of 2000, who came thither to solicit relief in wood and eatables, as out of door paupers." Many of the homeless were immigrant families from Ireland. Women and children were offered food and blankets, but the men "were ordered to go and earn a living." As a consequence of the credit squeeze, however, businesses were not hiring. The normally active wharves around Lower Manhattan, with their shouting stevedores moving crates and barrels of goods from around the world, grew quiet. The hundreds of stores that had emerged from the ashes over the past year were at a standstill. What goods that could be had were priced at gouging levels. The city was ready to explode.[5]

The eruption began as a call for protest. In early February posters were printed and hung around the city:

BREAD, MEAT, RENT, FUEL! THEIR PRICES MUST COME DOWN!

The Voice of the People Shall be Heard, and Will Prevail!
The People will meet in the PARK, Rain or Shine
All Friends of Humanity, determined to resist
Monopolists and Extortioners, are invited to attend.

In response to the call, thousands of working-class New Yorkers began to gather in the early afternoon of February 11. The conservative press scoffed that "the worst passions" of a mob made up "chiefly of foreigners" threatened the power and wisdom of Wall Street. But the riots were based on real misery that had taken hold throughout the poorer communities of New York, and would not be quelled easily or quickly. The Flour Riots, as they became known, wracked the police and political leaders in a demonstration of a basic fact: the opulence of New York and Liverpool was built on the backs of working white and Black people on both sides of the Atlantic.[6]

With more than five thousand people gathered in front of City Hall, speakers like labor radical Alexander Ming denounced the rich and their control over the lives of laborers. Ming directly challenged one baron, Eli Hart, who Ming claimed was hoarding more than fifty thousand barrels of flour that the poor could use to make bread. At the end of his speech, burly men lifted Ming onto their shoulders and carried him to Tammany Hall. The crowd then marched down Broadway until they reached Hart's flour warehouse on Washington Street. Three large doors marked the front of the warehouse, and within minutes the protesters had broken open the middle one, removed two dozen barrels, and spread the flour in the street.

Police officers led by the ubiquitous chief constable Jacob Hays arrived, but rioters grabbed their wooden clubs and broke the barrels in half. Mayor Cornelius Lawrence appeared to try to calm the protesters, but they threw flour at him until he left. The rioters then took out more flour barrels and bags of wheat and tossed papers and desks out the window. Other warehouses across Lower Manhattan felt the crowd's wrath into the night, and dozens were arrested. The next day, as the arrested demonstrators were paraded in court, several violent attempts were made to rescue the prisoners. It was mayhem on Wall Street.[7]

Some in the press acknowledged the plight of the city's working class and called for leniency. As one paper argued, newspapers "must not permit the corrupt Wall street press to monopolize the sympathy of those good citizens" who were protesting but not involved in violence. "We are engaged in a holy cause," the *New York Herald* declared, "against the deep, damnable, juggling corruptions of the whole Wall Street press." New Yorkers should trust "Recorder Riker and the Court of Sessions" to identify and punish the rioters without a wholesale denunciation of the workers' miserable situation.[8]

Reports of bank failures, business closings, and laid-off workers blared from the headlines. News from New Orleans cotton markets was dismal, as cotton prices spiraled downward and bales sat rotting on the docks of ports in the United States and Great

Britain. Tales of several failures among the largest houses in New Orleans shocked and alarmed Wall Street brokers and financiers. By March, rumors of banks collapsing in England spread panic across the Atlantic.[9]

New York's African Americans watched the economic turmoil and social unrest among the white working poor with a great deal of trepidation. Would Black neighborhoods be next to feel the wrath of immigrant mobs? Would abolitionists come under attack again in a new and devastating wave of anti-Black violence as the city had experienced in the summer of 1834? Ruggles, Van Rensselaer, and other Black leaders kept a watchful eye on the protests.

Anti-Black riots weren't their only worry; other New Yorkers with official capacities seemed to have resorted to questionable practices. Ruggles accused the Alms House, a city-supported homeless shelter, and its director, Losee Van Nostrand, of operating a slave-trading business that victimized the poorest Black residents of Manhattan and Brooklyn. Toward the end of 1837 and into the spring of 1838, Ruggles followed what he called a "strange occurrence" when a Black woman and two children were removed from the Alms House in the middle of the night and taken to Bridewell. The next day the family had disappeared, and Ruggles hurried to interview Van Nostrand, who was "cautious and uncommunicative." Ruggles tried to persuade the Alms House overseer to reveal where the family had gone and worried that Van Nostrand was "sending free born citizens of this state to the South as slaves, because they were poor and needy." Ruggles was right to be concerned, because reports had emerged that African American cadavers were secretly being bought and sold for medical research. Newspaper readers learned that the bodies of four of their citizens had been stuffed into barrels and shipped to South Carolina for medical research. White city newspapers made light of the business, headlining their stories "Pickled Negroes" and "Human Pork."[10]

As trade with the southern cotton producers stood still and the financial crisis paralyzed Wall Street, Boudinot and Nash stepped

up the efforts of the New York Kidnapping Club to make money. The Panic of 1837 only increased the hunger for victims.

At the same time, Ruggles himself came under withering attack from the conservative Wall Street press. The *Morning Courier*, published at 56 Wall Street, led the charge. "A black scoundrel named David Ruggles," an editorial declared, was guilty of "gross insolence upon this community." Editor James Watson Webb was particularly irked that Ruggles, whom the paper called a "brawling troublesome fellow," constantly criticized Riker, Boudinot, Nash, and the kidnapping club. "We have, of course, nothing to do with the negro," but his example means "that every sable vagabond is at liberty to libel the officers of government, the city authorities, and all others." The Wall Street press remained concerned that abolitionist agitation would anger the South and further hamper commerce, and they censured abolitionists like Ruggles for placing the interests of Black people over trade, the Constitution, and the Union.[11]

Conservative New Yorkers within the business elite realized that contrary to Governor Marcy's claim that the antislavery movement was dying, in fact the crusade was very much alive. White and Black abolitionists were busy making plans, setting up newspapers to promote the cause, and hiring writers and editors. The New York Anti-Slavery Society office had established a prominent presence across from City Hall Park on Nassau Street, and with funding from wealthy benefactors like Arthur Tappan, New York's abolitionists tried to reinforce their movement in case their fears of an attack came to fruition. For example, the society tried to recruit white abolitionist James G. Birney, a Kentucky-born successful planter and slave owner who had begun to doubt the morality of bondage in the 1820s. By the following decade he was living in Cincinnati and editing an antislavery paper called *The Philanthropist*. Birney's status as a former slave owner who through his own conscience had come to believe in immediate abolition seemed to lend credence to claims that moral persuasion was the right path for the antislavery movement.

Soon the New York Anti-Slavery Society was recruiting Birney to live and work in Gotham. Society secretary Henry B. Stanton wrote to Birney and tried to convince him to move to New York: "The field is the nation. From N.Y. you can exert an influence upon the whole field . . . you can put your stamp upon the abolitionism of the whole region." Stanton emphasized the city's emergence as an influential and connected city, which made it the ideal place to promote abolitionism in the Northeast. "Half of the moral power of the nation lies within 24 hours easy ride (mostly steamboat) of New York City. There the fulcrum must be placed by which we are to overturn the nation." Just as Wall Street gloated about the growing wealth and economic power of Manhattan, so too did abolitionists promote the city for the same reason.[12]

Antislavery sentiment appeared also to be slowly making headway in the halls of Congress. Former president John Quincy Adams, son of the second president, now representing Massachusetts's Twelfth Congressional District, spent much of the winter and spring of 1837 bringing abolitionist petitions to the floor of the House of Representatives. While Ruggles and other Black activists appreciated Adams's efforts on behalf of the antislavery movement, Wall Street wrung its hands in fear of southern reaction. As the *Journal of Commerce* complained, "It is painful to see a man who has shared the highest honors which the country can bestow, thus throwing away his influence, for no imaginable good." The elder statesman's appeals to abolition could only sow "strife and confusion," especially among the slaveholding states. Didn't the nation have enough to worry about with trade ground to a halt and the poor rioting in the streets? "It would be well if our very existence as a nation were not to be put at hazard by the efforts of a set of men who value the Union less than the rights . . . of the slaves," the *Journal of Commerce* moaned.[13]

WITH POVERTY AND UNEMPLOYMENT crippling the city, tensions between the Black community and the police deteriorated further. Relations between the New York constables, from Chief Constable

Hays's sprawling office down to Boudinot's beat in the Third Ward, and African Americans had almost always been fraught with tension, but in the wake of the panic even routine interactions became filled with violence. In one instance, Philip Doyle, an Irish city marshal and street inspector in the Fourth Ward, tried to serve a warrant on a Black man named Allen, accused of stowing away on ships from New York harbor. When Doyle went to serve the warrant on board the brig *Cumberland*, he was accosted by several Black men who threw Doyle into the forecastle. After a long while they let Doyle out, but he returned with reinforcements and arrested the whole group.[14]

The city's exasperated Black leaders called for another mass meeting to be led by leading African American professionals and merchants like Edward V. Clark, Henry Davis, and Philip Alexander Bell. Born free in New York, Bell became one of the city's leading editors.

Although they had a long list of grievances with the police, African American activists decided to work on one major goal. With

Prominent editor and activist Philip Alexander Bell. *(Schomburg Center for Research in Black Culture, Manuscripts, Archives and Rare Books Division, The New York Public Library)*

PHILLIP A. BELL.

the increase in kidnappings during the Panic, Bell demanded an explicit right to call witnesses in cases of accused runaway slaves. Gathered again at Phoenix Hall on Chapel Street, hundreds of Black citizens signed their names, declaring in a petition to the New York State legislature that "the undersigned fathers and mothers, and men and women of color of New-York" had been subjected to a rash of kidnappings without so much as a hearing, let alone a jury trial. In March, just a month after the Flour Riots rocked Wall Street, hundreds of activists in Manhattan and Brooklyn, together with white abolitionist allies like attorney Horace Dresser, petitioned the state legislature for the right to a trial by jury in all fugitive slave cases. Nearly one hundred fifty men and one hundred women from Brooklyn signed the petition in support of jury trials and sent the document to Albany. Alas, the motion was defeated, and it would be years before African Americans accused of being runaways would earn the right to a trial by jury.[15]

Even more ominous for African Americans, Boudinot and his fellow actors in the kidnapping club were becoming ever more efficient, especially since they did not have to worry about defending themselves or their actions before a jury. Still blandishing the writ that he had received from Governor Marcy five years before, Boudinot and his fellow officers turned their attention to their next victim.

Sixty-three-year-old Jacob Davis had a balding head and a gray beard and was nearly lame due to sore joints accrued over a lifetime of hard work. For several years he had lived in the city, marrying a woman who gave birth to their first child, and attending a Baptist church each Sunday. Davis's wife, though, was mentally unstable and repeatedly threatened to tell the police he was a runaway. One day in the spring of 1837 she followed through on the threat: Davis was arrested by Nash and Boudinot after being claimed by a Virginia slaver named Henry Herman. Declared a slave by Recorder Riker, Davis was about to be sent south when it became clear that Herman didn't want him after all. The Virginia master was hoping

that by claiming Davis he might spark a movement among the old man's friends in the Black community to buy his freedom.

Remarkably, Boudinot volunteered to serve as the mediator in the deal. An elected member of the New York police force became a broker between Herman and the friends of Davis. Boudinot stated the terms of the deal: if the abolitionists would pay Boudinot $260, plus expenses, he would let Davis go with a deed indicating his free status. Boudinot would pocket $110, while Herman would get the $150 he requested. When that deal fell through, the Colonization Society asked if he wanted to be sent to the African colony of Liberia. The society offered to buy his liberty and sail him across the Atlantic. But Davis demurred, saying he would rather return to southern slavery than to a strange continent he knew little about. So Boudinot renewed his offer to the abolitionists and the Black churches, who raised more than $300 to purchase his freedom.[16]

While imprisoned in Bridewell, Davis befriended another inmate named William Dixon, one whose storied case would shake the Black community to its very core. Like many of New York City's thousands of working-class African Americans, Dixon rose early one April morning in 1837 to head to work. Though he had worked as a sawyer, painter, and in other odd jobs, his current employment as a whitewasher demanded an early rise, and he could not afford to be late. At thirty-seven, Dixon was six feet tall, powerfully built with a high forehead, and had the confident bearing of a commander or monarch. Though unusually regal in appearance, Dixon was like many New Yorkers who lived near the wharves along the East River: he worked hard, sang in the choir at Zion's Church on Sundays, left before sunrise, and came home after the sun went down.[17]

Even as they tried to live and work in peace, though, African Americans constantly looked over their shoulder, and with good reason. Today William Dixon's neighborhood lies between Chinatown and Little Italy, but before it became surrounded by ethnic restaurants that exemplify the modern multicultural metropolis,

New York was a microcosm of the national turmoil over free-dom and slavery. And as Dixon and his fellow Black city residents knew, at any moment their lives as free citizens could be instantly transformed into a swirling nightmare of courts, slave masters, constables, and lawyers, all working together to pull them into the vortex of southern slavery.

Would this be the morning he would be seized and thrown into southern slavery? When Dixon kissed his wife early that morning, he knew that every step potentially brought him closer to danger. But what choice did he have? He had to work. He had to earn money to pay for rent and food.

On April 4, 1837, Dixon's luck ran out and he was arrested just as he crossed the threshold of his home. Alas, he had fallen into the crooked hands of Nash and Boudinot. In minutes New York police officers had seized Dixon and stashed him in a New York prison, where he remained shackled for a week until he was finally brought to the New York Hall of Justice before New York City recorder Riker.[18]

Early in the afternoon of April 11, Dixon stood before Riker. Though his voice shook with emotion, Dixon stood with "grace and dignity" in front of the hearing. "It is hard, your Honor," Dixon told Riker, "it is hard to be thus treated in this land of liberty. I am an innocent man. I am a freeman. I have a wife that I love. It is hard to be torn from my family, and thrust into prison like a dog—merely because, being a *colored* man, I claim to be a *freeman*." Though he spoke clearly, his eyes filled with tears. As solitary as he might have felt at the moment, though, he was not alone. Several hundred of the city's Black citizens had heard of Dixon's arrest, and those who could not find a seat in the crowded courtroom stood impatiently outside.[19]

Dixon and his sympathizers placed their fate in the hands of antislavery lawyers like Horace Dresser to keep them free with any legal arguments they could muster before Riker. The details of the arrest quickly became known. Dr. Walter Allender claimed Dixon was really his property Jacob Ellis, who had run away from Baltimore in 1832. Allender had enlisted New York lawyers John

A. Morrill, a prominent member of the Democratic Party, as well as Thomas Phenix, who had recently been a city district attorney. Often accused runaways were whisked away from the alleyways and wharves of New York without so much as a hearing, but at least Dixon now had the chance to convince Riker that he was not a runaway.

Dresser and Dixon knew Riker would be hard to convince, but they gathered half a dozen witnesses who claimed that they had seen Dixon in Boston and New York long before 1832. A frustrated Morrill and Phenix told Riker that the witnesses were lying and submitted that documents demonstrating Dixon's free status were counterfeit. As the lawyers parried, the Black observers in the courtroom remained calm and respectful. "You could not collect the same number of whites in this city," one white abolitionist in the room declared, who "would have been so quiet and orderly." The first day of the trial adjourned, and Riker ordered Dixon taken back to prison.[20]

Just as Dixon was being manacled, though, several Black men yelled, "To the Rescue!" and tried to seize Dixon from custody. Black men and women who had gathered by the hundreds in City Hall Park rushed to the scene. Several police officers, including Boudinot, joined the melee. Looking out of his window, Justice Bloodgood witnessed the struggle between the police and the would-be rescuers, and he also rushed in. Dixon was secreted away by his liberators and concealed in a cellar on Duane Street. One African American slammed a police officer with a whitewash brush and nearly tore his ear in two. Boudinot pulled out his pistol, held it squarely in the protester's face, and fired, though the gun failed to go off. A "stout" Black woman seized Bloodgood around the neck in a crushing bear hug while another protester grabbed him by the heels and wrestled him to the ground. As Bloodgood lay on all fours, a number of protesters kicked him in the rear end.

Dixon had run away from the police at the first sign of trouble. A couple of protesters handed him a dirk and a spring knife, which he placed in his pocket as he ran down Chambers and Hudson Streets, with Boudinot and his fellow officers in hot pursuit. Dixon

reached a jeweler's shop on Reade Street, darted up the adjacent alley, and jumped through a coal vault. Constable Hays tracked Dixon down.[21]

A few days later, when jailer and deputy sheriff Fountain and Boudinot were taking Dixon from Bridewell, which was located near City Hall, to Riker's courtroom, they were followed by around one thousand African American protesters who had had enough of kidnapping. While white abolitionists like William Lloyd Garrison continued to maintain that moral persuasion was the backbone of antislavery, Black people themselves were beginning to doubt the power of that argument to change their lives. As the crowd grew more rowdy, a Black protester named James Parm suddenly rushed the police and Dixon, and began trying to wrest Dixon from Boudinot's grip. Another police officer grabbed Parm, and the crowd then attacked the officers. It seemed like a civil war had broken out in the streets of Lower Manhattan before Dixon was tracked down and found and taken back to Bridewell. As one white onlooker commented, "This is enough to abolitionize us all."[22]

Conservative New Yorkers, and even some Black authorities, were shocked and disgusted by the mob's attempt to thwart the proceedings. Reverend Samuel Cornish, editor of *Freedom's Journal* and *The Colored American*, two of the city's most important Black newspapers, wrote a lengthy apology to the white legal and political authorities. Cornish told his community to rely on the work of the New York Committee of Vigilance and its band of lawyers, and to avoid congregating outside of City Hall every time an accused fugitive was arrested. Clearly apologizing to judges like Riker and Bloodgood, Cornish considered himself a member of the Black elite and denounced "the ignorant part of our colored citizens." He especially chastised Black women who "so degraded themselves" at the rally; "we beg their husbands," Cornish condescendingly wrote, "to keep them at home for the time to come, and to find some better occupation for them." But Cornish also made clear that he was not apologizing to the "negro catchers" Nash and Boudinot or the New York lawyers

who supported the claims of southern slavers. When they die, Cornish remarked bitterly, "the grave worms will refuse to eat their rotten flesh."[23]

Not surprisingly, Cornish's apology to Judges Bloodgood and Riker went unappreciated, as became clear a week later. John Bloodgood, one of the justices of the peace for New York, was an overly opinionated and irascible judge who kept two large pistols on his desk in court. During Dixon's trial, Bloodgood took the opportunity to assail the Black rioters who had tried to rescue Dixon: "I should have liked no better sport than to shoot a half dozen damned n——. Damn their souls! I should have liked to send the damned n—— to hell!"[24]

When a new hearing opened in June, attendees of both races thronged the courtroom and repeatedly interrupted the proceedings to denounce either Dixon or the slaver Allender. Since both sides could produce witnesses testifying to the free or enslaved status of the accused, such hearings often devolved into a humiliating account of the suspected runaway's physical characteristics. In Dixon's case, he had an umbilical hernia that Allender had offered as evidence of his slave past. Allender compared the hernia "to a small egg, with the small end cut square off," a description confirmed by a New York doctor hired to examine Dixon. Through his lawyer, Dixon officially asked that his case be removed to the New York Supreme Court, declaring that he did "hereby *respectfully and solemnly* PROTEST against any further proceedings before the said Recorder." In the meantime, Ruggles and other Black activists began raising money to pay for Dixon's legal defense. Ruggles organized a collection for Dixon at an antikidnapping rally at Broadway Hall. As soon as he was able to make bail, Dixon fled with the help of the city's Underground Railroad until he secretly crossed the border into Canada, the real land of the free, where he could remain safe from the pursuit of the New York Kidnapping Club.[25]

The story of William Dixon reminds us that all of New York, from the bankers and insurance executives of Lower Manhattan to the poorest tenants of Five Points, was well aware that the periodic

crises over fugitive slaves and the kidnapping of free-born citizens were tearing the city apart. It may have occasionally saddened the heart of even the most ardent and aloof Wall Street merchant, but every so often the life of a person of color had to be sacrificed in order to placate white southerners. New Yorkers did not need reminding. The nation had grown to more than seventeen million people, but the connections binding the country together, links that were personal and familial as much as they were financial, meant that New Yorkers and southerners came into constant contact. Considering how vast the nation had become, it might still be surprising how often familiar faces bumped into each other far away from home. One chilling incident, involving one of the ringleaders of the New York Kidnapping Club, proved that such chance encounters could be treacherous.

Not long after William Dixon's trial and escape to Canada, Daniel Nash traveled to Savannah, Georgia, no doubt on an errand for a slave owner. Not long after arriving in that southern port city, Nash instantly recognized someone he knew from back home in New York: John Hopper, the son of well-known abolitionist Isaac Hopper. John had traveled to the South on business, not to cause any trouble regarding slavery, but Nash was ready to pounce.

After his evening tea, John Hopper had retired to his comfortable room in Savannah's prominent City Hotel. Within minutes of entering the room, Nash and more than a dozen drunk ruffians broke the door open, with Nash yelling, "This same Hopper, his brother and damned old father [and] David Ruggles, a damned n——, whom they treat as a brother—I'd give my own life to have him here—are the very leaders of Abolition in New York City." Just as Nash finished his brief speech, Hopper was punched in the face by one of the intruders. Right there in the hotel room they proceeded to put Hopper on trial for promoting abolitionism in the South. A large bloodthirsty crowd had gathered downstairs and outside of the hotel, waiting for a mere whisper to join the lynching.[26]

In search of any piece of evidence that might indicate his guilt, the men ordered Hopper to open his trunk, and when he didn't

move fast enough they snatched the keys away and forced it open, tossing clothes and other personal belongings around the room until they had discovered a suspicious bundle of pamphlets. Southern postmasters had just recently been flooded with antislavery pamphlets of northern origin, and protesters had angrily burned any such antislavery documents they could find. All of the pamphlets were harmless, save one that Hopper had been given by a clergyman during a stop in Charleston. Published by the Quakers, the booklet addressed colonization and specifically Sierra Leone. The ruffians believed that though it was hardly incendiary, the booklet was exactly what they were looking for.

Almost immediately the men shouted downstairs that they had found a trunk full of abolitionist booklets, telling Hopper to say his final prayers. The hotel's owner appeared and, worried that "my property will be destroyed," implored the men to take Hopper outside to the waiting crowd rather than risk any damage to the hotel. He turned to Hopper and said, "Young man, you are in a very unfortunate situation. You should never have left your home—but it is your own doing and you deserve your fate." Hopper proclaimed his innocence, and as the hotel owner went to fetch the mayor, the barkeeper brought Hopper a note. Scared for his life, almost resigned to his death by lynching, Hopper read the note: "His only chance of escape is by jumping out of the window!!" Hopper, though, knew this was likely a ruse, since "we were in the 3rd story [and] the street below was thronged with a drunken and infuriated mob."

Hopper had little choice but to go downstairs with the vigilantes. "I considered my fate inevitable," Hopper lamented, "and I determined to meet it with as much fortitude as possible." At the foot of the stairs, Hopper was met by Savannah's mayor and several of the city's political leaders, who were only able to calm the frothing mob by promising to place Hopper in jail, a move that likely saved his life.

While Hopper slept in a Savannah jail, Nash began to sober up but was no less vile and persistent in his charges against his fellow New Yorker. Nash told Savannah's authorities that Hopper's father

was "a great friend to the n—" and his brother a "n— amalgam-ator." In fact, Nash declared, "nine-tenths of the Northern men were abolitionists, but were ashamed to own it." Only after con-vincing Savannah's leaders that the so-called abolitionist pamphlet in his trunk promoted colonization, and not abolitionism, was he allowed to quietly slip out of town. Though eight hundred miles away from Gotham, John Hopper had fallen victim to the New York Kidnapping Club, barely escaping the South with his life.[27]

Once back home, Nash knew that he might be fired from his job as a city marshal after so nearly costing Hopper his life. Nash, however, claimed boldly that if the mayor fired him, "I'll make a business [of kidnapping]—I'll catch them whenever and wherever I can find them." As suspected, Nash was called into the mayor's office and dismissed. As Nash left the office with his pal and fel-low member of the New York Kidnapping Club John Wilder and stepped outside, he saw Ruggles waiting by the building. "Now, Ruggles, you have done something," Nash sneered, "but I'll be damned if I don't go at it now, harder than ever. I'll make a busi-ness of it now. It don't require a warrant from the mayor to catch n—s." Wilder grabbed Nash's arm and said, "Damn 'em, Nash. We'll see you righted." And the two left for Tammany Hall.[28]

As he had promised, Nash continued to join Boudinot, Wilder, and Virginia sheriff Edward Waddy in pursuing victims like George Thompson. Thompson worked as a gardener in Manhattanville, just a few blocks north of where Columbia University now stands. One late evening while he was asleep, he heard a knock on the front door that all Black residents had learned to fear. Thompson rose up, told his wife and five children to keep calm and quiet, and pulled the curtain aside to see an unknown Black man on his doorstep. Thompson knew it was cold outside so he unbolted the door, and before he could react, Boudinot, Nash, and Waddy had thrust open the door. Thompson reached for his gun, but Boudi-not grabbed a pistol in each hand and yelled, "Now raise a hand, and I'll see who will shoot the strongest." The gang began drag-ging Thompson out in his nightclothes. Waddy was from Virginia, and so when they were taking Thompson to Bridewell Prison,

Boudinot turned to Waddy and said, "Ned, you must not be seen here. Keep out of the way." Boudinot worried that working side by side with a Virginia sheriff would be suspicious. Waddy obliged, saying that he would "take $1200 for him, but shall take him back first." Boudinot, John Lyon, Nash, and the other members of the New York Kidnapping Club would no doubt get their cut as well.[29]

At first the keeper of Bridewell refused to imprison Thompson without an official approval, so Boudinot grabbed the cell door keys off the wall himself, threw his victim into prison, and walked away with the keys. Boudinot acted like he owned the place, and no one dared to stop him.

With Thompson lodged in Bridewell, Boudinot ventured into City Hall to obtain a certificate from Riker to take Thompson into slavery. Remarkably, years after Governor Marcy first authorized Boudinot to arrest the runaways from Virginia, Boudinot was still using the same document. In fact, the first paper had been so faded and worn by overuse in scores of fugitive slave cases that Boudinot had the document redrawn and authorized by Marcy on more sturdy parchment. It mattered not that the kidnapping gang had used the warrant to arrest many more African Americans than just Ben and the original runaways who had escaped from the docks of Norfolk in a whaleboat.

After leaving Thompson in Bridewell and checking in with Riker, Boudinot left City Hall and walked through City Hall Park. As Boudinot strolled through the park with its budding trees and springtime flowers emerging from their winter slumber, the city constable must have felt smugly satisfied that he was about to reap the profits of yet another victim. As he was walking, though, Josiah Hopper, an antislavery druggist who kept a store at Broadway and Franklin, noticed the constable and approached him. The Hoppers were well-known abolitionists in the Northeast, as Nash knew when he tried to have John Hopper lynched in Savannah. Josiah Hopper called Boudinot a kidnapper and (according to Boudinot) tried to strike him. Boudinot grabbed Hopper and pulled him into the police station to charge him with assault, but Hopper claimed that it was Boudinot who had committed assault. A

frustrated Recorder Riker, growing weary of fugitive slave cases and the attendant constant battles they caused, charged them both with assault. Yet another trial ensued.[30]

After having been involved in sending so many Black New Yorkers to the South, Riker was reluctant to get involved in Thompson's case. The courtroom was packed with African American activists like Ruggles, all of them watching the proceedings with a careful eye. Even the sheriff seemed to question Boudinot's five-year-old warrant, but Riker advised the sheriff to keep Thompson in jail until the matter was completely settled. At that moment, an elderly Quaker gentleman from the Hopper family rose in Riker's courtroom and asked to speak. Naively thinking that Riker might not have been fully aware of the extent of Boudinot's use of his well-worn warrant from Governor Marcy, the elder Hopper told the court that New York had been terrorized by kidnappers for years. Riker again refused to intervene.[31]

Since Riker washed his hands of the Thompson case, Boudinot then brought Thompson before Judge John T. Irving, who served with Michael Ulshoeffer on the Court of Common Pleas. Irving, the brother of Washington Irving of "The Legend of Sleepy Hollow" fame, authorized Waddy and Nash to bring Thompson into Virginia slavery. When Nash returned to New York, he told the New York Kidnapping Club that he had stayed to watch Thompson's trial for stealing the original small boat back in October 1832 that launched the exploits of the New York Kidnapping Club. Thompson was swiftly found guilty, Nash reported, and sentenced to be whipped and burned on his hands. In fact, Nash boasted that he had assisted in branding Thompson's hands with a hot iron.[32]

New York's political and legal systems acquiesced to this kind of abuse, Black citizens argued, because the city's economy was so dependent upon the southern cotton trade. The North was selling its soul, intellectuals like Samuel Cornish declared, in exchange for profits. Wall Street had made "deep and damning concessions . . . to the hydra system of slavery." When the northern states, "maddened with the greediness of gain, and the wildness of

Editor and activist
Samuel Cornish. *(New-York
Historical Society)*

speculation," allowed the Fugitive Slave Clause of the Constitution
to paper over the kidnapping of Black children, Cornish maintained, "prostration and ruin were inevitable and to be expected."[33]

RUGGLES EVEN UNCOVERED EVIDENCE that New Yorkers were actually
keeping slaves confined within the city. At the start of the summer, the activist found the evidence and then sent a warning to
antislavery newspapers that "not one in a thousand of your readers can be aware of the extent to which slavery prevails even in the
so-called free-state of New York." Ruggles found out that David
Stanford, one of the directors of the Brooklyn Bank and a member of the Methodist Episcopal Church, was using a loophole in
state law to keep people enslaved. According to the law, travelers
and businessmen could bring their enslaved property into the
city and state, as long as they intended to leave. This permitted
the constant influx of southern slaveholders to enter the city.

Slavers settling in the city were permitted to keep their chattel for up to nine months before the law required such enslaved people to be set free. But as Ruggles discovered, New York slave owners could just take their property across state lines and bring them back, resetting the clock every nine months! Ruggles revealed that he knew of at least eleven such cases in the city by the middle of 1837.[34]

In the meantime, the illegal transatlantic slave trade continued unabated. The British sent dozens of ships to patrol the African coast, but even the world's most powerful navy could hardly stem the tide. "The slave trade," remarked the *Journal of Commerce*, "is carried on to a greater extent than ever, and all under the Portuguese flag." With their long history of engaging in the lucrative slave trade, a business that brought them back and forth across the Atlantic and up and down the coasts of Africa and the Americas, Portuguese slave traders often operated under the guise of legitimate trade in products like Madeira wine. Many ships even carried dummy dry goods in order to buttress their captains' claims of engaging in legal business.[35]

Given the hysteria and anger among white New Yorkers, one would think that the city was run by and for Black activists like Ruggles. At the end of the spring, posters were plastered in prominent locations throughout Manhattan. This time the handbill demanded at the top of its masthead in large letters, "FREEMEN AWAKE!" Ruggles walked by one of the posters and the words likely sent shivers down his spine. The bold text clearly aimed its anger at him and fellow Black activists:

> The Constitution of our Country is in danger! The Abolitionists are up, and threatening the dissolution of the Union . . . NO AMALGAMATION! The whites are starving, while the blacks are fed.

Ruggles himself was named, as were other abolitionists. Word had it that none other than Nash was behind the handbill, which featured the well-worn rumor about race mixing.[36]

Only a few hundred showed up for Nash's rally, and the crowd was quickly dispersed by Chief Constable Hays, but during the summer and fall of 1837, Ruggles was dismayed that the kidnapping cases were piling up. Boudinot and Nash seized victims faster than the courts could render decisions to send them into slavery. By September it was becoming clear that the judges were fed up. Ruggles and abolitionist attorney Dresser learned that Edward Watson was being held in New York illegally as an "apprentice," and that his abductor intended to sail Watson on board a brig bound for South Carolina to be sold as a slave. Representing the New York Vigilance Committee, Dresser hurried to Judge Irving to obtain a writ of habeas corpus, but Irving suddenly claimed he was sick and going to bed. They then rushed to Judge Ulshoeffer's at 52 Lispenard just down from Ruggles's office. After listening for a minute inside his home, Ulshoeffer complained that he was hungry and wanted his dinner; he walked to the foyer and said, "There's the door—this is my house." Before they could find a judge to issue the writ, it was too late. Watson was headed to South Carolina slavery.[37]

As the economic panic continued to grip the city, slowing dramatically the once-booming trade with the South, tensions between the police and the Black community, and between the white working class and the poor neighborhoods of color, simmered. And the New York Kidnapping Club took full advantage of the anti-Black fervor, using its presence among the ward constables to bully anyone who dared stand in the way.[38]

BY THE AUTUMN OF 1837, six months after the financial panic had first struck and as the leaves in City Park piled up on the muddy walkways, the normally buzzing wharves around Lower Manhattan were still disturbingly quiet. There had been hope that the cotton trade between the South and England would pick up when the cotton harvests began in summer and early fall before cold weather could endanger the quality and yield of the crop. But the credit and financial crisis seemed only marginally improved

and, in fact, would not recover significantly for years to come. For men like Henry C. Wright, a white atheist and editor who stood prominently against slavery, the cause of the economic disaster lay with Wall Street's "truckling to the dictation of southern slave-holders." "The merchants of Wall and Pearl streets in New York," Wright declared, "are cursing the day they ever bowed down to the southern Moloch, slavery." A malaise that would last for years had settled like a heavy fog on Manhattan.[39]

In addition to suffering themselves from the economic crisis, Ruggles and the Black community had to contend with the prevalence of disturbing cases like that of William Dixon. It was hard to be optimistic as the new year dawned. Before Christmas, a large gathering "of the aggrieved and depressed" citizens of color took place at Asbury Church. Leaders like Edward V. Clark and Edward Crosby called the meeting to order, and Ruggles stood in front of the church to read a declaration of sentiments modeled on the nation's Declaration of Independence: "When a people find themselves . . . cruelly held up to the public as objects of persecution . . . and when money holds out its lure to endanger their liberties and lives, it becomes them to resort to every right and lawful mode" to protect themselves. Ruggles and other Black activists had steadfastly maintained that if self-defense required violence, then it was justified: "We cannot recommend non-resistance to persons . . . when their liberty is invaded and their lives endangered by avaricious kidnappers." Ruggles had been consistent on this point: when arrested or accused of being runaway slaves, Black people had every right to use violence to defend their freedom.

To Ruggles this stance had always made sense, but the resolution sparked debate among those gathered at Asbury Church. Reverend Theodore S. Wright, one of the city's most prominent Black voices, and other clergy like Charles B. Ray and Jacob Matthews, objected to the use of violence as inconsistent with the principles of peace as advocated by the American Anti-Slavery Society. Ruggles rose to disagree respectfully, replying that self-defense was entirely "consistent with liberty, humanity, and justice." In fact,

The Colored American had just reported on a case in which a woman named Lucy, who had been jailed for being a runaway, had killed herself by hanging. So desperate was Lucy to resist a return to bondage that she literally had to pull and hold her legs up in her arms so that she would choke to death. Ruggles knew of Lucy's suicide, understanding that no one would submit willingly to slavery. Wright still objected and motioned to strike Ruggles's advocacy of violence in self-defense.[40]

Wright's motion was voted on three times before it was defeated, but the growing split within the Black community over whether violence could ever be justified was becoming a chasm. For Ruggles, it seemed logical, even obvious, that one should resist to the point of violence. He had seen too often Boudinot and Nash team up to employ brutal power to abduct men, women, and children over the past few years, and he was forced to consider how he would respond if they followed through on threats to kidnap him. He had long ago decided that he would use any means necessary. But as Reverend Wright argued, the official stance of the American Anti-Slavery Society, the main national abolitionist organization that William Lloyd Garrison had helped to found, was nonviolence. Ruggles and Wright maintained a cordial friendship, but it was clear that they represented different poles of opinion when it came to the crisis of kidnapping in New York.

One point that those gathered at Asbury Church could agree on, though, was that the New York Kidnapping Club continued to operate with impunity. Though judges like Riker and Ulshoeffer had grown weary of the constant stream of fugitive slave cases that flooded their courts, Betts, Riker, Nash, Boudinot, Wilder, and Waddy, Ruggles told the audience at Asbury Church, "compose the kidnapping club" that had been wreaking havoc on their community for years.[41]

All of this added up to the continued worsening of the position of Black people in Gotham. They wanted to work, feed and house their families, and form their own churches and societies in and around Manhattan. Black communities had also begun to

form just outside New York, in places like Jersey City, the Bronx, and Brooklyn. Looking to escape the machinations of Boudinot and Irish Democratic ruffians, Black New Yorkers crossed the Hudson and East Rivers in search of amity and autonomy. As the small but growing Black community in Brooklyn was soon to realize, however, crossing a river did not guarantee either peace or freedom.

No End in Sight

RUGGLES HAD TRIED EVERYTHING HE COULD THINK OF TO STOP THE rash of kidnappings plaguing the city and yet every month—and sometimes every week—it seemed a new report flashed across Manhattan. He had called meetings, marched in protests, called lawyers, sat in jail himself, and printed notices and editorials in city newspapers. He had helped to found the New York Committee of Vigilance and had proclaimed the urgency of action and the right of self-defense. Ruggles had even called out publicly by name the members of the New York Kidnapping Club.

But the unremitting work of the gang persisted. In the month between early December 1837 and January 1838, twenty-six new cases beset the city. Justice Betts still presided over federal maritime cases involving the slave trade; Boudinot, sometimes aided by his friend Nash, continued to patrol the streets of Lower Manhattan in his relentless quest for more victims; the fugitive slave laws remained firmly in place, and New York had no jury trial requirements in cases of alleged fugitives; the federal government still relied on police officers, sheriffs, and marshals to enforce those laws; and Wall Street bankers, insurance company leaders, and

merchants remained committed to defending the Union and its compromise over slavery.[1]

Equally disturbing was the fact that the New York Kidnapping Club had begun to extend its malign influence far beyond Lower Manhattan, spreading like a plague into the small towns and rural areas outside the city. Acting on a tip, Boudinot thought he had found a member of the original group that had escaped from Norfolk back in the summer of 1832. Greenwich resident Peter John Lee, enticed away by a man he thought was a friend, left home and crossed into Rye, New York, just north of Manhattan where Boudinot, Nash, and other members of the New York Kidnapping Club pounced on him. Sheriff Edward R. Waddy had traveled from Virginia to extend the reach of slavery into northern communities and worked alongside Nash and Boudinot to capture Lee. Within hours, Lee was placed in shackles, taken back to New York City, and with Waddy dragged back to bondage.

David Ruggles and William Johnston, acting as secretaries of the Committee of Vigilance, wrote to prominent lawyers to request their help in defending Lee. In a remarkable series of letters, they hired leading white attorneys, pressed public officials to acknowledge the invasion of slavery into supposedly free soil, and rallied the Black community to protest such a brazen violation of basic civil rights. Johnston was adamant that the warrant was illegal and wrote to attorney Theodore Sedgwick:

> I understand that Judge Jay advised the abandonment of the case of Peter John Lee under the impression that the Governor's warrant was valid. The production of that instrument on the case now before Judge Urwin gives a very different view of the case. If therefore the affidavits together with a copy of the warrant is sent to Westchester we may succeed in proving its insufficiency. As you have had some correspondence with the Mayor of NY on the subject will you procure the affidavits from him—if he has the original and not copies in order that they may be sent forthwith to Westchester.

Here was a Free black man writing to and working closely with some of the leading white attorneys and politicians in the city, defending an accused runaway slave and trying to prevent his apparent return to bondage. After lengthy deliberations, Nash was fined over $1,000 but Lee was sent into southern slavery.[2]

Outraged that Boudinot and Nash were now spreading their kidnapping pestilence beyond the shadows of Wall Street, Ruggles began publishing his own magazine. On and off for the next few years, Ruggles would hunker down in his home office on Lispenard Street to set the type, work the levers of his printing machine, and sell copies of the *Mirror of Liberty*, despite his failing eyesight. The magazine's title reflected the fact that Ruggles wanted to point out the hypocrisy of a nation so intent on viewing itself as a beacon of freedom while turning its gaze away from kidnapping and slavery.

From the very first issue, Ruggles evinced the passion and intellect that made him such a potent force. For a subscription price of one dollar a year, Ruggles promised a "free and independent journal" that "will never attempt to treat questions of public interest in a manner to avoid giving offence to men, when principle is involved." Ruggles's new magazine garnered nationwide attention in the antislavery press. Garrison praised the work of "our indefatigable colored brother."[3]

The inaugural issue of the *Mirror of Liberty* featured a story about slavery in Brooklyn that had been months in the making, one so shocking that Ruggles felt he would not be believed unless he recorded the event in minute detail.

BY THE 1830s, BROOKLYN was fast becoming a suburb of Manhattan, a place where wealthy New Yorkers could trade crowded neighborhoods for more bucolic estates by traveling across the East River on one of Robert Fulton's steamboat ferries. Also home to an important navy yard, Brooklyn neighborhoods like Williamsburg, Fort Greene, and Brooklyn Heights witnessed the building

of factories, shops, and restaurants that would begin to attract even more residents. Brooklyn's population doubled between 1820 and 1830, reached nearly fifty thousand by 1840, and would number a quarter million just before the Civil War. Poet and journalist Walt Whitman covered the city for the *Brooklyn Daily Eagle*, and, while it remained in the shadow of Manhattan, the town was becoming an important destination for middle-class and working-class Irish immigrants and African Americans.

Black Brooklynites could be found in Fort Greene and thriving neighborhoods like Weeksville building vigorous communities that by their very nature undermined racist claims that people of African descent were somehow ill-suited for civility. By the 1840s, African American schoolchildren could enroll in the Colored School, the town would soon employ its own police force, and Black churches had sprung up to welcome congregations. White

A winter scene in early Brooklyn. *(Brooklyn Museum, from the Brooklyn Institute of Arts and Sciences)*.

and Black churchgoers could hear Henry Ward Beecher, one of the nation's leading and most controversial white abolitionists, explain why slavery was a moral blot on the nation that needed to be erased immediately. Weeksville exemplified the sense of community that could develop when African Americans could boast of their own schools, churches, and businesses. At the same time that the New York Kidnapping Club was terrorizing Black Manhattanites, and as Ruggles began publishing the *Mirror of Liberty*, James Weeks, a Black stevedore originally from Virginia, bought land in the Bedford Hills area of Brooklyn that soon embraced some five hundred African Americans. They built the Berean Missionary Baptist Church and other public institutions, printed their own newspaper, and established charitable associations and social and intellectual organizations to enhance their communities.[4]

Today, visitors to the corner of Atlantic Avenue and Henry Street in the heart of Brooklyn arrive for visits to doctors' and dentists' offices, or to lunch at one of the many ethnic restaurants nearby. Just down from the commercialized piers along the East River, the corner of Atlantic and Henry is a shopping and dining center in the Cobble Hill neighborhood. But in early 1838 that corner was the home of Daniel K. Dodge, a Savannah slaveholder who had moved north several years before. There was nothing unusual about southerners moving to New York or any northern city, for that matter, nor was it unusual for northerners to venture south to make a new life. Dodge was different, however, as Ruggles found out. When Dodge and his wife had moved to Brooklyn permanently, they took one of their slaves with them, and then had two more shipped north a couple of years later. As shocking as it may seem, the Dodges kept three Black people enslaved for as many as four years, right in the center of Brooklyn.

Ruggles was dumbfounded when he learned of the slaveholding Dodges. He had seen almost everything, he believed, and he was rarely shaken by the nuanced and twisted ties between New York and slavery. But this was different: the Dodges didn't even pretend to take their enslaved property across state lines to bring them back after the nine-month window, as other New Yorkers

(and George Washington when the presidency sat in Philadelphia) had done. The Dodges kept slaves in the city throughout the year, within the confines of their spacious walk-up, and without any apparent interference from the police.[5]

That is, until Ruggles found out.

Ruggles left his home on Lispenard early one evening, took the ferry across the East River to Brooklyn, and knocked on the Dodges' front door. A butler answered, and Ruggles was escorted to the basement, where he waited for Mrs. Dodge to appear, since her husband was away. After a few awkward moments standing in the basement, Ruggles soon met with Mrs. Dodge. Ruggles asked if the family was holding slaves in violation of New York State law. Mrs. Dodge claimed to agree with Ruggles that slavery was an evil institution, and she became animated when she told Ruggles that emancipation in the South was "a hard matter." The three enslaved people in the home, Jim, Charity, and Jesse, must have heard the commotion because they joined Mrs. Dodge and Ruggles in the basement. Jesse was the mother, Charity the daughter, and Jim the young brother.

As Ruggles recounted in the *Mirror of Liberty*, Mrs. Dodge turned to the three enslaved people and said, "Jim, Charity, and Jesse are as free as anybody. Ain't you!"

Jesse replied, "Ah! I do not know that, missee. I hear when master come back, he send us back" to Georgia.

"That is a mistake, ain't it Charity," Mrs. Dodge asked as she pivoted to the younger woman.

"I don't know, I hear so, missee," came Charity's reply.

"Haven't I told you that you are free?"

"You told me to say so if anybody ask me, but you beat me here as much as ever, missee."

Ruggles chimed in, and, directing his comments to Charity, said, "Why, if Mrs. Dodge brought you here to be free, she would not treat you ill, but, on the contrary, she would be kind to you and pay you wages."

Charity scoffed. "Wages!" She could hardly contain her disbelief.

It was true that no wages were paid, Mrs. Dodge admitted, "but I take good care of you."

Charity scoffed again. "I have lived here four years and never received a dollar, and this homespun frock and linsey woolsey petticoat that I stand in, is my best dress."

"Come, I won't have so much talk, Charity." Mrs. Dodge, still speaking to Charity, pointed to Ruggles and said, "I suppose you have been after this person, to take you away?"

Before she could reply, Ruggles reentered the conversation: "I have only come to see that they receive that protection which is afforded them under the laws of this state. They are as free as I am; after remaining here nine months, they have a right to demand wages for every hour's service they have performed in your family during their residence in this state."

Mrs. Dodge finally admitted that they were her slaves, leading one of the Dodge daughters to appear and beg Ruggles not to take them away.

"If they are held as slaves," Ruggles replied, "and are willing to go, they can leave you, and I will protect them."

Now concerned that Ruggles was going to make off with her "property," Mrs. Dodge ran to the nearby home of a Dr. McClennan. McClennan crossed the Dodges' threshold and went to the top of the basement stairs. "Hallo there what are you about?" he yelled down to Ruggles, who was then engaged in talking to Jesse about how they came to live in Brooklyn as slaves. Ruggles told Mrs. Dodge that Jesse's story did not match hers, and by then McClennan was even more irritated after being ignored for several minutes. McClennan charged Ruggles with intruding on the home, and Ruggles returned the charge. Ruggles had remained calm and polite through the entire exchange, but McClennan claimed he had been called by Mrs. Dodge to remove a "disorderly person." "Find such a person here," Ruggles retorted, "and I will aid you in his removal." McClennan, his voice rising in anger, told the activist, "I wish you would leave sir," and Ruggles responded by asking the doctor to leave. A physical confrontation would not

have made sense from the doctor's perspective, given that Ruggles was several inches taller and considerably bulkier than McClennan. Suddenly, McClennan realized he was talking with the notorious radical Black activist, whose fame had evidently crossed the East River. For several more minutes, Mrs. Dodge, Ruggles, and McClennan discussed the state laws regarding slavery. Mrs. Dodge continued to insist that she treated the three enslaved people with kindness and humanity, and Charity raised an eyebrow.

Mrs. Dodge turned to Charity. "You know you are subject to fits and will suffer if you leave me."

"Yes, I know I had fits from your beating me on the head, missee."

"Hush, you impudent jade, how dare you speak so to your mistress?"

"I suppose I must speak the truth, missee."

Dr. McClennan joined in, asking Ruggles: "Can't you leave them until Saturday, when Mr. Dodge will be home?"

Ruggles replied with continued calm and self-control. "They are perfectly free to do as they please; if they choose to remain, they can; I employ no force to remove them; if they go with me, I will protect them."

Charity had already made up her mind. "I is free as a rat, and am going; if I was to stop here, I should find myself dead tomorrow morning. I know you missee." Charity gathered her clothes, which were mere rags, and left with Ruggles.

Over the next few days, with Charity stashed safely at an antislavery home in Manhattan, Ruggles attempted to speak with Daniel Dodge. On one occasion Ruggles could see through a basement window that Jim and Jesse were locked in a room. Ruggles learned that the Dodges were determined to take their two remaining enslaved people back to the family plantation.

Yet rather than rally to Ruggles's defense in bravely confronting the slaveholding Dodges, conservative New York papers harshly criticized the activist for interfering. Editor C. F. Daniels, who published the *New York Gazette* at 67 Wall Street, praised Dodge as a man of good character who had been unfairly attacked by

Ruggles, who called the Black protester "an insolent black fellow" and "a nuisance and a vagabond." Daniels claimed that Charity was "entirely incapable of doing anything to maintain herself, and will of course become a tenant of the Alms-house." For Wall Street editors and businessmen, the Dodges were the ones to be praised for having taken care of Charity, and they seemed unconcerned that the Dodges were holding slaves in the supposedly free city of Brooklyn.[6]

Unfortunately for Ruggles, Charity quickly descended into poverty, and the abolitionist was blamed for her misfortune. Ruggles managed to find her a boardinghouse and a place to work, but "such was the state of her morals" that she could not keep a job. Then she met Solomon Reddix, a man she befriended in the boardinghouse, and quickly became pregnant. The Wall Street press had a field day once they realized that not only had Charity been "inveigled" from her "charitable master" in Brooklyn, but that she had fallen into despair. And who was to blame? Not the Dodges, who had carried Charity from slavery in Savannah to slavery in Brooklyn, but Ruggles. The *New York Gazette* denounced Ruggles, promising its readers that the paper would keep them informed of Charity's plight.

For his part, Ruggles quite rightly pointed out that he was not responsible for everything Charity did after she left the Dodges. Ruggles confronted Reddix, who refused to marry Charity but did promise to help support the baby financially. Ruggles spent some of his money to get Charity situated. He then drew up a bill for four years of wages, amounting to hundreds of dollars, and sent Charity to Brooklyn to recover her pay since she had toiled for the Dodge family, who of course refused to pay her anything.

Ruggles pointed out in the *Mirror of Liberty* that in the past three years he had found no fewer than fourteen slaves living in Brooklyn, which he called "the Savannah of New York." But conservative New York papers like the *New York Gazette* refused to credit Ruggles for working to free these enslaved people, instead attacking him for interfering in the private affairs of wealthy families and placing vulnerable people like Charity on the public dole.[7]

RUGGLES'S FOCUS THEN TURNED back to Lower Manhattan, where amid all of the depressing news in the Black community, Ruggles and his allies could at least count one bright development. In the spring of 1838, Richard Riker left the position of city recorder, which he had held for more than twenty years. From that powerful post, Riker had tormented Gotham's Black community, and except for a few circumstances, made it exceedingly easy for Nash, Boudinot, and others in the New York Kidnapping Club to send the accused into southern slavery. Now approaching the age of sixty-five, Riker returned to private practice, and his appearance in court as an advocate generated murmurs among the other lawyers. Riker was a celebrity in Gotham. As the *Hudson River Chronicle* noted, "Though far advanced in life, it is said that he pleaded with all the impassioned earnestness of a young barrister who had just commenced his career." As the tone of this newspaper notice indicates, Riker was respected within the New York Democratic Party and considered an elder statesman deserving of great respect within the white community, even though Ruggles and abolitionists considered Riker their archnemesis.[8]

In fact, city Democrats persuaded Riker to run for mayor just after he had stepped down as recorder. As the trees along Broadway began to bud out and the weather was finally warming after a long winter, New York's Democrats gathered in a great meeting in City Hall Park, just a few yards away from where Riker had presided in court. As the pro-Whig *Morning Herald* complained about the political rally, "The loafers of the Five Points, of the Astor House, of Wall Street, will meet" to look "down upon the soft bosoms of the pretty girls as they pass along." Scorning the Democrats for their embrace of the white laboring class, the paper sarcastically proclaimed:

Rogues and Rowdies attend!

Perpetuation of principle!!

Mobocracy in their might!!!

Recorder for Mayor!!!![9]

But the former recorder wanted to return to private life. The many cases of fugitive slave renditions that had come before him had clearly worn on Riker over the previous two decades. He had been attacked as a kidnapper, as an uncaring tool of the southern slaveholder, and he had failed to get direction from the state supreme court in cases of suspected runaways. Dick Riker had had enough.

But so, too, had the city's abolitionists. In late May, Black and white activists gathered for the second anniversary of the New York Committee of Vigilance at the Third Free Presbyterian Church in Manhattan. African Americans were cautiously optimistic that Riker's retirement might improve their safety, but they were also cognizant that the kidnapping club relied on many more judges and lawyers to protect the interests of southern slave owners. Reverend J. H. Martyn rose to give a lengthy speech denouncing "the pusillanimous and disgraceful conduct of the magistrates, subordinate officers and members of the bar in the city of New York, who 'go with the South,' against suffering humanity, from Judge Betts down to Ex-Recorder Riker, and from officer Boudinot down to the degraded Nash." Riker might have left the bench, but New Yorkers like Martyn worried that proslavery and pro-South sentiment remained entrenched in the minds of political and legal authorities.[10]

For his part, of course, Ruggles was more than happy to see Riker exit the public arena. Writing in his new magazine the *Mirror of Liberty*, the radical activist announced that "it affords me inexpressible pleasure, to be enabled to inform the friends of human rights" that Riker was leaving the court. Families across Manhattan and Brooklyn would rejoice, Ruggles believed, in knowing that the recorder could no longer send their loved ones into southern slavery. Never one to mince words, Ruggles took the opportunity to "congratulate humanity, liberty, and justice" on the retirement of "so execrable a magistrate." The city's Black residents were not sure if Riker's replacement in the recorder's office would be an ally of civil rights, but they could hardly imagine that the office could be any less sympathetic to their interests.

Although Riker left the scene, any hopes that Ruggles might have held regarding the end of the kidnapping gang were quickly dashed. In the summer and fall of 1838, three highly publicized cases rendered moot any optimism among the city's growing Black community.[11]

A copy of Ruggles's *Mirror of Liberty*. (Beinecke Rare Book & Manuscript Library, Yale University)

THE THREE CASES OF alleged fugitive slaves scarred the city for many years, as Black New Yorkers like Ruggles would refer to them again and again in angry editorials. And it all began with the man who perhaps more than any other had helped make New York into a key port in the illegal transatlantic slave trade. Nathaniel Gordon, already a noted slaver as New Yorkers learned in the *St. Nicholas* case back in 1836, is a notorious name in American history. During the Civil War Nathaniel Gordon Jr. would be executed for the crime of slave trading. But long before President Abraham Lincoln would refuse to intervene in the hanging of Nathaniel Gordon Jr. for human trafficking in 1862, Gordon's father was arrested for the same crime. Originally from Portland, Maine, members of the Gordon family were small-time slave dealers, importing one or two people from Africa or Havana in their roles as ship captains, in clear violation of US laws against transatlantic human trafficking.

Captain Nathaniel Gordon Sr. supplemented his usual shipping commerce by buying, selling, and transporting enslaved people, and no doubt by 1838 he had already made considerable money along the Atlantic seaboard. But by the summer of that year, his luck nearly ran out. Docking in New York harbor in June, Captain Gordon's brig *Dunlap* became the focus of a months-long heated struggle that not only attracted national press, but also threatened to divide New York's Black and white abolitionist movement. At the center of the struggle stood the indefatigable David Ruggles.

The fight began when George Washington came to Ruggles's office on Lispenard Street. Though the man bore a famous name, he was as desperate and downtrodden as the real George Washington was revered. This Washington had been enslaved on the island of Guadeloupe in the Caribbean, toiling for the family of Lambert Bercier, a New Yorker with deep family ties across France, the Caribbean, and Gotham. Bercier tricked Washington into boarding the ship, and with Gordon's help locked the father and husband in the ship's forecastle. Washington, the Bercier family, and other passengers and crew voyaged from Guadeloupe

to New York aboard the *Dunlap*, captained by Nathaniel Gordon. As the ship waited in quarantine just outside the harbor, Bercier handed Washington a new outfit and told him to get dressed. Washington would be disguised as a sailor on Gordon's ship to avoid suspicion.[12]

Washington soon learned from the other crew that New York had outlawed bondage, so he whispered to others about his perilous situation aboard the *Dunlap*, who told him of Ruggles and the Committee of Vigilance. Disgusted and angry after hearing the tale, Ruggles marched down to the wharves and confronted Bercier, who admitted he had paid good money for Washington in Guadeloupe and that he was not about to set the man free. As frustrated as he was, though, Ruggles almost always tried to work through the system by informing city officials in the hope that their indifference to the plight of Black folks would be overcome by the public shaming Ruggles promised if the authorities failed to act. US District Attorney William Price heard the report and issued a warrant for the arrest of both Bercier and Gordon, who were jailed on $10,000 and $5,000 bond, respectively.[13]

The differing bail amounts reflected a belief among the legal authorities that while Bercier clearly had bought Washington fully intending to keep him in bondage, Captain Gordon might not have known that Washington was enslaved. Ruggles didn't buy that claim for a minute. Remarkably, at the urging of white abolitionists like the attorney Horace Dresser, Ruggles interviewed Gordon and Bercier in Bridewell to hear their side of the tale. There was the radical Ruggles bravely visiting a slave owner and a slave trader in prison. Gordon insisted that he had no idea that Bercier had purchased Washington, but Ruggles knew that Gordon was lying, and in any event should have been much more aware of laws against slave trading than the French-born Bercier.[14]

Assistant District Attorney Hamilton and US Deputy Marshal Rapalje handled the prosecution, but Ruggles had little faith in either of these men, whom he deemed tools of southern masters. Hamilton never failed to insult Ruggles in person, but "though reproached and stigmatized" the radical refused to "be deterred, or

yield a single inch," to serve "the cause of my downtrodden, bleeding countrymen." Unfortunately, neither Hamilton nor Rapalje bothered to detain or even interview the *Dunlap*'s crew, meaning that Ruggles himself had to track down witnesses in support of Washington's claims. He finally identified Robert Smith, the brig's cook, who was willing to testify, but none of the other seamen turned up.[15]

As Ruggles wrote letter after letter and interviewed a number of people in the case on behalf of Washington, Ruggles was stunned to learn that white attorney Dresser swallowed Captain Gordon's claims of innocence. The *Dunlap*'s owner promised to contribute a substantial amount of money to the Committee of Vigilance if Ruggles would drop the case against Gordon and let the ship go free. Dresser wrote Ruggles a lengthy letter offering his advice to "let up, and make them pay as large a sum into the treasury of the Vigilance Committee" as they could. Dresser really seemed to believe Gordon anyway and thought that a New York jury would never convict him.

Ruggles could not believe that Dresser would willingly take what amounted to a bribe to drop the case, and while Dresser had been a good friend and an important antislavery ally, the issue threatened to divide the two friends and was emblematic of the racial and interpersonal tensions that could arise within the abolitionist movement. Ruggles responded to Dresser's advice by stating flatly that he viewed the promise of payment as a payoff and as a matter of principle would not accept it. Dresser took this as an insult, and Ruggles maintained his opinion that "the captain is as guilty as Bercier." He wanted to see the case through to the end, even if that meant an acquittal for both. The activist certainly had no faith in DA Hamilton, who Ruggles asserted "has no heart, no soul, and no principle."

As Dresser predicted, the grand jury quickly declined to indict either Bercier or Gordon, but that didn't stop the Wall Street merchants and their allies in editorial offices from disparaging Ruggles. The *New York Express* called the whole Bercier-Gordon affair a case of the Black man kidnapping whites and avowed that such interference would remain "embarrassments to commerce,

of trading and freighting vessels between the Free States and the West Indies, or Southern Ports." The business community declared that it would "not put up with" Ruggles and other Black abolitionists meddling in commerce.[16]

The lengths to which Ruggles would go, whether or not it disrupted trade with the slave South, became even clearer in the summer of 1838 when he learned that three New Jersey men had been kidnapped from New York harbor. Tricked into boarding a steamship called the *New Castle*, Isaac Wright, Robert Garrison, and Stephen Dickerson were declared missing by their distraught parents. Stephen had written a letter to his forty-five-year-old father, Stephen F. Dickerson, recounting their kidnapping and desperately seeking help from New York.[17]

The details of Dickerson's horrific experience within the bowels of the slave system as he passed from one slaveholder and southern con man to another are redolent of Solomon Northup's trials, recounted in his memoir *Twelve Years a Slave*. Dickerson, Wright, and Garrison were sailors, an especially precarious job, especially when ships called at southern ports, because men were liable to be seized as potential slaves. Early in the fall of 1837, the three men sailed on board the steamboat *New Castle* and landed at New Orleans about a month later. For the next three months they sailed between Louisiana and the Florida port of St. Marks.[18]

Near Christmas Day in 1837, the *New Castle* docked not far from the famous United States Hotel, a New Orleans landmark that embodied the commercial spirit of the Louisiana city. Another sailor approached Dickerson, Wright, and Garrison and told them they all had to head into town to buy some hemp, used to wipe down the deck, the steam engine, and other parts of the ship. But before they could protest, a slave trader named Botts had the three men tossed into Harper's Jail. A shocked and dismayed Dickerson knew that he was now ensnared within the dark and shadowy southern web of slavery. Botts strode into the jail and began peppering the men with questions: Were they free? What streets in New York did they live on? Who were their neighbors? Through the questioning it became clear that Botts knew full well

that Dickerson and the others were born free. After they answered truthfully, Botts had the men tied to a ladder facedown on the ground and whipped thirty-five times. Botts then turned to the men and muttered that if they ever spoke about New York again, they would be whipped mercilessly.[19]

After three weeks in the jail, Dickerson was forced on board another steamboat, the *Bunker Hill,* and his tormentor again appeared with chains in hand. Botts took the men to Vicksburg and placed them with an auctioneer named Rudisill. In humiliating fashion, Rudisill forced the men to walk around Vicksburg for about an hour, with one carrying a red flag and the other ringing a bell to garner attention. Wright was sold first, and Dickerson became distraught at the sight of his friend being sold. "The separation was painful," Dickerson recalled, since they had comforted one another throughout the ordeal.

Sold to a Kentucky slaver, Dickerson worked as a domestic servant for three months, and then worked on a country farm. "I now began to think I should never see my native city or my friends again," Dickerson lamented. "My distress became intolerable." He ate "Indian bread and salt meat" and employed farming skills he had learned up North, but he longed for a return to his parents in New York. "The thoughts of home often rushed upon my mind, when I was at work in the field, and when I laid down to sleep." For two years, Dickerson worked on Richard Percival's Kentucky farm, until one day when he met a farmer named Thomas Vantreese, who allowed Dickerson to pick fruit from his sumptuous orchard. Dickerson decided to confide to Vantreese his real background, and the Kentucky farmer admitted that he thought Dickerson might be free. Vantreese contacted a New York lawyer named Cradock who confirmed Dickerson's sordid tale of kidnapping.

With the help of the local sheriff, Dickerson then traveled back to New Orleans, ever watchful for the treacherous Botts, and met a lawyer named Elwyn, who had formerly lived in New York. After a lengthy interview, Elwyn became convinced that Dickerson was telling the truth and drew up papers that could vouch for Dickerson's freeborn status. Percival reappeared and promised to help

Dickerson return home to New York, but once back in Kentucky Percival demanded $200 from Dickerson to set him free. Not knowing what to do next, Dickerson signed an IOU for the money and began working on the steamboat *Shylock*, captained by Samuel McEwen. "I was fully aware," Dickerson later told his family, that he was being manipulated. But he did not know how to get out of slavery's sticky web.

After being cheated out of wages on one steamboat after another, Dickerson finally boarded the *Natchez* and arrived in New York, almost three years since he had been kidnapped. "I cannot express the joy I felt on getting home," he recounted. "My father had been overwhelmed with grief, and had almost given me up as lost forever." His companion Isaac Wright had also managed to escape, but several years later Robert Garrison remained trapped somewhere in the dark recesses of slavery.[20]

While Dickerson was being moved from one slave trader to another along the Mississippi River, the unrelenting Ruggles, enraged at the kidnapping of three young men, began investigating. He learned that the steamship's captain, James Dayton Wilson, had just returned to his home and Ruggles demanded his arrest. Wilson claimed that while he had left the ship, Thomas Lewis had come aboard and kidnapped the young men and sold them at the slave market in New Orleans. A slaveholder in Memphis admitted he had the men but had purchased them not knowing they had been kidnapped and promised to free them with proof.[21]

By July 1838 Ruggles had found out that Lewis had escaped jail in Tallahassee, where he had been convicted of decapitating a man with a bowie knife. Lewis had left the South and returned to New England, working as a seaman on the ship *Lieutenant Tracy*, which sailed between Providence and New Bedford. Ruggles took a train to Philadelphia, found information about Lewis's job aboard the cutter, and followed the trail to Providence and Newport before frantically making it to New Bedford. Arriving at the Massachusetts port, Ruggles found out that Lewis was due to leave again in just two hours, so he hustled to the police station and had the kidnapper arrested. In the name of justice, Ruggles had

crossed half a dozen states and traveled for days on end at his own expense, just to track Lewis down.[22]

The Wall Street press again blasted Ruggles for interfering in commerce. Ruggles's "crime," in the eyes of men like newspaper editor C. F. Daniels, was that he had caused Captain Wilson to be arrested for kidnapping, even though, as it turned out, Wilson may not have known about Lewis's plans. "It is about time to know whether we are in Africa or America," newspapers angrily declared. Despite the hostility of the press, the city's Black community mobilized to raise money for Dickerson's return. In fact, Stephen Dickerson Sr. was active in the public meetings and demonstrations that demanded action from city officials to rescue his son. Once Dickerson Jr. and Wright returned to New York, African American leaders arranged jobs for both men at the furniture store of L. and H. Parker on Chatham Street.[23]

WORKING TIRELESSLY ON SO many cases like those of Dickerson and Wright over the past couple of years, Ruggles had begun to feel the battles taking a physical toll, and his eyesight grew dimmer with each passing month. As he advanced in age, his health was failing, even though he would turn just thirty years old in 1840. But his role in so many cases over the past few years was also wearing thin on white political leaders and the editors who supported them. It seemed Ruggles had gone too far in the minds of city merchants, and they would soon exact revenge.

The chance to pounce on Ruggles came in early fall 1838, when an enslaved man named Thomas Hughes fled from a Louisiana gambler. Born in Richmond, Hughes (like many enslaved southerners) found out at an early age that his father was also his master, who had sexually assaulted his slaves. When still an infant, Tom was sold along with his twin sister and mother (Rachel) to his father's brother. The modern sensibility is shocked at the callous nature of slaveholders' familial relationships, the uncaring way in which white men could rape enslaved women and then sell off their own sons and daughters. But such was the nature of family

life in the Old South. One wealthy white woman, South Carolina's Mary Chesnut, admitted that "like the patriarchs of old, our men live all in one house with their wives and their concubines, and the mulattoes one sees in every family exactly resemble the white children." While still a child, Tom endured the selling of his sister and mother to a distant plantation; Tom never saw them again. As a teenager, Tom himself was sold to his master's son. In other words, Tom had been purchased by his own half brother, who was so cruel that Tom often asked how one brother could treat another with such meanness. The whole fiction of southern honor, masculinity, and patriarchy rested on a massive social conspiracy in preventing such questions from being uttered in public, and for his transgression Tom Hughes was handcuffed, tied to a horse's belly, and sold to a slaver in Kentucky.[24]

While enslaved in Kentucky, Tom heard that his father had also moved to the state and was every bit as rich as he had been in Virginia. Probably in hope of arranging a lucrative sale, Hughes's "owner" allowed Tom to see his father and beg him to be purchased and set free. "I told him of the miserable life I was leading," Tom told his father and former master, "subject to the will of any person who might become my master; but to all my entreaties he turned a deaf ear, and in public would not speak to me as he passed me." Tom stayed nearby for two weeks, hoping that at least he could persuade his father to reveal the whereabouts of his mother and sister. But to Tom's disappointment his father cared so little about Rachel and his offspring that he hadn't even bothered to record the name of their purchaser.

In the meantime, Tom had been sold yet again, this time to a New Orleans gambler named John Darg. Believing he had little to lose at this point, Hughes looked for a chance to make his escape. When Darg announced that they would be taking a trip to New York City, Hughes knew that his opportunity had arrived. Just twenty years old in 1838, Thomas Hughes had been sold numerous times, had been dragged back and forth across southern state lines, and had witnessed the selling of his mother and sibling.

That was enough suffering and misery for a lifetime and more. As he later recalled, "I resolved, before I left New Orleans, never to return a slave."[25]

Despite all of the injustices he had endured, Thomas Hughes demonstrated that unlike the white men who had owned him, he was a man of principle. White abolitionists in New York would later claim that Tom's decision to take money from Darg was a reflection of the lack of morals that bondage promoted in southern African Americans. White antislavery activists would shake their heads and claim that stealing and other immoral acts were part and parcel of the lives of enslaved people who had been raised in the midst of an unjust system. "All of the tendencies of slavery," one white abolitionist later wrote, "are calculated to blunt the moral sensibilities, and to destroy that power of discrimination between right and wrong." The irony is that Hughes was more decent and principled than all the white men he had met put together. And as far as right and wrong went, the whole moral universe had been turned upside down in the southern families he knew. He fled and took Darg's money out of desperation, believing that one day he would pay back the money.[26]

As soon as he fled, rolls of cash in hand, Hughes befriended a fellow African American named Henry Clark, a waiter at a Broadway restaurant, who took Hughes to the home of white abolitionist Isaac Hopper. Hopper consulted Ruggles as well as other abolitionists like Barney Corse and Horace Dresser, and they all agreed that Hughes should spend the night at Hopper's house while they figured out their next steps. None of the men knew Hughes had taken the money from Darg, but they were pretty sure Hughes was a runaway.

The next morning at sunrise Hopper was eating breakfast and reading the *New York Sun*. There, in the morning paper, he spotted an ad offering an award of one thousand dollars for the "apprehension and return of a mulatto man" who had taken several thousand dollars from his master. Darg had raced from his hotel on Varick Street and immediately placed the ad. Somehow

Hopper knew that his house guest was the target. He had pledged to take in runaways, and Hopper had suspected that Tom was a fugitive, but he could not countenance thievery and told Hughes he would have to leave and return the money.[27]

Hughes hung his head and admitted taking the money from Darg, but he claimed he had only seized the rolls of cash from Darg's trunk to buy his way to freedom. He had given some to Henry Clark in exchange for his help, and he had entrusted more of the cash to a man who pledged to help him reach Canada. None of that mattered to the Quaker Isaac Hopper, who could understand fleeing from the injustice of slavery but not the desperate necessity of stealing. Tom returned more than six hundred dollars of the cash to Darg, but the rest had been lost in the desperate attempt to flee. This was excuse enough for New York City's police. Within forty-eight hours of Tom having taken the money, Hopper, Ruggles, and Corse had been arrested.[28]

The first trial combined the indictment of Hughes, Corse, Ruggles, Henry Clark, James Sloan Gibbons, and Hopper, all of whom were charged in October 1838 with accessory after the fact, essentially for knowingly harboring Hughes after he had stolen the money from Darg. Corse and Hopper were well-known abolitionists, while Gibbons was a banker from Philadelphia married to Abigail Hopper and a committed antislavery activist. They were being charged along with Black defendants Hughes, Clark, and Ruggles. Since Riker had stepped down as city recorder, Robert H. Morris now presided over the Court of General Sessions. The district attorney called several witnesses, including Darg's wife and police officers, who testified that Corse and the others had conspired to hide Hughes even when they learned he had stolen a substantial amount of money. The defense drew evidence from several affidavits, including two from Ruggles and abolitionist lawyer Horace Dresser.[29]

The trial dragged on into March 1839, but the jury was clearly having trouble arriving at a verdict. After three days of on-and-off deliberations, the jurors declared to Recorder Morris that

they could not reach a decision and the court declared a mistrial. Believing they still had a chance to make an example of Ruggles and other abolitionists, however, the district attorney was determined to try the case again. Testimony continued on into the fall of 1839, a full year since Hughes had first been arrested. Again the jury failed to reach a verdict on Corse, Ruggles, Clark, Hopper, and Gibbons, but Hughes was found guilty and sentenced to two years at Sing Sing.[30]

The members of the New York Kidnapping Club, fed up with Ruggles and his constant agitation, seized their chance to throw Ruggles into prison. The police and the Wall Street press claimed, with no evidence, that Ruggles had encouraged Hughes to steal the money, and Ruggles was arrested soon after Hughes was captured. For two days Ruggles sat in a small cell surrounded by men arrested for public intoxication. In the meantime, the police went to work to prove Ruggles and the other abolitionists were just as guilty as Hughes. The police were active agents in the New York Kidnapping Club, and abolitionists knew that they could not be trusted. "Corruption pervades every department of our *police system*," one antislavery man claimed; they are little more than "reckless marauders." The problem was that the Wall Street press also fanned the anti-Black and anti-abolitionist fervor. C. F. Daniels of the *New York Gazette* led the charge against Ruggles and openly called for him to be sent into southern slavery, referring to him in the newspaper as a "sooty scoundrel" and the "official ourang outang of the 'Anti-Slavery Society.'" It is little wonder, then, that ordinary white New Yorkers reading these attacks harbored such animus toward Ruggles and his allies. When the trial against Ruggles began, one juror loudly proclaimed "that he would *never acquit an abolitionist!*" Initially, Ruggles was held on three thousand dollars bail, but when his friends gathered enough funds to post bail, the judge raised it to five thousand dollars.[31]

As part of their efforts against Ruggles, two New York police officers, Henry W. Merritt and Ebenezer Peck, cornered Catherine Clark, the wife of Henry Clark, who had befriended Hughes

shortly after his escape. In her early twenties by the fall of 1838, Catherine could not read or write but she knew that Merritt and Peck were trying to trick her into testifying against Ruggles. Merritt would, in a couple of years, be fired for corruption in a highly publicized trial for having taken bribes, abused prisoners, and received stolen goods. He was rotten to the core, but the New York Kidnapping Club had put him in charge of gathering evidence against Ruggles. The officers first locked Catherine in jail, hoping to intimidate her into lying, and then later ransacked her home. Peck threatened her, called her a liar, and stalked her every movement. Catherine, however, did not cave, and though the district attorney declared that the New Yorkers had to convict Ruggles, Hopper, and Corse, there was no evidence that they had persuaded Hughes to steal from Darg. The case against the abolitionists had dragged on for months, but Ruggles was once again a free man, which meant little to the New York police force on the lookout for any minor misstep.[32]

After Hughes had served his sentence, his torments continued. Darg returned to New York and tricked Hughes into returning to the South. Before they had left for New York, Thomas had fallen in love with and married another enslaved person named Mary. Knowing Tom's feelings, Darg promised that he could live with Mary and that he would not be a slave but a domestic servant. Darg took Mary all the way to New York to reunite with Thomas and promised that the couple would both live freely as husband and wife. Darg knew how to manipulate Tom, who went South "solely with the hope of living with Mary." Deep down Hughes knew better, but with few friends in New York and the wish to be with Mary so strong, he went with Darg. Once they reached Baltimore, Darg jailed Tom and told him he had sold Mary. "I cannot describe how I felt," Tom lamented. "I feel very sorry that I could not live with her and be free, but I had rather live in the State Prison all my life than to be a slave." In just a few simple words, Thomas Hughes had expressed the sentiments of so many thousands of African Americans determined to emancipate themselves despite the risks.[33]

As DEDICATED AS HE remained to the cause of human rights, Ruggles himself began doubting whether New York was making any progress in becoming a safe harbor for African Americans. On the contrary, it seemed that the richer the city became, the more Wall Street advanced in wealth and power, the more dangerous Gotham had become for Black people. New York was developing into the metropolis that would make it one of the world's great centers of capitalism, but financial success did not breed humanitarianism, and the city struggled mightily every day with the tensions wrought by the police, Tammany Hall Democrats and their Irish working-class supporters, and the people of color who also sought to make New York their home. Unfortunately, just when they needed leadership the most, the Black abolitionist community in New York began to fracture, and, not surprisingly, at the center of that schism stood David Ruggles.

New York and the
Transatlantic Slave Trade

B Y THE END OF THE 1830S, THE PROSPECTS OF ENDING KIDNAP-
pings and slavery seemed more remote than ever to
Ruggles and his fellow antislavery radicals. Many leaders
on Wall Street joined with the Democrats in Tammany Hall to
forge a united proslavery and pro-South front. The New York
Kidnapping Club continued to patrol Manhattan, Brooklyn, and
other communities surrounding Gotham. And to make matters
worse, the group of Black abolitionists working hardest to battle
against those forces was itself in disarray.

Just when the picture appeared bleak beyond hope, one
change in state law in 1840 instantly reshaped the relationship
between Black New Yorkers and the police. The passage of a new
law requiring a jury trial in cases of accused runaways, a law for
which Ruggles and his fellow abolitionists had long clamored, and
which Boudinot and Nash had long feared, changed the dynamics
on the streets dramatically. No longer could officers arrest alleged
fugitives and take them out of the city without notice or due process, as they had so many times over the previous decade. In fact,
the implementation of jury trials in the cases of accused runaways

significantly slowed the work of Boudinot and the New York Kidnapping Club, all but bringing its dark history to a close.

Before the jury trial law passed the New York State legislature, though, Black New Yorkers confronted a demoralizing split within their ranks. As selfless as he could be in the struggle against kidnapping and racism, Ruggles could also be a very difficult person. Radical agitators like Ruggles often made more enemies than friends, and even his closest supporters in the African American and abolitionist communities found him argumentative, sensitive to criticism, and self-righteous in the extreme. In fact, by early 1839 Ruggles found himself at odds with much of New York's antislavery establishment, especially with newspaper editor Cornish of *The Colored American*. Ruggles had already chafed against what he perceived to be Cornish's snooty scorn for the Black protesters in the wake of the Dixon and Darg affairs, but by 1839 the personality differences between the reserved Cornish and the excitable Ruggles added to the very real policy variances between them.

In the end Ruggles's hastiness permanently doomed his relationship with Cornish. Without the editor's approval, Ruggles persuaded the typesetter for *The Colored American* to include a defamatory notice, and the paper was sued for libel. Ruggles

The masthead of *The Colored American*. (*University of Detroit Mercy*)

himself was no stranger to the courts, having already been sued for calling one individual a robber and murderer. In this more recent case of John Russel, Ruggles claimed in an article titled "Humanity Weeps" that Russel was guilty of importing enslaved Africans into New York from Gambia in the brig *Governor Temple*. In fact, Ruggles was reprinting a letter he had received from a seaman who had identified Russel as the owner of a slaver. According to the information, Russel and the captain of the ship had forced on board "three native Africans" who had "neither money nor clothes" and Russel knew that these men, one named Robin and the other two both named Joan, were being enslaved and tried to sell them in New Orleans before taking them into New York harbor. Russel sued Ruggles, Cornish, Philip A. Bell, and Robert Sears, all men associated with the paper, for damages in the city's Court of Common Pleas. In publishing the libel, Ruggles had placed the entire newspaper and its editors in jeopardy. Cornish was beside himself and blamed the Vigilance Committee and its treasurer Ruggles; he published an editorial critical of the activist, who responded with a heartfelt letter. "This comes to you from a *deeply injured* and afflicted friend," Ruggles's letter to Cornish began. He went on to lament Cornish's "*anti-Christian spirit*" when "you . . . reached over the Committee to stab me." Ruggles was hurt and he wanted Cornish to know.[1]

But Cornish's supporters came vigorously to his defense. Just after Ruggles had published the second issue of his magazine the *Mirror of Liberty*, a Cornish supporter penned a letter highly critical of Ruggles. The magazine issue was "all DAVID RUGGLES—'Him first—him last—him middle—him without end.'" According to the letter writer, who signed it simply as "AN ABOLITIONIST," Ruggles suffered from a "tottering reputation," even among the city's Black residents: "There is not a colored man in New York, but who begins to see through this *vigilant* man." It seemed that Cornish was not the only abolitionist who had tired of Ruggles.[2]

Meanwhile, Cornish's legal bills defending himself against the libel suit mounted to nearly $1,000 by July. Much of the money was owed to New York attorneys Robert and Theodore Sedgwick,

who sent invoices to a number of abolitionists seeking payment for legal services. Ruggles pledged to "foot the bill, if I have to sell my old socks for the money." But the truth was that Ruggles didn't have the money even if he wanted to cover the costs.[3]

The sensitive Ruggles was deeply wounded, not just by Cornish's attacks, but even more by the assertion that his own community had turned against him. Ruggles defended himself, to counter the "*envy, hatred, and malice*" that characterized Cornish's verbal assaults, and "though the struggle will be *Greek against Greek*," he promised to win back his reputation. For the next several months the two men dueled in the press, each attack more vicious than the last, and by mid-1839 the differences between two of New York's leading activists had become irreconcilable. The spat in fact spilled into the Black citizenry, as supporters lined up behind one man or the other.

In late July a "Great Public Meeting" convened leaders to mediate the dispute but accomplished little, and Ruggles resigned from the Vigilance Committee. In fact, the enmity between Ruggles and the committee turned ugly when he sued its leaders, including the respected Theodore S. Wright, for $2,500 in unpaid wages and expenses. Ruggles complained in his suit that he had labored on behalf of the antislavery cause for the past three years, uncompensated for all his hard work. An empaneled group of three men, including Horace Dresser and Arthur Tappan, decided that Ruggles was in fact due a large part of unpaid wages, though far less than Ruggles had requested. The case ended with Ruggles collecting about $500. The case was over, and so was the relationship between Ruggles and the Vigilance Committee.[4]

Ruggles then turned to the one venue that was his and his alone, the one place where he could express his pain and outrage without having his comments filtered through another editor. The third issue of his *Mirror of Liberty* focused on vindication and—in no small way—on vindictiveness. In page after page, he defended his actions in the Darg case and in the handling of the Vigilance Committee's funds, offering testimony from allies within the Black city leadership like Henry Graves and Nathaniel Thomas,

who signed their name to a public appeal on behalf of Ruggles that he gleefully reprinted.

As vigorous as he was in defending himself, Ruggles spent equal energy attacking Cornish and former friends like William P. Johnson, who became "Mr. Judas Johnson." Philip A. Bell, *The Colored American*'s junior editor, was guilty of "treacherous imbecility." That newspaper, in Ruggles's heated opinion, was "one of the most odiferous sewers that is suffered to infest a community." Ruggles then tried to go around his erstwhile friends and call Black Gothamites to a "National Reform Convention." Thomas Van Rensselaer accused Ruggles of calling the meeting in "a hasty manner, and without . . . any general consultation." At the same time, Van Rensselaer had begun organizing his own "Manhattan Anti-Slavery Society."[5]

Just how sharp the divisions had become in the Black community became clear when a controversy over race and segregation erupted over Van Rensselaer's fancy new restaurant. Black businessmen who tried to cater to both Black and white customers were in a tough bind. They wanted to welcome Black patrons but were always wary of offending white customers who resented mixing with people of color, especially when it came to social events like dining. One summer night, two leading African Americans, Charles L. Reason and Alexander Crummell, visited Van Rensselaer's restaurant, only to be taken to eat in the kitchen. Outraged by such an insult, the two men berated the owner for segregating them, and Van Rensselaer responded with equal venom. Philip Bell similarly went to eat at the restaurant and then was taken behind a screen. This was a distraction the movement could ill afford, but for Bell and his insulted friends, the issue was worth the battle. Newspapers again were the battlefield, as editors clashed over to what extent Black business owners should accommodate white racism.[6]

The Black abolitionist movement had begun to fracture, and soon the white abolitionist community would, too. The American antislavery movement had benefited a great deal from the brave toil of leaders like Garrison, but the cause had also attracted a

small but determined and passionate number of followers with differing views. Garrison and his followers remained dedicated to a peaceful path of moral suasion to convince whites of the irreligious and immoral nature of holding human beings as property. Other antislavery voices, like that of former Kentucky slaveholder James G. Birney and his adherent Henry B. Stanton (husband of feminist Elizabeth Cady Stanton), wanted to enter the political arena to fight against bondage within the governmental systems founded by the Constitution. Garrison thought the Constitution was tainted by its legal protections for slavery and believed that members of the abolitionist community should remain aloof from partisan politics.

That division over whether to engage in the political arena divided the American antislavery movement just when Blacks needed whites to remain united. As African American New Yorker Charles B. Ray wrote to Birney, Black leaders hoped that whites would "bury the hatchet, & do nothing to reflect upon our holy cause in our beloved though slavery ridden country." Alas, it was too much to be hoped for, as Birney ran for president and Garrison left the country to attend the antislavery meeting in London. Into the breach stepped the New York Kidnapping Club.[7]

African American businessman and leader Charles B. Ray. *(From Carter Godwin Woodson's* The Negro in Our History, *Wikimedia Commons)*

By 1840, the New York Police Department, together with allies in the Irish working class, the Democratic Party, and Wall Street, combined their strengths to fight against those calling for Black civil rights. Boudinot and Jacob Hays still dominated the police force in Lower Manhattan, daily terrorizing people of color for profit. Wall Street businessmen and their journalist backers in the press like Gerard Hallock of the *Journal of Commerce* continued to scorn and harass anyone who even thought about placing concern for Black lives over the need to appease southern slaveholders and uphold the cotton trade.

But African American voices were fighting back against a racist press, and they particularly resented the constant support for southern slaveholders expressed in the pages of Wall Street's *Journal of Commerce*. Cornish at *The Colored American* angrily denounced the "unrighteous and insulting remarks" the paper frequently directed toward Black residents and condemned Hallock and his paper for "the uniform consistency of that journal, in its subservience to the measures and interests of the slave-holding south." Other Black observers accused the paper of "warring on American citizens of color." This became even more credible when, to the horror of Black New Yorkers, the *Journal of Commerce* reportedly included in its pages ads for the sale of slaves.[8]

The Democratic Party of New York could also be counted on to defend the Union, the prosperity it fostered, and the constitutional compromise over slavery. With the help of powerful pols based in Tammany Hall, Democrats maintained a machine-like efficiency when it came to voting and elections. They had been locked in a heated political war with the opposition Whig Party since the days of Andrew Jackson, and the hyperpartisanship continued into the 1840s.

That ruthless efficiency and willingness to use violence in support of the party were embodied in Isaiah Rynders. Born in 1804 in Waterford, New York, Rynders tried his hand at a number of occupations but was most known as an avid gambler and frequent knife fighter on Mississippi River steamboats in the 1820s and early 1830s. He reportedly killed a man after a card game in

Mississippi and fled to Gotham around 1837. Known for a booming voice, a powerful memory that allowed him to recite scenes from Shakespeare's plays, and a tendency toward wild gesticulation, Rynders made an immediate and commanding impact on New York. Just as Boudinot, Riker, Nash, and other leaders of the New York Kidnapping Club were shaping their perverse business, Rynders arrived. It was good timing for Rynders, but bad timing for the city's African Americans.[9]

Rynders organized his band of blowhards and thugs into the elite-sounding Empire Club, but they were known among everyday residents by more earthy names, such as the "Plug Uglies." Under Rynders's charismatic leadership, the Empire Club intimidated political opponents, beat up Black citizens and abolitionists, conducted outright election fraud, and harassed speakers who dared to cross Tammany. In fact, the machinations of Rynders and his gang likely resulted in the election of an American president. Rynders and the Empire Club had pushed opponents away from the polls and lined up Irish voters to cast ballots for Democratic candidate James K. Polk. Since the margin in New York was so narrow, and since the state was needed to push Polk over the finish line, Rynders rode high as the man

Isaiah Rynders of Tammany Hall. *(New York Society Library)*

who defeated Henry Clay and the Whigs. In fact, New Yorkers elevated Rynders to near-mythic status for having swung the election to the Democrats. Rynders's influence helped him win a job working for the party in Washington, where he moved his brawling politics for a brief time before returning to New York. He even attended Polk's inaugural party, where he was championed as "the ruling spirit of the stormy Democratic elements of the redoubtable and formidable Empire Club" and "the feared opponent of the Whiggery in the city of the Knickerbockers." His elevated political status did not calm his street-level gangsterism, and by the following spring after the election, Rynders was again embroiled in a pistol-wielding brawl.[10]

While Rynders wreaked havoc on the Democrats' opponents, city officials were equally dismissive of African Americans' growing anger over their mistreatment. Riker's replacement, Robert H. Morris, had proven only slightly more conscientious when it came to Black civil rights. Morris had served as an assistant to the US attorney in New York, and his father was a prominent judge, but Morris owed his job as city recorder to Democratic governor and anti-abolitionist champion William Marcy.

It didn't help at all that though the mayoralty toggled between Democrats and Whigs throughout the 1830s and 1840s, none of the city's mayors devoted much time or attention to kidnapping or fugitive slave renditions. Abolitionists like Ruggles were suspicious of both political parties, but at least the Whigs at the state level seemed better at hiding their disdain for people of color. Many of the most prominent politicians, including William Henry Seward and Thurlow Weed, were Whigs; Seward, in fact, helped to coin the phrase "higher conscience" to describe his views on the Fugitive Slave Clause of the Constitution. There was no denying that the nation's founding document required northern states to return runaways. The clause was clear and unequivocal, even though the enforcement mechanisms were far less settled. There was no use pretending that the Constitution was antislavery, but Seward and other abolitionists argued that their sense of right and wrong, their strong belief that slavery was immoral, was more

important than adherence to man-made law. They felt a higher duty to obey their conscience.

By the early nineteenth century, considerable tensions had emerged between state government and city officials, tensions that had only escalated in the 1830s. Perhaps most importantly, the contrasting ideology of politicians elected at the state and municipal levels generated friction and mutual resentments that made reigning in the kidnapping club even more difficult. Many of the state's most conservative politicians, including those most pro-South, represented Gotham, from Isaiah Rynders to mayors like Cornelius Lawrence and Isaac L. Varian. Upstate New York, especially after evangelical fervor swept through in the 1820s and 1830s, held some of the North's most ardent antislavery cities, including Rochester, which would become the home of Frederick Douglass. These New York upstate counties sent men like Seward and Weed to the State House and to Congress, and they were behind the most important anti-kidnapping legislation passed in the state before the Civil War.[11]

With the backing of Whig governor William Henry Seward, the state assembly passed two important laws in the spring of 1840. The first required a trial by jury for all cases of suspected run-aways, an urgent reform that abolitionists like Ruggles had been demanding, and that was clearly aimed at the noxious antics of police officers like Boudinot and Nash. At least if an actual trial was required, Black citizens could prevent their loved ones from being kidnapped in the middle of the night and placed on a boat or train to southern slavery before the sun rose. Examples of such trials had taken root in ancient Greece and Rome, had become an important common-law right in early modern England, and had been enshrined in the Bill of Rights in the Constitution. But as free states struggled to enforce the Fugitive Slave Clause and later laws passed to render the clause effectual, New York's African Americans who were vulnerable to abduction were only rarely granted such trials. But by 1840, Connecticut and Indiana had already passed similar laws, and now finally New York joined them. Just as important, the new law punished kidnappers with a

maximum sentence of ten years, a hefty reprimand that optimistic legislators hoped would deter slave catchers from taking the risk.

Ruggles was skeptical that the new laws would really make a significant difference. In fact, Governor Seward would soon appoint Boudinot commissioner of deeds in New York, which allowed him to earn additional salary while he still held his job as constable of the Third Ward. Still, Ruggles leaned toward the Whig Party, since New York Democrats and their base of support in Tammany Hall were so stridently anti-Black. But Ruggles also knew that Boudinot and Nash were committed members of the Whig Party, which told him all he needed to know about that political organization. In fact, both members of the Kidnapping Club were accused of political corruption in the late 1830s. Nash, charged publicly with buying votes and lining up repeat voters, strongly denied what he called "false and unfounded" allegations. His partner in crime Boudinot came to his defense and signed an affidavit saying that he had sent Nash on an errand in Ohio, no doubt related to runaways. Ruggles didn't trust any of them, or politicians in either party.[12]

Much to Ruggles's surprise, though, the new law stuck. Kidnappings and fugitive slave arrests would continue until the Civil War, and Boudinot remained a fixture on the police force, but the new jury trial law severely curtailed the actions of the New York Kidnapping Club, which had always depended in part on arresting accused runaways and processing them as quickly and quietly as possible before activists or conscientious legal authorities could intervene. When Ruggles and the Black community were able to marshal their substantial numbers into protests and mobs, Boudinot and Nash resented the attention and commotion. The jury trial and the anti-kidnapping laws made a significant difference in New York and marked the beginning of the end for the kidnapping gang.

JUST AS THE NEW YORK Kidnapping Club was on the wane, however, an equally troubling rise in the transatlantic slave trade took center stage. As we saw in Chapter Four, the use of the Port of New

York to build slaving ships, to outfit slavers with all manner of supplies from iron shackles to casks of water, and to support slaving
voyages through investment and insurance, was hardly new and
had been taking place in New York for decades after Congress had
made the slave trade illegal in the early 1800s. Much to the dismay
of Ruggles and his allies, New York customs officers had done little
to stop the practice. Yet the new wave of slaving was different. In
the 1840s and 1850s, New York became one of the most important ports in the illegal trade in kidnapped Africans. How a city
that was becoming a world-famous financial center, a metropolis
that would in a few decades witness the construction of the Statue
of Liberty in that same harbor, would also be home to the illegal
slave trade is one of the great ironies in American history.

Scores of New York captains, businessmen, and seamen were
involved, and probably hundreds of ships were engaged in the
slave trade before reaching a peak in the 1850s. Before African
Americans could breathe a sigh of relief over the passage of the
jury-trial and anti-kidnapping laws, New York politicians, policemen, and public officials ignominiously allowed the city to become
synonymous with the brutal and deadly slave trade.

The slaving ships seemed to come in pairs or in groups, perhaps in hopes of using their numbers to ensure success. One
night in mid-June in 1839, around two o'clock in the morning,
under dark skies and with a mist blowing off the water, three ships
appeared in New York harbor. The lead ship, with its name the
Buzzard emblazoned on its wooden sides, displayed the flag of the
British navy. The two other ships, the *Clera* and the *Eagle*, sported
Spanish flags but appeared to have American crew aboard. The
mystery deepened when it became clear that the original Spanish
crew had all perished from malaria and that New York native Captain Hooker of the *Clera* was also near death. The ghostly ships
were clearly built in America, but why were they being guided into
the commercial waters off Manhattan?

Before any questions could be answered, other ships appeared
in the harbor shepherded by British vessels, so many that the *New
York Herald* complained that "the thing is getting to be an everyday

occurrence." The *Wyoming*, captained by John Edwards, arrived in mid-July, and the murky history of the brig slowly became clearer after its appearance in New York harbor. Edwards ran another brig between Havana and New Orleans, and then bought the *Wyoming* expressly to transport slaves from Africa. Captain Edwards had staffed the *Wyoming* under an American flag with a Spanish crew and several Spanish slave traders and left Havana for the West African coast. In April 1839 captain and crew arrived at the mouth of the Gallinas River in Liberia, between Cape Saint Ann and Grand Cape Mount, a notorious hub of the illegal transatlantic slave trade.

The British navy, determined to suppress the slave trade, patrolled the waters off the West African coast, including hotspots like the Gallinas River. Suspicious of the *Wyoming*, a British captain boarded the ship and found ledgers, irons, water casks, and other telltale signs of the ship's intentions. When the ship had left New York seven months prior, the city was proud of its shipbuilding heritage. In fact, a beautiful painting of the *Wyoming* hung in the editorial room of the *New York Herald*. But the shameful mission of the brig created anger and frustration among the more liberal-minded residents of Gotham, who thought the trade in human bodies much more abhorrent than the abstraction of slavery itself. New Yorkers might be able to look the other way regarding slavery as it existed in the South, but they angrily demanded an end to the illegal importation of more captives.

Who was to blame for this embarrassment, where haughty British navy captains chastised Americans for their eager participation in the transatlantic slave trade? The answer to the mystery of slave ships like the *Clera*, the *Eagle*, and the *Wyoming* was soon revealed, as the captains were arrested and placed in debtors' prison not far from New York's City Hall. Over the coming months, the details would be unveiled, and the conspiracy involved a wellborn American diplomat; the triangular slave trade linking New York, Havana, and West Africa; and the complicity of an American political system that had grown accustomed to making deals to keep its fragile Union intact.[13]

About two hundred slave ships, almost all of them built in New York, Philadelphia, or Baltimore as sturdy brigs, were constructed by firms that received huge bribes to remain silent and oblivious. One small firm received hush money amounting to hundreds of dollars at a time, and a major shipbuilding business in New York hauled in a quarter of a million dollars in one season. The American-built vessels were incredibly fast, designed to outrun patrol ships and under favorable wind conditions could even compete with the speed of steamers. Just after construction, the ships were loaded with cargo and sailed to Havana with American papers and manned by American seamen. Once in Cuba, the ships were sold and the American crews discharged; a new crew of Spanish, Portuguese, and a few Americans were hired, but the American captain remained in command. The ship also took on a Spanish captain as a passenger. After crossing the Atlantic, the Spanish captain replaced the American captain, and the Spanish flag was raised.

All along the western coast of Africa and particularly at the mouth of major rivers, elaborate signaling systems warned slave traders of British patrols. Lookouts along the shore lit torches at the tops of the tallest trees, and then slaves were taken on board in the middle of the night.

The slave ships were an unimaginably horrifying sight for the men, women, and children taken from their native lands and brutally transported to another continent. Imagine being a six- or seven-year-old child, captured and chained with other strangers of all ages who spoke a hundred different languages. The shock and fear of being kidnapped from your family were almost overwhelming, but the fear of what was happening next proved equally scary. Were you being rounded up to be eaten? To be sexually and physically abused? To be taken to some land far from home? The fear of the unknown would be debilitating even as you remained chained and imprisoned in one of the many castle-like fortresses that slave traders operated all along the West African coast. As you sit among strangers in the prison, the worst still awaits.

Sometime during the summer (you would have lost track of the days and weeks) a large brig with foreign letters spelling

Ulysses painted on its wooden hull, and bearing a Portuguese flag, approaches the floating prison in which you have been sitting for several weeks. You don't know this, but the *Ulysses* is on its eighth transatlantic slave-trading voyage, having already transported thousands of people into bondage in places like Brazil, America, and Cuba. This time you are one of 556 people of all ages who are forced aboard the brig. You are led naked in chains into the bowels of the great ship and ultimately into a dark compartment only two and a half feet high. You are wedged into the small space so tightly that your body is pressed on all sides by other bodies. You barely have enough room to turn over at night. And there you will lie for the fifty days it will take to reach your destination thousands of miles from where you were born.

Within days of this Middle Passage between Africa and the New World, the small compartment is filled with the stench of feces, urine, vomit, and sweat, which will be ankle-deep by the time you next see land. Almost everyone is naked, except for a few of the stronger African male captives who have traded clothing and some modicum of better treatment in exchange for wielding whips to keep the rest in order. You are fed barely enough to survive, and only allowed a pint of water per day. The traders have carefully calculated the provisions in their ledgers, ensuring that, like all good capitalists, they will have a healthy profit by the journey's end. You wonder what kind of devils would subject fellow human beings to such cruelty.[14]

Abolitionists in places like New York asked the same question. As abhorrent as owning human beings and forcing them to toil in cotton fields was to many Americans, the actual buying and selling of people seemed much worse, and the slave trade, the continued uprooting of children and their families long after the practice was outlawed, seemed especially egregious. The question for abolitionists back in New York was: Who was approving the sale of the ships in Havana so that the complicated maneuvering and refitting of the brigs could continue unabated?[15]

Nicholas P. Trist boasted a pedigree that linked the most prominent Founding Fathers in the Democratic Party. The grandson

of a confidant of James Madison, Trist studied at West Point and then studied law with Thomas Jefferson. Trist married into the Jefferson family when he wed the president's granddaughter, and by the 1830s he had firmly established himself as a leading Democratic operative, including a stint as Andrew Jackson's personal secretary, a job that had landed him a plum post as the leading diplomat in Cuba.

Ensconced as the US consul in Havana, the proslavery Trist immediately set his sights on a large sugar plantation, but lost the investment. Throughout the 1830s, Trist earned money from signing and approving documents that masked the sale of American ships that all knew were destined to become slavers, and according to British critics Trist also secretly signed documents that made it appear that African-born enslaved people hailed from Cuba, to skirt the ban on the transatlantic slave trade.

British naval officers were the ones who brought Trist's dubious actions to light. British commissioner Richard Madden wrote a lengthy letter to American abolitionist William Channing, which was printed and widely distributed as a pamphlet that revealed Trist's nefarious activities in Cuba. As word spread of Trist's abetting the slave trade and placing the interests of Spanish and Portuguese slave traders ahead of the commercial interests of American merchants, Trist found himself in hot water back home. City papers reported that Trist was despised even by the American merchants in Havana, who had "no confidence in his wisdom or his goodness." The shocking and widespread involvement in the transatlantic trade, represented in the public mind by the ongoing controversy over *La Amistad*, showed that there were hundreds of *Amistad*s abducting thousands of Africans in the triangular trade between Havana and American ports like New York, decades after Congress had outlawed the practice. Explosive reports, driven mostly by British documents and published newspaper articles, were reprinted and read in New York.[16]

African American opinion leaders like Ruggles were outraged, of course, and so too were other abolitionists as well as northeastern shipbuilders and masters who saw their business reputations

besmirched. In September 1839, a grand meeting of shipping interests, from builders to merchants, met at the Second Ward Hotel on Nassau Street in Manhattan. Speakers at the assembly denounced Trist, but others thought the charges against him were mere rumors. What seemed to irritate the shipmasters most of all was the fact that Trist seemed protective of Spanish and Portuguese interests at the expense of America's, since slaving was adversely affecting legitimate trade. Non-slaving captains engaged in legal business were constantly being harassed and detained by British patrols.

New York shipping firms were making hundreds of thousands of dollars every year, and the real anger arose when Trist threatened that profit. But the heat was sufficient by the end of 1839 that even Wall Street editors were advising the consul "to come home and defend himself against the war that has been hotly waging upon him for some months." He was removed from his Cuba post, but the damage to his reputation proved ephemeral because in the coming years he would be sent to Mexico to negotiate the sale of a huge swath of territory that would become the southwestern states of Utah, Colorado, Wyoming, California, Nevada, New Mexico, and Arizona, further proof of the intertwined nature of the rise of American capitalism and power with the ever-growing clout of American slavery.[17]

RUGGLES READ ABOUT THE controversies over Trist and the slave trade in New York papers, reading with dismay the stories from faraway places like Africa and Cuba that he knew he would likely never see. Ruggles considered all people of color his brethren, no matter where they lived on the globe, and it pained him to think that the condition of his brothers and sisters had improved only marginally. True, the abolitionist movement seemed to gain more credence in the eyes of white allies, especially as the treacherous and cruel actions of Boudinot, Nash, Pettis, and other associates of the New York Kidnapping Club continued to generate controversy. Thanks to the new jury-trial law, their most infamous activities

would gradually diminish. But the abolitionist press reported on the arrests and kidnappings of suspected runaways into the early 1840s. Every month, papers offered shocking tales of children lost or loved ones disappearing, warning Black families with headlines that blared "LOOK OUT FOR KIDNAPPERS." *The Colored American* declared during the summer of 1841 that "our city is infested with kidnappers. There are villains now prowling in our streets, who are keener than blood-hounds on the track of a negro."[18]

For Ruggles, the reports were no doubt demoralizing, but during that same summer of 1841, he was embroiled in his own battle against Jim Crow laws in public transportation that consumed what little physical energy he had left. State and city laws in the free states allowed private companies that ran railroads, ferries, and stagecoaches the right to create separate compartments for whites and Blacks. The so-called dirty car on trains was reserved for Black travelers, who paid the same amount for their tickets but were excluded from "whites only" seating. This was true in racially conservative cities like New York but also in areas of New England where abolitionists had been particularly vocal. More than a hundred years before the heroic Rosa Parks refused to leave her seat on a Montgomery bus, helping to spark the modern civil rights movement, a similar struggle over racial segregation rocked Black communities in New York and New England. And as usual David Ruggles was at the center of the action.

The long-simmering controversy over Jim Crow in public transportation actually erupted in early 1841 when prominent Black businessman Thomas Downing found himself beaten and abused for taking a seat in the whites-only car of the Harlem Railroad. This train had become notorious in New York for its maltreatment of Black passengers. Downing managed a church refectory on Broad Street and was well respected even in the white community as the owner of a popular oyster restaurant in Lower Manhattan. The conservative *Journal of Commerce* credited Downing with quick action in Lower Manhattan during the Great Fire in December 1835, which likely saved more than a million dollars' worth of

New York restaurateur Thomas Downing. *(Photographs and Prints Division, Schomburg Center for Research in Black Culture, The New York Public Library, Astor, Lenox and Tilden Foundations)*

THOMAS DOWNING
Thomas Downing, one of the pioneers of New York city. He at one time owned the property at No. 3 Broad street, now occupied by the Morgan-Drexler building, a structure valued at $3,000,000. Born in 1791, he knew intimately every New Yorker of prominence up to the days of the Civil war. It was he who saved James Gordon Bennett's New York Herald from going under by advancing a loan of $10,000 to Bennett.

buildings from burning. But none of this standing in the community mattered much when Downing was dragged from a white car on the Harlem Railroad in early 1841. He was so badly beaten that he sued the railroad and the agent who threw him off, but a jury refused to punish the white agent or the company.[19]

Black New Yorkers continued to test Jim Crow segregation even after Downing had been abused, and Ruggles was among the most prominent travelers to test the law. Traveling from Manhattan to New Bedford, Massachusetts, to testify in a slave-trading trial, Ruggles bought a ticket for two dollars and sat in a whites-only car. A conductor approached Ruggles and told him to move to the "dirty car," but the activist refused. A few minutes later the railroad superintendent appeared with three other men, and they grabbed

Ruggles, tore his clothes, and tossed him onto the platform. He demanded his trunk, which had been placed in the baggage car, but the agents refused and the train left with his trunk still aboard.[20]

An indignant Ruggles sued the railroad company, and there was ample evidence that the activist had been assaulted. The judge, however, refused to listen to Ruggles's claims of segregation, saying that no white man would want to ride in a railroad car with Black passengers, and that the railroad had every right as a private company to set its own rules. The *Boston Times* newspaper called Ruggles "an insolent negro" who "did wrong in entertaining a place where he knew his presence was not wanted." Ruggles complained bitterly that he had been "found guilty of wearing a colored skin."[21]

A few weeks later some of the most prominent Black activists in America were in the same predicament as Ruggles. Frederick Douglass, who would become famous in 1845 when he published his autobiography, had not yet emerged as the leading Black voice of the nineteenth-century civil rights movement. But just after his friend Ruggles had been thrown from a car in New Bedford, Douglass was on his way to an Anti-Slavery Society meeting and bought a ticket on the Eastern Railroad at the Newburyport station north of Boston. Douglass and a white abolitionist named J. M. Buffum took their seats, when they were immediately confronted by a group of railroad agents demanding that Douglass move to the Black car. Buffum objected, as did several other passengers, who said that they did not mind Douglass sitting in their car, even taking a vote by a show of hands to demonstrate.

The agents persisted. Douglass said, "If you give me any good reason why I should leave this car, I'll go willing." The other passengers yelled, "Give him one good reason!" Finally, the agent muttered, "Because you are black." The frustrated agent brought a bunch of ruffians back, who screamed, "Snake out the damned n——!" They beat the white abolitionist traveling with Douglass and grabbed Douglass and threw him in the dirty car. Several other clashes with Black passengers defiantly taking seats in whites-only railroad cars erupted in the summer and fall of 1841, including

one involving antislavery activist Mary Newhall Green, who was carrying her baby, and the prominent Black abolitionist Charles Lenox Remond.[22]

The summer of protests against Jim Crow had worn on Ruggles, whose eyesight continued to worsen. For a time, he discovered a lotion that dramatically improved his vision, but his eyes soon darkened again, and he began planning a trip to Paris to visit an ophthalmologist, an expensive trip Ruggles could hardly afford. Given the $250 bill he held for his legal defense in the Darg case, combined with other monies he spent to aid victims of the New York Kidnapping Club, Ruggles had expended hundreds of dollars of his own scarce funds in support of the cause of human rights, to the detriment of his own physical and financial welfare.

With his health deteriorating, he left behind Manhattan forever and moved to western Massachusetts to try to recover his health. Friends in the antislavery crusade tried to raise funds to help. In a poem titled "An Appeal to Abolitionists in Behalf of David Ruggles," fellow abolitionists in *The Liberator* called for aid:

> Say ye, shall he who labored
>   So faithfully, so long
> To free the weak and helpless
>   From cruel hands and strong . . .
> The eyes that blessed the hopeless,
>   Are now with blindness dim—
> "He hath been sight to others,"
>   Who will be sight to him?[23]

Despite such pleas, Ruggles would live out his few remaining years in Massachusetts, far removed from the Manhattan battles over Black lives that had cost him so much.

Though he still had many supporters in New York and New England, the turmoil over his recent fight with Cornish and the Vigilance Committee led him to the brink of exhaustion, and he was beginning to feel alienated from his adopted home in Manhattan. While he was being vilified by Cornish and the leaders of

the committee, Ruggles at the same time was being feted by the antislavery communities in and around Boston, which in 1841 and 1842 was aflame with indignation over the fugitive slave case of George Latimer. A self-emancipated man from Virginia, Latimer had fled bondage to make a life in Boston, only to be captured by slave catchers and put on trial. Massachusetts residents were outraged over this violation of their rights as a state to outlaw slavery. Together with others across the free states, protests over fugitive slave recaptures generated a powerful northern states' rights politics that would represent a new and important shift in thinking. Boston's abolitionist community even began publishing a newspaper called *The Latimer Journal*, and several "Latimer Meetings" appeared across New England in righteous remonstration against the arrest of runaways and the kidnapping of free people.

The abolitionist press, including Sidney Gay's *National Anti-Slavery Standard*, were angry that kidnapping continued to plague the city. In fact, they began formulating a northern free state ideology that mirrored the states' rights philosophy of the slave South. Didn't New York and other states have the right to keep slavery out of their borders? What did the law mean if southerners could cross into free states to seize whomever they saw fit to accuse of being a fugitive? "The dignity of our State" was at stake, according to Gay and fellow abolitionists, and fellow New Yorkers in the police force, the halls of city government, and the courtrooms were finally beginning to see the validity of Gay's argument.[24]

Primed by the Latimer crisis, Massachusetts antislavery campaigners persuaded Ruggles to leave New York and make his home in Northampton. Suffering from ill health and fatigue, having been arrested and beaten for his radicalism in Gotham, Ruggles considered the possibility that life in a small town would prove reinvigorating and even perhaps help restore some of his lost eyesight. Boston-area abolitionists like the equally formidable William C. Nell called meetings to support Ruggles's struggling journal, *Mirror of Liberty*, and tried to persuade the New Yorker to move north. Nearby, in New Bedford, Frederick Douglass and other prominent abolitionists also declared their support for

Ruggles and his journal, raised fifty dollars and promised to raise more, and praised Ruggles for his role in a recent fugitive slave case. Douglass himself became an agent for Ruggles's journal.[25]

The pull to Massachusetts was strong, and sometime in 1842 Ruggles moved permanently to Northampton to join a communitarian group and to found a "water cure" hospital in which patients could relax and recuperate in a spa-like environment. Ruggles's days as a fierce critic and foe of what he had labeled the New York Kidnapping Club were behind him forever, but he could not leave his determination to fight slavery and kidnapping when he moved to Massachusetts, and in a few years he would help to found the Colored Citizens Association in his new state.

Until his death at the end of 1849 from some kind of intestinal distress, Ruggles maintained a close relationship with leading Black abolitionists like Sojourner Truth and Frederick Douglass. Though he had seemingly mellowed in his final years, after decades of sacrificing his own health to battle Boudinot, Riker, and Nash and the other members of the New York Kidnapping Club, Ruggles was no less committed to fighting racism and segregation in western Massachusetts, including a stint as agent for Douglass's antislavery newspaper *The North Star*. Ruggles would no longer duel with the New York police officers who arrested Black residents at will; no more would he surreptitiously walk the alleyways of Lower Manhattan or the docks along the East River in search of kidnappers and slave traders. His days of fighting the entrenched commercial interests of Wall Street as they tried to maintain positive business ties with southern slaveholders were over.[26]

BY 1840, WALL STREET had begun the long, slow climb out of its economic depression, a recovery exemplified by the erection of new and extravagant buildings in Lower Manhattan. Deep in the marble quarries of Quincy, Massachusetts, workmen toiled in the summer sun to carve out eighteen massive columns. Each weighing about thirty-three tons and fluted in the neoclassical style, the columns would be transported down the Atlantic coast to New

York, where they would be erected at the imposing façade of the
Wall Street Exchange building. The columns were so colossal that
a nine-ton cart had to be specially constructed to carry them four
miles from the quarry to the port at Quincy Point. Seventy oxen
were hitched to the cart, pulling each $4,000 column to the edge
of the sea. Once completed, the New York Exchange would cost
well over one million dollars to construct, but in the eyes of Wall
Street financiers the building would serve as a fitting monument
to the dizzying physical and financial growth of the city itself, and
indeed, the nation. The city's growing number of Black business
owners did not feel included in this celebratory moment, as the
new exchange was clearly mostly if not exclusively for the benefit of white merchants and bankers. In fact, Black Wall Street
began to organize its own "Union Commercial Association," led
by restaurateur Thomas Van Rensselaer.[27]

Just as the columns of the new exchange were being lifted into
place, the New York Kidnapping Club was slowly dying. Although
he remained a member of the New York police and would soon
be appointed captain of the Third Ward, Boudinot declared bankruptcy at the end of 1842, just after Ruggles had decamped to
Northampton. Though he likely garnered thousands of dollars
in his role as a slave catcher and kidnapper, Boudinot had been
involved in questionable land speculations. Then, in September
1842, Richard Riker, whose decisions as city recorder for nearly
thirty years on behalf of southern slaveholding claimants sent
untold numbers of people into bondage, died at the age of seventy.
Despite his legacy of devastation and racism, he was remembered
fondly by the commercial press of the city, which credited Riker
with maintaining the bonds of Union through the Constitution's
Fugitive Slave Clause and the political framework it provided for
the city's rapid growth and prosperity. Courts in the city shut down
in his honor, and papers as far south as New Orleans and Charleston noted his passing.[28]

Though the kidnapping club was receding, the abduction of
free African Americans and the arrest of the self-emancipated
persisted. Arrests and abductions were unrelenting. Slave-hunting

lawyer Fontaine Pettis sustained his practice on behalf of slaveholding clients, boasting that he now had "agents in all the principal
places of negro resort in the free states." Though the state had
passed laws approving jury trials for all cases of accused fugitive
slaves, New York City politicians remained steadfast in support of
renditions and the national compromise with the South. Abolitionism waxed and waned in northern communities throughout
the 1840s and 1850s, but most white New Yorkers stood firmly
against racial equality and Black civil rights.

With a population of half a million people, how could the
removal of just one individual change the character of a city? And
yet, with Ruggles gone, New York was indeed a different place.
Part of the reason was the nature of Ruggles's activism: it seemed
like he was more than just one person since he was constantly on
patrol in the streets and along the wharves of both Manhattan
and Brooklyn. One minute he appeared before a judge in City
Hall; the next he stood in the middle of Pearl Street to confront
Boudinot and corrupt officers. Though within the city lived scores
of Black and white antislavery activists who fought against racism
and police violence, Ruggles was a one-man army who struggled
day and night against the kidnapping club.

With Ruggles removed to Massachusetts, New York's abolitionist movement was in important ways liberated from his heavy hand.
Manhattan would now have the chance to develop a movement
more suitable to a global capital, not so deeply dependent on the
work of one person, but a more organized and sustained effort
to combat the city's worst tendencies toward indifference. Black
leaders like Louis Napoleon stepped up in Ruggles's absence, calling out those who kidnapped accused runaways and those who
tried to sneak into New York enslaved people from other states. In
one of the more celebrated antebellum cases over slavery, Napoleon openly challenged in court the ability of a Virginia family
to enter Gotham with their slaves (among them six children) in
tow. With the help of abolitionist attorney John Jay, Napoleon and
other Black New Yorkers won an important victory. Much to the
shock and anger of white southerners across the slave states, the

city's Superior Court ruled that once they crossed into New York, the enslaved "property" of the Lemmon family became free.[29]

The question was which side would ultimately claim victory. Would Gotham remain a Democratic Party and Tammany stronghold, one not just indifferent to Black lives, but indeed openly hostile? Would politicians continue to employ the NYPD as a political arm to criminalize Black bodies and to enforce the desire of southern slaveholders to recapture runaways? Or would New York begin to embrace the kind of multiracial and multiethnic democracy that Ruggles had wanted so desperately?

These were not just questions for one city; Americans more generally grappled with these same controversies. How could northern states keep slavery out of their borders but remain true to their constitutional obligations to return runaways? This very question was destroying the Union, as southern states continued to clamor for legislation protecting slavery, and some in the free states in the North and Midwest began to question the moral implications of their legal responsibility to return the self-emancipated. New York City lay at the heart of the nationwide schism.

Ironically, a new law passed to quell the national crisis over slavery and freedom only widened the schism. In 1850 Americans were forced to confront one of the worst laws ever passed by the United States Congress. The Fugitive Slave Law struck absolute terror in Black communities throughout the North and Midwest and accomplished what the kidnapping club couldn't do on its own: breathe new life into the arrests and abductions of Black New Yorkers.

"Blessed Be Cotton!"

THE FUGITIVE SLAVE LAW AND NEW YORK CITY

DESPITE THE LONG RECORD OF ABUSE, NEW YORK'S AFRICAN American community had been hopeful in the late 1840s. Businesses released from the 1837 Panic flourished, especially in new communities in Brooklyn as well as the Seneca Village neighborhood in Manhattan. Thomas Downing continued to manage his popular oyster restaurant on Broad Street, but he was now joined by Black restaurateurs like Lawrence Chloe and Stephen Simmons. T. S. Boston and M. J. Lyons opened a photography studio on Beach Street, while Philip A. White and James McCune Smith continued to run pharmacies. African American leaders like Charles Reason and Charles B. Ray formed the Society for the Promotion of Education Among Colored Children. Black-owned businesses like ice cream parlors, printers, undertakers, watchmakers, and engravers buoyed a lively and stable Black community.[1]

African Americans even had reason to anticipate that cracks might be developing in the alliance among Wall Street, the Democratic Party, and public officials like the police. Their hope came in the surprising form of yet another young man who refused to

accept the federal government's definition of him as a piece of property.

Since he was a boy, George Kirk had toiled on the land of Charles Chapman, a sprawling Georgia cotton plantation along the banks of the Ogeechee, a blackwater river a few miles south of Savannah. In recent years, though, the twenty-two-year-old Kirk had been hired out to work in the stables of Savannah, a situation that gave him a modicum of independence and the excitement of urban society. When Chapman called him back to the plantation, where he knew he would have to scrape by with a small daily ration of corn and where the backbreaking work of hoeing the fields awaited, George decided to steal away on a ship bound for the North.

He managed to remain concealed, wrapped up in one of the sails, for the entire first day of the voyage, but on the second day one of the sailors discovered George and brought him before Captain Theodore Buckley, who was outraged that he'd stolen passage. Buckley wanted to throw George off the ship in Charleston, but an intense headwind kept the *Mobile* bound for New York, and the ship made landfall around midnight in late October. George was secreted away under lock and key while Captain Buckley decided what to do with him.

The following day, as the *Mobile* was being unloaded, George started screaming for help, and the Black stevedores working on the Manhattan wharves soon began congregating alongside the ship. Before the dockworkers could act, Buckley managed to cut the ship loose and float back out into the harbor, but the commotion had caught the attention of the city's Black leadership, who called for Buckley's arrest as a slave trader.

Hundreds of African Americans stood vigilant outside City Hall as New York once again braced itself for a tumultuous case of a fugitive. As familiar as the broad strokes of this case would be to Black New Yorkers, however, the George Kirk affair would prove different from the cases of Henry Scott, Hester Carr, William Dixon, and Stephen Dickerson, other men and women whose arrests had scarred race relations. In fact, the matter of

George Kirk proved an important harbinger for the future of New York abolitionism.[2]

Though Captain Buckley had tried to avoid the mob of angry Black protesters gathered at the wharf around the *Mobile*, he was taken to City Hall and charged before Judge John W. Edmonds with slave trading. Immediately Buckley countered that he had no idea that Kirk was secreted away on his brig, and that he was no slave trader. However, Buckley also made clear that he intended to take Kirk back to Savannah and his owner once his New York business was complete. New York's abolitionists were just as determined that Kirk remain in the free states.

Black activists and their white allies in the legal community finally found in Judge Edmonds a sympathetic ear. Edmonds had been a city recorder like Riker, but there the similarities ended. In his late forties, Edmonds had earned a reputation as a reformer, particularly in the state prison system. Most importantly for Kirk, Edmonds was dubious about the morality of the Fugitive Slave Clause of the Constitution. Edmonds decided that the law required that either the master or someone demonstrably acting on the owner's behalf be present to carry away a fugitive, but Captain Buckley was neither Kirk's master nor did he have proof that he acted on behalf of Chapman. In a decision that brought cheers to the racially mixed courtroom as well as the throngs outside, Edmonds ruled that Kirk was a free man. Abolitionist writer Lydia Maria Child was so overjoyed that she called Kirk "the living gospel of Freedom, bound in black."[3]

As much as Kirk's friends welcomed his release, the city's merchants and politicians thought that Edmonds had decided the case on a technicality, and they feared trade with the South would grind to a halt over the controversy. They had reason to be afraid. In fact, southern papers were watching the case every bit as closely as Wall Street and Tammany Hall feared. How would the city redeem its commitment to the Union and to southern slavery? Pressed by Wall Street interests, the mayor became directly involved. Though Judge Edmonds had declared Kirk free, Captain Buckley obtained a warrant for Kirk's arrest signed by the mayor himself.[4]

New York mayor Andrew Mickle made his fortune by marrying into one of the city's largest chewing tobacco firms, and as he became a fixture on Wall Street, he worked his way through the ranks of the Tammany machine, and proved more than happy to assume the role expected of northern Democrats. Mickle's next move shocked even the most cynical observers of urban politics. There would be a second trial.

As daylight broke in City Park on the morning of November 4, 1846, only a few Black protesters had gathered, but by the time Judge Edmonds took his seat on the bench at ten in the morning more than fifty angry Black residents had coalesced near City Hall. Somehow the crowd heard that Captain Buckley possessed the mayor's warrant, and suddenly the protesters tried to storm the courtroom, though they were repulsed by a hundred police officers sent to the court to keep order. Over the protests of Tammany Hall Democrats and Buckley, Judge Edmonds once again declared Kirk a free man, and Kirk was whisked out of the court, through the park, and onto Nassau Street. Black protesters shouted "Hurrah!" and wept with joy. Kirk was lodged in one of the only safe harbors in Lower Manhattan: the Anti-Slavery Society office.

Late in the afternoon, as the NYPD kept an uneasy peace with African Americans guarding the Anti-Slavery building, a cart pulled up and a large crate was taken from the building. The police were not tricked, and they opened the crate to find Kirk hiding inside. This time Kirk was taken to Tombs Prison while the appeals continued. All other arguments exhausted, Buckley now claimed that Kirk had to be arrested for assault and battery for supposedly having attacked him while docked. Mayor Mickle demanded bail in the large sum of a thousand dollars. Remarkably, under the guise of maintaining order, Mickle ordered nine hundred members of the NYPD to arrest Kirk. Never before had a northern city deployed such a large police force to act as the arm of southern slavery, and many members of the public were shocked that so many of their officers were unleashed to take a single man into bondage. The next day headlines blared the embarrassing news that their mayor had sent "the New York Police on a Slave Hunt!"[5]

This time, it seemed that Wall Street and Tammany Hall had overplayed their hand. In their desperate attempt to placate Captain Buckley and appease southern masters, Mayor Mickle and the Democrats generated widespread public resentment and indignation, even among white moderates. This was key. For if ordinary white New Yorkers were becoming indignant at the mayor's maneuvering, perhaps they were beginning finally to see the costs incurred by kowtowing to southern slave owners. The Fugitive Slave Clause of the Constitution required the return of runaways, but did New Yorkers really want the spectacle of their own mayor sending hundreds of city officials to capture one man, who (for all they knew) may not have even been a slave? That very question at the heart of all the success enjoyed by the kidnapping club and the slave traders was barely asked until now. Only the most ardent white abolitionists like Beecher and Garrison had joined Black antislavery radicals in calling the compromise between the free states and the slave states into question. Now, for the first time, it seemed like they were finally getting through to the rest of white New York.

Antislavery activists seized the chance to highlight the mayor's overreaction and to paint themselves as the reasonable and peaceful advocates of the city. "But a very few years ago," *The National Anti-Slavery Standard* declared, "and public sentiment would have been strongly against us, and the press would have been its faithful echo." But now even some of the conservative editors who had so carefully guarded the interests of trade and commerce were questioning New York's role in the national crisis over runaways. So while at first it seemed like Kirk would be just another wound to the city's record on human rights, the actions of Judge Edmonds, the growing and increasingly sophisticated abolitionist movement, and the bravery of Black activists seemed to be reshaping the battle for New York's soul.[6]

OPTIMISTIC PEOPLE OF COLOR took heart in the new allies that seemed to be forming in the ranks of the judiciary, and Judge Edmonds brought optimism to victims of the kidnapping club even as the

NYPD and the mayor's office seemed solidly in the grips of Tammany Hall Democrats. Yet there were cracks developing in City Hall, too. Whig politicians, often more sympathetic to the civil rights claims of Black residents, were slowly making headway in winning elected city offices. Between 1847 and 1853, the Whigs captured the mayoralty in three out of four elections.

Perhaps more importantly for the daily lives of African Americans walking the streets of Brooklyn and Manhattan, there were signs of division within the police force. Boudinot, Nash, and the other notorious members of the police were still visible and active. Residents, whether they were runaways or born free, still constantly peered over their shoulders for fear of being arrested or abducted. But a new generation of officers emerged who might counter the worst tendencies of the force. The reason for such hopefulness became evident in another case of an arrested runaway in December 1848.

One chilly morning at around 8:30, Joseph Belt, light-skinned and only twenty-one, walked down Duane Street with his friend Thomas Peck. Before they could react, a carriage abruptly stopped next to them and out jumped a handful of rough men who grabbed Belt and Peck, claiming that the two friends were wanted for robbery. As we have seen, kidnappers and slave catchers often used such subterfuge because if they seized someone for being a fugitive, the captive might use violence to escape. But the real motive became clear when Peck and Belt were loaded in handcuffs into the carriage. One of the ruffians looked at Peck and uttered, "He ain't the one, let him go." Right then Belt knew the real reason he had been taken. Peck volunteered to stay with Belt, but Joseph asked Peck to leave the carriage and alert the Black community of his apprehension.[7]

Several months before, Belt supposedly had fled John Lee's Maryland farm and made his way first to Lynn, Massachusetts, and then into New York. Lee hired two slave hunters, Charles Bird and Sidney Clayton, for two hundred dollars to track down Belt, and by late December they had found their prey. Bird and Clayton sailed Belt to Gravesend Beach on Long Island, where Lee

awaited. As soon as he saw Belt, Lee told him "he would give it to him when he got back" to Maryland. To throw off the pursuit of any rescuers, Bird and Clayton bought train tickets to Philadelphia, creating a false trail.[8]

What the men from Maryland did not count on, though, was the tenacity of two police officers with a conscience. Soon after Belt had been snatched away, Officers Russell Hulse and Samuel Wolven were sent to arrest the abductors, and they arrived just in time. As the officers approached the room where Belt was being held, Lee quickly uncuffed Belt and told him to jump out the window. Belt refused and instead sought the officers' protection. As Lee admitted, if the officers had been a half hour later, the Maryland slave catchers would have made off with Belt.[9]

Luckily for Belt, his case came before John Edmonds, the same judge who had demonstrated such sympathy to George Kirk. Though they were heartened by Judge Edmonds's decision in the Kirk hearing, the city's African Americans were determined to continue to press the legal system to hear their pleas, and they crowded the courtroom when Belt came before the judge.

To the delight of those African Americans assembled in the courtroom, Judge Edmonds declared that Clayton and Bird had no right to seize Belt without due process. Equally new and important, Edmonds went out of his way to praise the work of NYPD officers Hulse and Wolven. The sudden but crucial turn of the legal system was not lost on the city's Black leaders: the bench and the police, instead of abetting the abduction of Black residents by Boudinot and the New York Kidnapping Club, had actually proved essential to rescuing Belt. No doubt Ruggles had followed the case closely from his new home in Massachusetts, and no doubt he was amazed at the dramatic shift in the courts. New York's Black citizens rejoiced at a mass meeting, declaring defiantly that "no colored persons ought to allow themselves to be arrested as a slave upon any conditions, pretenses, or grounds whatsoever, at the risk of life itself." Just as Ruggles had long advocated, Black New Yorkers were now asserting that they would fight kidnapping or slave recaptures with violence if necessary.[10]

As Ruggles and other Black leaders knew, the fight was far from over. The 1850s would witness some of the most egregious violations of Black civil rights that the city had ever seen, and the illegal slave trade in New York harbor would persist with renewed vigor during the middle of that decade. But at least now there was evidence that the courts and the police force were not unified in their disdain for Black residents. At least now African Americans could hope that a rising sense of justice on the bench and in the police districts could counter the work of darker forces that sought to undermine the Black community.

Also heartening was the fact that the antislavery movement was gaining new traction in New York City. In fact, abolitionists from around the country bravely gathered in the heart of Gotham for a large convention in early 1850. The meeting of the American Anti-Slavery Society drew activists from around the nation to the Tabernacle in Manhattan, including Garrison, Douglass, Abby Foster, Wendell Phillips, and many others. They had come from New England and the Midwest, entering what was still one of the most pro-South bastions in the free states.

Prominent abolitionist Abby Kelley Foster. *(From* A Life for Liberty *by Sallie Holley, John White Chadwick, University of California)*

The pious and pacifist Garrison rose before the gathering to deliver a stirring speech about Christian brotherhood and the religious undergirding of the antislavery movement. Abolitionism, the editor of *The Liberator* declared, was "the greatest Christian movement of the age." Just as Garrison was delivering his talk, Isaiah Rynders, the boisterous and brawling leader of Tammany Hall and the Democratic Party, shouted out from the floor that churches across the country in fact sanctioned and supported bondage. This was true, of course; some of the most vocal advocates of slavery, especially in the South, were clergymen who found ample support for bondage in the Bible. Garrison asked Rynders to wait until he had finished, and the abolitionist went on to attack slavery and offer resolutions on the corruption of American politicians who had defended enslavement. At this Rynders rose again and shouted that he refused to listen to the abuse of the country, and he rallied his many supporters in attendance, who also shouted and hissed as Garrison tried to maintain order. Rynders and several of his men rushed the platform, and his allies in the crowd yelled "Hurrah for Rynders" and "Out with the n—!" Abolitionists in the audience asked Rynders to tone down his profanity, since many women populated the hall. Astride the platform, Rynders bellowed, "I doubt very much whether white women who cohabit and mix with the woolly-headed negro are entitled to any respect from a white man." A lone abolitionist, disheveled with a long beard, then rose to sing "Hallelujah" in the gallery before he was drowned out by the ruffians. A folk music group called the Hutchinsons also began singing, but Rynders shouted up at them, "You long-haired Abolitionists, if you don't stop singing, I'll come up there and bring you down." One of Rynders's men then seized the podium to argue that African Americans were not human, "but belonged to the monkey tribe." Rynders and his men laughed and applauded. Police Chief Matsell stood right by Rynders, a single officer to protect the rights of the convening abolitionists, and did nothing to interrupt or control Rynders.[11]

The nation's most prominent person of color, the brilliant Frederick Douglass, who had recently gained fame for an autobiographical

account of his enslavement in Maryland as the "property" of his white father who was also his "owner," then took the stage to address the society. Douglass started by asking, "Look at me, and answer— am I a man?" Clearly challenged, Rynders yelled out, "*You* are not a black man. You are only half a n—." In a flash Douglass retorted, "I am half-brother to Captain Rynders!" The crowd roared with laughter, and Rynders later admitted that Douglass's shot stung bitterly, but Rynders and the Democratic Party rabble of the Empire Club successfully disrupted the society's proceedings the following day. A few months later Rynders would deliver a racist screed in the form of a July 4 oration, declaring that southern slaves were better treated than the northern members of the white working class.[12]

The American Anti-Slavery Society, realizing that New York was a dangerous place to hold meetings, withdrew and never formally returned. The *New York Globe* crowed that Douglass and the abolitionists deserved Rynders's abuse because they had violated cultural norms by allowing Black men and white women to sit in the same audience. Garrison and other speakers deserved to be shouted down because they had attacked the country and its leaders and laws. For his part, Douglass remembered the incident painfully for the rest of his life, lamenting the "demoniacal" treatment he received in a city that seemed "an enemy's land—surrounded on all sides" and criticizing his attackers as the "bloodhounds of slavery." For the near future, abolitionists would mark Gotham as a place of virulent racism and abuse. The widely publicized fervor over the meeting threatened to undo all of the recent positive developments in race relations exemplified by the Kirk and Belt cases.[13]

Embarrassed by the turmoil of the antislavery convention, New York's Black community reminded political and legal authorities that the dignity of the city was at stake over slavery and the cases of alleged fugitives. In the 1830s and early 1840s, David Ruggles had led that effort. But as vital as he was to that struggle, Ruggles often drained the energy of the movement in side squabbles and internecine conflict. Into the leadership vacuum left by Ruggles's removal to New England, a new and potent cadre of

Black leaders, combined with the increased visibility of civil rights veterans like James McCune Smith and Charles B. Ray, would emerge to take on the racial conservatives in city government and in the Chamber of Commerce. As City Hall and Wall Street placed the interests of slaveholders and the cotton trade above the interests of Black citizens, African American leaders risked their lives to make sure all of New York knew the costs.

THOSE COSTS WERE EVEN more obvious in the wake of a new Fugitive Slave Law passed to facilitate the recapture of women and men who refused to live in bondage, and the law generated a potent wave of outrage that set the nation on the path to civil war. The debate over what became the Compromise of 1850 began innocently enough as an attempt by political leaders in Congress to settle issues that had been vexing the nation for decades, including the problem of escaping slaves. Because running away was by nature a clandestine endeavor, we don't know really know how many enslaved people left slavery to make new lives in the free cities of the northern United States or Canada, but we know that there were enough men, women, and children escaping slavery over rails, aboard ships, and by foot that by 1850 the southern states believed that the number of fugitives had reached crisis proportions. With each new canal, road, and railroad, as the nation itself grew in complexity and mobility improved, running away from bondage, though still potentially deadly, became a better risk. After the violent events surrounding the Kirk and Belt cases were widely publicized in southern papers, slave owners demanded even more vociferously that the free states meet their responsibilities to recapture runaways, and the result of this demand was one of the most detestable laws ever enacted by Congress.

Details of the congressional debates over the compromise measures began filtering into an increasingly alarmed Black community in New York in the spring of 1850. Particularly worrisome were intimations that the compromise might include a dangerous new fugitive slave provision to mollify southern slaveholders.

Denied the ability to cast a ballot, African American leaders again called a mass meeting to express "the sentiments of the Colored People of New York City." Led by businessmen like Thomas Van Rensselaer and George T. Downing as well as church officials and intellectuals, the meeting targeted John C. Calhoun and other "enemies of the colored race" for failing to allow a trial by jury in the federal bill over fugitive slaves. By continuing to protect and defend slavery, the antislavery resolutions declared, the compromise would not settle the controversies but instead lead to even greater anxiety and distress. Their predictions proved prescient.[14]

Political leaders like the aging Henry Clay and Daniel Webster, along with relatively young up-and-comers like Stephen Douglas, were shocked when the Fugitive Slave Law passed as part of the Compromise of 1850 became the root of such overwhelming anger in the free states. In fact, the Fugitive Slave Law reaffirmed the Constitution's clearly stated request that free states return runaways. But when the law became public in September 1850, northern observers were stunned that they were now legally required to participate in recaptures.[15]

Specifics of the act infuriated many free-state voters who had previously taken the position that slavery was merely a southern problem. The law in fact required citizens to assist actively any attempts by law enforcement to arrest accused runaways, and threatened prosecution of those who resisted such arrests. From the perspective of white southerners, citizens in states like New York were simply being asked to help in enforcing well-established law. But northerners reacted with justifiable anger at being made accomplices in southern slavery. How could moderates or conservatives credibly argue that bondage was solely of concern to the South when free cities were now being called upon to aid the recapture of fugitives? Echoing the modern controversy over "sanctuary cities," antebellum New Yorkers begrudged the new law's requirement that they turn away runaways seeking aid and comfort and instead actively help in their return. Another stipulation of the new law seemed to put a thumb on the scales of justice by rewarding marshals more financial compensation for

declaring the accused to be runaways instead of declaring them to be free.

Many white citizens in cities from Boston to San Francisco abhorred the law, including many New Yorkers. The abolitionist community, of course, opposed the Fugitive Slave Law as a license to kidnap Black people, and thousands of African Americans fled across the northern border to settle in Canada to put themselves out of reach of US authorities. Even many white New York politicians seeking a moderate course had to admit that the new law seemed to make slavery a national institution. Massive protests erupted across the free states from Maine to California as whites increasingly came to realize that what abolitionists called the "Slave Power" had stretched its reach into the heart of their own neighborhoods.[16]

In New York City, an outraged and anxious Black community gathered for a massive meeting just days after the new law was announced. The older vanguard of the city's African American leadership, including men like Theodore S. Wright and Samuel Cornish, joined with a generation of emerging leaders to denounce the compromise measures. Charles B. Ray rose before the mixed-race gathering to proclaim that Black people were once again being sacrificed for the financial enrichment of Wall Street. "We do not rejoice in any moral triumph today," he sadly reported, "but only in the triumph of gold." Henry Walton Bibb, editor of *The Voice of the Fugitive*, decried the law for creating a "slave market at the North" and invited enslaved people to settle in Canada. Bibb declared the law nothing more than "high handed kidnapping."[17]

In July, at the State Convention of Colored People meeting in Albany, the convention had formed a committee to study the wording and implications of the Fugitive Slave Law. Their first objection focused on the law's requirement that "the freemen of the North [had] to deliver up fugitives from slavery," a stipulation that contrasted with humanistic interpretations of the Bible that stressed treating strangers with kindness. It seemed immoral to the committee that the new legislation "is in direct and impious

opposition to those laws of God which command deeds of humanity and mercy." The committee also declared that the Fugitive Slave Law violated the Declaration of Independence's claim that all men were entitled to life, liberty, and the pursuit of happiness. Finally, the convention lamented that the Bill of Rights protection of trial by jury and habeas corpus were absent from the law and so in violation of the Constitution itself.[18]

Even as the Fugitive Slave Law generated unprecedented resentment in New York's Black neighborhoods, conservative forces were equally determined to uphold the compromise measure. Clay, Webster, Douglas, and President Millard Fillmore had envisioned the Compromise of 1850 as a final settlement of the growing divisions between North and South, and they believed that successful implementation of the Fugitive Slave Law required full and unhesitating cooperation from the free states in returning runaways. If that cooperation was unmet, political leaders feared, the great American experiment in democracy was doomed

A poster warning the self-emancipated of slave hunters in the city.
(*Rauner Special Collections Library, Dartmouth College*)

to failure. In New York, as elsewhere, the Fugitive Slave Law would have to be enforced or the Union would collapse.

That view of the Union's fragility, centered in Tammany Hall and Wall Street, helps to explain why so many businessmen in both political parties rallied to defend the compromise. Wall Street's *Journal of Commerce* declared the new law "glorious news" and a one-hundred-gun salute celebrating the compromise was fired from the banks of the Battery. As editor Hallock noted in his paper, no one was happier to hear of the new laws "than capitalists whose means are always at a greater risk in troublesome times." Wall Street could not be more pleased that Black lives were being forfeited to keep the Union and the valuable cotton trade intact.[19]

Hallock used several columns of his paper to refute the "higher law" claims of abolitionists, who argued that God's law and the virtues of morality and conscience trumped any laws devised by man. Congress had passed the Fugitive Slave Law, but abolitionists refused to obey its strictures. Soon after passage of the new legislation was announced, outraged northerners listened to sermons, read editorials, and bought pamphlets that described the law as a gross violation of northern states' rights to keep bondage outside their borders. People from Maine to Michigan resented being made accomplices to this new slave-hunting system, and they angrily declared their intention to disobey the law. But conservatives argued that individual senses of morality had to give way to the force of law. "A man who does not admit that there is authority outside himself," one editorial asserted, ". . . is the highest being in the universe." Thanksgiving sermons rang from pulpits in New York and Brooklyn defending the Fugitive Slave Law and scorning those who believed that the rights of Black people were somehow more important than keeping the Union together.[20]

As one of Wall Street's leading voices, the *Journal of Commerce* both shaped and represented the pro-business agenda, much like today's *Wall Street Journal* presents the views of the business community. In fact, editor Hallock constantly reminded his readers that the only way they could continue to reap tremendous profits was by increasing the number of cotton bales from the slave states.

Gerard Hallock, editor of
the *Journal of Commerce*.
*(Library of Congress, Brady-
Handy Photograph Collection)*

In the wake of the Fugitive Slave Law, Hallock surrendered column after column of his paper to news of the pro-Union meetings
that he claimed were "spreading like wild-fire" across the Northeast. If some were outraged by the moral implications of the new
Fugitive Slave Law, others were equally incensed that abolitionists promoted disobedience. Whites in New Haven, Connecticut,
held a massive "Union Meeting" where they signed petitions and
rallied in defense of the new law. They downplayed slavery as a
legacy of the nation's founding and openly recognized that their
prosperity depended on a Union with slaveholders.[21]

One sermon declaring adherence to a "higher law," delivered by
Leonard Bacon, attracted Hallock's eagle eye. In a scathing review
of the sermon in the *Journal of Commerce*, Hallock denounced the
sermon and all others who maintained obedience only to what
they sanctimoniously called a higher law. Such "perverted consciences" would end only in anarchy; if any man could make his
own law, if he could decide which laws he would follow and which
ones were inconvenient, law would hold no meaning. Hallock

drew a distinction between divine law, which governed "moral action," and earthly laws designed to address "political action." What Bacon and Seward assumed as morality, Hallock believed, was really thinly disguised antislavery political ideology.[22]

To counter the higher-law claims of men like Bacon and Seward, Democrats held a massive "Union Meeting" at New York's Castle Garden, a large circular building in the Battery that during the 1800s had become a major entrepôt for immigrants. Speakers rallied Irish workers, Wall Street cotton magnates, and pro-Union sympathizers to declare "it the duty of the North and the whole country, to obey it in good faith." Ten thousand men, the speakers proclaimed in what sounded like a declaration of civil war, could be "summoned any twenty-four hours to enforce" the Fugitive Slave Act. Some of the city's most powerful businessmen, including Moses Taylor, head of the City Bank of New York, demanded that New Yorkers get behind the Fugitive Slave Law. The city's prosperity was at stake. The meeting at Castle Garden helped to create a new and powerful pro-business group that would champion the new Fugitive Slave Law. Composed of leading Democrats as well as Wall Street magnates like Moses Taylor, the Union Safety Committee denounced those who considered their own consciences a better guide to the law than the nation's Constitution. As the committee declared in late 1850, "aggressions . . . have been committed upon the Constitutional rights of the South by the northern fanaticism." It was time to enforce the law or the Union was doomed.[23]

Hallock repeatedly told readers that the Union was imperiled by maudlin appeals to the plight of Black people. In a telling editorial titled simply "Cotton," Hallock argued that the crop united the disparate regions of the country, joining the interests of southern slave owners together with those of northern merchants and bankers. In fact, were it not for cotton, the nation might have developed differently or even split apart given the vast distances between east and west, north and south. Were it not for cotton, the centrifugal forces of rapid growth and narrow local interests might have flung apart the interests of different states and

weakened the Union. "To all this," Hallock avowed, "Cotton is the great counteracting element." Remarkably, the editor attributed America's growing power and prosperity not to democracy, the genius of the Founding Fathers, or even the Constitution. It was all down to the binding interests of cotton, around which both the New York financiers and the small yeoman cotton farmers in Alabama could unite. Hallock summed up his editorial with a single telling phrase: "Blessed be cotton!"[24]

During the Democratic meeting at Castle Garden, Moses Taylor and other Wall Street leaders defended the compromise measures as necessary to maintain the business ties with southern slavery that had made the city one of the wealthiest in the world. But they went even further, arguing that slavery was a benign institution that had existed in all of the great historic civilizations. Meeting president George Wood told the audience that any claims that "slavery is, in itself, sinful, is . . . entirely unfounded." A remarkable and profoundly important scene unfolded: New York's leading bankers and merchants, some of them laying the foundation for the tremendous wealth from which the city continues to benefit today, stood before throngs of Democratic Party loyalists, defending slavery and slave catchers in the heart of Lower Manhattan. The new Union Safety Committee would counter the antislavery Vigilance Committee. On the streets and in the neighborhoods, along the docks and wharves, the Union Safety Committee and the Vigilance Committee were poised to clash over kidnapping and fugitive slave recaptures.[25]

For some white members of the new and fervent evangelical Protestant denominations, Wall Street's genuflection to slaveholders was too much to take. For New York's expanding abolitionist movement, it seemed that under the new law northerners were rendered subservient to the wishes of slave masters. As white New York abolitionist James G. Birney argued, "This is addressed to you as <u>freemen</u>. But how long you will remain such depends on the rebuke you give the majority in congress who passed at the last session, several infamous laws, the direct object of one of which is further to enslave others, the indirect effect of them

all, to oppress and substantially to enslave you." Birney and other activists wanted their fellow New Yorkers to see how slavery's syco-phants in Congress had seized control of the federal government against the laws of free states like New York.[26]

Farther north, among the small farms and towns upstate, Baptists and Methodists led an exponential growth in Protestant Christianity that was particularly powerful in the "burned over" dis-tricts of upstate New York but that also seeped into popular culture in Gotham. By 1850, the city embraced more than two hundred places of worship of various denominations, including more than a dozen Catholic churches as well as nine synagogues. Presbyteri-ans still boasted the most followers, but Baptists and Methodists were not far behind. Not all, of course, questioned the wickedness of slavery; Phoebe Palmer, a leading Methodist promoter of the notion of "Christian perfection," stressed individual conversion and said little about broader injustices like slavery. But evangelical leaders like George Barrell Cheever angrily denounced the con-trast between faith and the pursuit of wealth through slavery. He urged his congregation in New York "to remember the claims of the oppressed and enslaved humanity" even as they worked toward their own personal salvation.[27]

Cheever and other evangelicals questioned whether the forces of justice and humanity were losing badly in their battle for the soul of New York. When Cheever considered that the city's pros-perity had been built on cotton picked by the hands of enslaved people, he thought that fellow evangelicals like Palmer had been too often silent. They were as much to blame as the "millionaires, mammon-worshippers, and respectable and Christian cotton-conservatives" in politics and in business.[28]

The city's Black evangelical congregations did not need a "great awakening" to tell them slavery was evil. Encouraged by religious leaders like Peter Williams and his wife Molly Williams, African Americans joined Baptist and Methodist churches in large numbers. By 1850 they had built nearly twenty churches in New York and could claim about a quarter of the city's Black faithful. But Cheever, Peter Williams, and other religious leaders

who questioned the legitimacy of slavery, the compromises inherent in the Constitution, or the righteousness of the new Fugitive Slave Law were swimming against a powerful tide that washed past the slave-trading ships docked in the city's wharves and into the cramped alleyways of Lower Manhattan. With President Fillmore and the federal government solidly behind the compromise measures, US marshals searched for cases that would show the nation that the Fugitive Slave Law would be enforced. Almost immediately two explosive cases rocked New York City.[29]

James Hamlet, a porter at a store on Water Street, was the first showcase victim, or as one antislavery editor put it, "the first blood." A female slaver from Baltimore named Mary Brown claimed that Hamlet had escaped two years prior. Hamlet was spotted by Mary Brown's son, who worked in New York as a clerk, and who had seen Hamlet several times around the city. In less than a day and without the benefit of a full hearing, Hamlet was found to be the property of the Brown family and, accompanied by several deputy marshals there to prevent a rescue by Black sympathizers, was placed on a ship bound for Maryland. Black activists around the country despaired that the Fugitive Slave Law was being put into ruthless and efficient operation. Frederick Douglass lamented that "we are all at the mercy of a band of blood-hound commissioners." Wall Street's *Journal of Commerce*, however, cheered the ease and calm with which Hamlet was arrested, found guilty, and taken away.[30]

Black New Yorkers were not about to look on approvingly as the bureaucratic machinery of the new law demonstrated its effectiveness. Acting on word from the Brown family that they would consider selling Hamlet, African Americans sprang into action and gathered eight hundred dollars to purchase Hamlet and set him free. They lamented that such purchases legitimated slavery by reducing freedom to a financial transaction, but the desire to free Hamlet overrode such concerns. Some fifteen hundred African Americans crowded City Park to welcome Hamlet home a week later, and activists rallied for Black civil rights in Brooklyn, Williamsburg, and other nearby towns.[31]

James McCune Smith could often be seen at the head of these rallies. Smith, the doctor for the Colored Orphan Asylum and close friend of Frederick Douglass, was just thirty-seven in 1850 when the new Fugitive Slave Law ignited such rage. Now, at the restless and angry meeting held in the wake of the Fugitive Slave Law, Smith rose before Black and white men and women to denounce Webster and Clay for supporting the measures. Smith solemnly told the audience that James Hamlet's wife had died because of the fear and tension surrounding her husband's arrest as a runaway. "Millard Fillmore, Daniel Webster, and Horace Greeley," he asserted, "should be summoned as witnesses" in her death because they were responsible.[32]

The ebullience that Black New Yorkers felt upon Hamlet's return was quickly dashed in another fugitive slave case a couple of months later, a case that proved much more scarring and devastating than Hamlet's. The case of Henry Long would live on in the city's collective memory long after he was returned to bondage in January 1851 and, perhaps more than any another event, convinced many New Yorkers of all races and genders that Washington's Fugitive Slave Law was no mere legal abstraction, but the very real grounds for a battle over freedom and survival.

Like James Hamlet, Henry Long would soon become another sacrificial victim for the Union. In his early thirties, Long worked as a waiter at the Pacific Hotel when in late December he was approached by US marshals and NYPD officers. They claimed that he was being arrested on suspicion of larceny, but they were lying: a doctor named William Parker, acting on behalf of Virginia slaver John T. Smith, claimed Long had escaped from Richmond in 1848. Within the hour, Long found himself in a New York jail, his fate in the hands of a commissioner appointed under the new Fugitive Slave Law. As one NYPD officer noted in his personal journal, "the n— slave Long is being examined." Long was assumed to be a runaway as soon as he was arrested.[33]

While the Union Safety Committee, the cotton traders, the NYPD, and some New York judges wanted to declare Long a fugitive as soon as possible, African Americans sought to slow down

Long's rendition. The city braced for another series of courtroom dramas, legal wrangling over technicalities, and press reports of every maneuver. In fact, kidnappings and recaptures had erupted so often over the years that the whole proceeding now had the air of performance and theater, entertaining perhaps, if so much were not at stake, including the fate of a real human being.[34]

During these show trials, lawyers for and against the accused runaway were accustomed to gathering witnesses to support their claims, but the courts almost always seemed to believe the white witnesses and to dismiss the testimony of African Americans. On the stand, supposed relatives of slaver John Smith were called to testify that they had known Henry Long back in Virginia and that he was the same person now appearing in court. All were prompted by attorney George Wood, the same man serving as president of the Union Safety Committee, who had volunteered to represent John Smith for free. In fact, one New York paper complained that "the strength of the New York bar has been virtually arrayed" against Henry Long. John Jay, the lawyer who had come to represent many accused runaways after Horace Dresser had served in that same capacity for so many years, called several Black witnesses to testify on Long's behalf. John Butler, a coachman who lived on Centre Street, swore that he had worked with Long since 1847, before Smith claimed he had absconded. Elizabeth Dixon stated that she had boarded Long at her home on Elizabeth Street in November 1847. Meanwhile, as the legal machinations ground on for more than two weeks, African Americans met at Zion Church and collected one hundred dollars to support Long's defense.[35]

Judge Andrew Judson, a Democrat who soon garnered national notoriety in another case for declaring that Black people would never rise from racial inferiority, decided Long's fate. In his ruling, Judge Judson made it clear that he believed the white over the Black witnesses. Several members of John Smith's family and several of his friends had testified that they knew Long to be a fugitive slave. Against such claims, John Jay had only gathered a few Black witnesses, like Dixon and Butler. If Long had truly been born in New York, Judge Judson declared, then "why are not his parents,

his brothers, his sisters, his neighbors, his boyhood acquaintances here to identify him, instead of John Butler?" With that the judge proclaimed Long a "fugitive from service" who should be sent back to bondage in Virginia.[36]

It seemed like a complete victory for the Union Safety Committee, for the cotton interests on Wall Street, and for New Yorkers in Tammany Hall. At the request of New York police chief George W. Matsell, Captain Isaiah Rynders, the notorious and violent racist denounced throughout neighborhoods of color, paraded Henry Long to the ferry, brandishing a rifle and swearing police vengeance on abolitionists. By this time, Rynders was one of the most powerful men in the city, and in the words of one New Yorker, "at his word money and men are ready for any undertaking." Just the year before, Rynders had participated in the deadly Astor Place Riot.[37]

Rynders ordered the officers to form two long lines, with an alley in the center, so that more than two dozen constables could guide Long to the docks. Unlike previous fugitive slave cases in which the Black community rose up to protest and even attempted to rescue the accused in collective action, Henry Long was taken across the Hudson River into New Jersey and onto the train to Richmond with barely any interference. As he rode the train, Long and the other passengers were serenaded by an enslaved man playing the violin. The musician had boarded the train in Washington along with a dozen other slaves who were being sold down South now that the Compromise of 1850 had outlawed the buying and selling of slaves in the capital city.[38]

Wall Street editors like Hallock took the acquiescence of the Black community as a good sign that boded well for successful prosecution of the Fugitive Slave Law. "They have probably learned," Hallock grumbled in reference to Black New Yorkers, "that rebellion is not so rife in this community as they were taught to believe; and that any attempt to resist by force, would rebound with terrible weight upon their heads." Later that spring, Police Chief Matsell was gifted a double-barreled gun inscribed with the thanks of the US marshal for his aid in capturing Long.[39]

Hallock was probably right that the city's Black community was somewhat chastened by the power that the new law seemed to wield, and Frederick Douglass himself lamented that protesters neglected to interfere in the slightest way with Long's recapture. In a low voice full of despair, his spirit shrouded in gloom, Douglass declared his dismay with the inaction. Equally dispiriting, Douglass argued, was the genuflection of members of both political parties. Whigs and Democrats alike acted now "as though slavery had ceased to exist," a collusion in favor of Unionism and a bowing to the requirements of the Fugitive Slave Law that once again sacrificed the interests of Black people, carelessly disregarding whether the accused were actually born free.[40]

Meanwhile, white southerners read about the Hamlet and Long cases with building anger. Telegraph wires took the news of New York abolitionism into the newsrooms of southern newspapers and then into the angry hands of white southern readers. In response to the expensive delay required to send Henry Long back to slavery, white southerners started a "Central Southern Rights Association," a boycott movement against antislavery merchants that threatened to sign up twenty thousand Virginia men. The signers pledged to avoid engaging in business with any New York firm that refused to denounce abolition. The so-called Non-intercourse Movement launched when newspapers began publishing the names of New York firms suspected of being less than ironclad in their defense of southern rights. Papers from Tennessee and Alabama to the Atlantic coast printed the names of merchants who had signed the pledge of the Union meeting at Castle Garden. The *New York Tribune* complained that any candidates who "are not worshippers at the shrine of Cotton" were doomed to defeat.[41]

Only politicians and candidates who pledged to defend slavery and southern trade were welcome on Wall Street. When Georgia senator Henry S. Foote visited Manhattan in February 1851, he was feted by the Union Safety Committee as one of the great protectors of trade between North and South. "He has been the guest of the City," a newspaper crowed, "and the lion of the hour."

Then Daniel Webster, one of the archdefenders of the compromise measures, visited New York City in April 1851 and received a hero's welcome from Wall Street right after he had been shunned in the capital of his home state. While Boston rejected Webster's request to speak at Faneuil Hall, New York's Union Safety Committee gave him the key to the city. Such obsequiousness toward Foote and Webster was intended to show southern slave masters where the loyalties of New Yorkers lay.[42]

When Henry Long reached Virginia, he was already a household name in his hometown of Richmond, but the whites living in the state capital were eager to re-enslave the famous runaway. Within days of his forced return to the South, Long found himself put up for auction by the notorious slave-trading firm of Pulliam & Slade, who featured Long in a catalog and mocked the fugitive as "an experienced tavern servant, having graduated at one of the principal hotels in New York." More than fifteen hundred people crowded the slave market near Richmond's City Hotel, but Long stubbornly boasted that he would soon join his wife back in New York. Unfortunately, Virginia was not about to let that happen. The auctioneer yelled that whoever bid the highest for Long would have to sign a guarantee to take him further south into Georgia.[43]

A few minutes after ten o'clock in the morning, Long was brought to the auction room and seated next to two women also up for sale with their four small children. The agitated Long forced a smile to hide his tremendous fear and unease. African Americans of all ages, included the women and children nearby, sobbed and wailed at the prospect of separation. A white man approached Long and sarcastically asked the famous fugitive if he was glad to be back in Virginia. "Well," Long replied, "I often thought I would like to come back some time, but I meant to come independently." Whites continued to taunt Long, asking him why the abolitionists in New York failed to save him, but he refused to evince the fear he felt inside. "Ain't you sorry you are brought back?" one asked. "Well," he answered, "the best of men have their downfalls."[44]

Soon it was time for the auction to begin. The auctioneer called out: "Whoever is going to buy n— will come down to" the office. Within a few minutes, one young man in his twenties had sold for nine hundred dollars. Next a nineteen-year-old boy of mixed race had brought eight hundred as his mother, an enslaved cook, sorrowfully looked on. When it was clear that he was destined for Danville, nearly one hundred fifty miles from his mother in Richmond, he sobbed loudly while his mother's face streamed with tears of her own.

By the early afternoon Long's turn came. Whites in the audience yelled "that damned n— should be strung up" for running away. Another young white man swaggered toward the center of the stage, claiming with brashness that he should buy Long just so he could give him thirteen lashes before breakfast. He slashed the air to provide a physical demonstration of his words. The auctioneer turned Long around like he was a piece of meat, asked him questions about his health and strength, then reminded the audience that upon sale he would have to be sold again in Georgia, a stipulation that drew a spontaneous round of applause. The bidding was brief, and Long sold for $750 to David Clayton of Georgia.[45]

That was not the last time the world heard from Henry Long. Later in 1851, his name once again appeared in papers across the country. It seems that once ensconced on a Georgia farm, Long "agitated among his brethren the question of their liberty." Yes, Long was causing trouble, telling fellow enslaved people of the years he spent in precarious freedom in New York, how too they might manage to escape, how the North harbored Black and white abolitionists who might aid a fugitive. He was arrested for making insurrectionary speeches to African Americans in Atlanta. The *Louisville Journal* smirked that this was to be expected. "A negro who has been associating with the free negroes in the Eastern cities for a year or two, is unfit for that species of servitude which is most desirable." Long was clearly causing trouble in the heart of the Confederacy. David Ruggles would have been proud.[46]

THE CONSEQUENCES OF THE rendition of Henry Long were grave and enduring. Individuals who had aided Long's defense like white attorney John Jay were blackballed from New York clubs and organizations. Some police officers, in the eyes of moderate whites like *New York Tribune* editor Horace Greeley, had acted with even less professionalism and decency than they had in the cases of George Kirk, Joseph Belt, and James Hamlet. Not only were the police employed to break up legitimate protests, but they had deliberately occupied as many seats in the courtroom as they could to take them away from Black residents who wished to attend the proceedings. Officers had also shouted insults to the small number of Blacks who were able to attend, and they heaped opprobrium on Black witnesses called to testify on Long's behalf. Alas, Judge Judson only paused the deliberations to chastise Black audience members and failed to call similarly to the white police officers or white friends of Tammany Hall who interjected invectives as the trial unfolded. The Long case was hardly a moment of pride for the NYPD, but Wall Street praised Judson and the court for doing their duty to keep the cotton flowing from southern plantations.[47]

One bright development in the aftermath of the Long case from the perspective of civil rights came in the continued maturation of organized Black abolitionism. In reaction to the Hamlet and Long trials, a group of African American businessmen and professionals that became known as the Committee of Thirteen assumed the role once held by Ruggles and the Vigilance Committee. Led by seasoned veterans like James McCune Smith and Philip A. Bell, the Committee of Thirteen was exactly the kind of leadership the city's Black community needed in the wake of the Fugitive Slave Law. Bell had earned the admiration of fellow African Americans as co-editor of the *Weekly Advocate* at the same time that the kidnapping club was at its peak. He would soon move to San Francisco but played a crucial public role in combating racism and abductions in the 1850s. Veterans of the kidnapping and recapture wars like Smith and Bell were joined on the committee by younger rising leaders like pharmacist William P. Powell, who

Physician and activist
James McCune Smith.
*(New-York Historical
Society)*

would go on to serve as a surgeon in the Union Army; Junius C. Morel, a Brooklyn teacher and editorialist who contributed to *Frederick Douglass' Newspaper*, and George T. Downing, a restaurateur who was the son of prominent businessman Thomas Downing.[48]

The Committee of Thirteen issued a new and important periodical simply titled *The Vigilance Committee* to call for donations and support from the entire Black community in New York. The first copy reminded readers that the New York Kidnapping Club had emerged back in the early 1830s thanks to the escape of enslaved people from Northampton County, Virginia, which in turn had prompted New York governor Marcy to release his "roving warrant" to Boudinot and Nash. In response, the city's abolitionists had managed to counter the kidnappers' machinations. In fact, the new newspaper declared, more than eighteen hundred people had been saved from the clutches of Boudinot and his allies in the 1830s and 1840s, including forty in one month![49]

The newly energized Vigilance Committee committed financial resources as well as countless man-hours to the cause. Their services included funding the legal defense of accused runaways, feeding and clothing those newly escaped, hiding and housing those in need, and secretly moving those in danger of arrest to safer areas outside the city. Theodore S. Wright, the president of the reinvigorated committee, had been the first African American to graduate from Princeton Theological Seminary and was the pastor at the First Colored Presbyterian Church on Frankfort Street just east of City Hall. Wright had also helped to found the interracial American Anti-Slavery Society in the early 1830s, and then the American and Foreign Anti-Slavery Society after a split with William Lloyd Garrison over the propriety of allowing women to serve in leadership positions. The Vigilance Committee's secretary, Charles B. Ray, had joined Philip Bell and Samuel Cornish in publishing the city's most important Black newspaper. Born free in Massachusetts, Ray originally enrolled in Wesleyan Seminary in Connecticut but was expelled after a short time because white students had so vigorously protested the presence of a Black student. He moved to Gotham just as Boudinot and the New York Kidnapping Club were beginning to terrorize Black citizens, and opened a prominent shoe store on Pearl Street. Together this new group of activists would lead New York's African American community as the nation inexorably drifted toward civil war.[50]

Thanks to the audacity of the cotton magnates on Wall Street and their political allies in Tammany Hall, who rallied to support the Fugitive Slave Law, a new and more organized abolitionist movement was coalescing to protect New York's Black community from kidnappings and recaptures, and to combat the powerful business and political forces that favored the Union. Black neighborhoods needed the protection, because the next few years would witness the reemergence of a frightening, furtive transatlantic slave trade. Over the past twenty years, Black New Yorkers and their allies had experienced a dizzying roller coaster of emotions, alternating between optimistic hopes that

the police and the legal system were beginning to see the moral imperative of civil rights and disappointment that any signs of substantial change proved ephemeral. Up and down, back and forth; one kidnapping case would appear cause for celebration, while the next would seem equally powerful reason to despair.

And in the tumultuous decade of the 1850s the rhythmic sway of hope and despair would reach new extremes. It would take all the energy that the Committee of Thirteen and the rest of the Black community could muster to combat the political and diplomatic might of a cruel and secretive group that rivaled the temerity of the New York Kidnapping Club. Known as the Portuguese Company, the group of transatlantic pirates would devote much of the 1850s to making the Port of New York a lynchpin in an illegal slave trade that linked the African coast and Cuba to the Empire City.

The Portuguese Company

F AR FROM SETTLING THORNY ISSUES LIKE THE RETURN OF RUNAWAYS, the new Fugitive Slave Law only worsened the growing hostility between North and South. White southerners suspected that free states like New York would not comply with the rules regarding the return of escapees, or somehow figure out how to let their "higher law" conscience thwart enforcement. Southerners also resented the closing of the slave trade in the nation's capital and the fact that the large territory of California had just entered the Union as a free state. But white southerners could always be counted on to defend slavery with hyperbolic rhetoric and fierce determination. That had remained true since the early 1800s. The most significant change in public opinion was taking place in the free states.

It was easy for ordinary whites to place bondage out of their minds, since they were not usually confronted with slavery. "Leave the South to deal with slavery; it is their institution and their problem to deal with" was a common refrain heard in the North. Democratic newspapers, even those that questioned the morality of bondage, echoed this cliché, telling readers that northern states had little to do with how white southerners decided to conduct

their affairs. In the wake of the new Fugitive Slave Law, though, that contention was becoming increasingly hard to sustain. The Fugitive Slave Law had accomplished what seemed impossible: it made the sectional crisis even worse and caused a fundamental shift in free-state public opinion. More than any single event or act, the Fugitive Slave Law convinced northerners that at some point soon they would have to confront the power of slave owners in American politics.[1]

When the Fugitive Slave Law passed in 1850, New York was in the midst of a population explosion, now numbering more than three quarters of a million people, and the building surge in Lower Manhattan had spilled across the East River into Brooklyn and northward toward the Bronx and Queens. Connecting those once far-flung satellites was a complicated network of carriage roads, ferries, horse paths, and waterways. The city had firmly established its importance to international finance and trade; factors and agents shipped southern cotton to England and New England, while banks and commercial houses near Wall Street reaped tremendous profits. In that sense New York's future was

Wall Street in the nineteenth century. *(The National Archives and Records Administration)*

clear: it would build taller and farther out, it would continue to establish lucrative links to remote markets, and the population would continue to balloon.

But while everyone expected that the city's growth would continue unabated, the unparalleled prosperity led by Wall Street failed to obscure New York's struggle to face the vulnerability of its poor and Black neighbors. The fundamental questions that had occupied sympathetic leaders in the 1830s and 1840s continued to vex them in the 1850s. Segregation, for example, remained a source of frustration among African Americans, especially on public transportation, as New Yorker Elizabeth Jennings found out. Jennings herself had grown up in a prominent Black New York family: her father, Thomas L. Jennings, was a leading abolitionist and respected tailor who had earned a patent for a method of dry cleaning. Elizabeth would soon follow in her father's activist footsteps, all because of one fateful day on which she found herself ejected from a New York streetcar. She had refused to sit in the "colored" car of the Third Avenue line.

Late for church, both Jennings and her friend Sarah Adams flagged down the driver of a streetcar, who told them to wait for the next one. Worried that she would miss the services, Jennings and Adams boldly told the driver that they would remain on the car. They all stood their ground for several minutes until the driver finally acquiesced and allowed the ladies to sit. As Jennings and Adams moved to sit, the conductor growled that "if the passengers raise any objections you shall go out." Jennings responded that she "was a respectable person, born and raised in New York," and that she had never before been so insulted simply for going to church, calling the conductor, Edward Moss, an "impudent fellow" for treating the two of them so disrespectfully. Now the conductor was infuriated and grabbed Jennings as she tried desperately to hold on to the window sash. He broke her grip and then she reached to grab onto his coat while the driver joined the melee. The two men pushed her partially out so that her head hung over the platform pavement and her legs remained in the streetcar. Jennings screamed "Murder!" while Adams yelled "You'll kill her!" A police

Elizabeth Jennings. *(Kansas State Historical Society via Museum of the City of New York)*

officer boarded the car and took Jennings out himself while she demanded to know his name and the car number. The officer, Jennings later recalled, "drove me away like a dog."[2]

Jennings's treatment had been echoed in previous cases of racial discrimination in public transportation, such as Ruggles's beating on a New Jersey carriage and Thomas Downing's harassment on the train to Harlem. In those previous instances, the Black community gathered to protest discrimination, but in Jennings's case the community was particularly alarmed and angered. Here a Black woman from a respectable household had been physically and verbally accosted on her way to church. Determined to be heard, they brought the case before a judge and jury in 1855, with the future president Chester A. Arthur in support of Jennings's case. In a stunning decision before the Brooklyn Circuit Court that represented a significant legal shift from the days of the recorder Richard Riker, the judge declared that Black riders had equal rights to public transportation as whites, as long as they were "sober, well-behaved and free from disease." To the modern ear, the ruling is condescending, but the Black community greeted it as a landmark ruling in favor of civil rights. The

jury was less convinced and reduced the damages award Jennings had sought, but the legal victory perhaps indicated that the days of city, state, and federal courts always deciding against people of color might be in the midst of changing. To press their claims against segregation further, Elizabeth's father, Thomas, together with other prominent Black businessmen like James McCune Smith, established the Legal Rights Association.[3]

In fact, the entire Black community in Gotham mobilized against segregation, not just through the Legal Rights Association, but through a series of rallies and mass meetings designed to capitalize on the court's decision to award Jennings damages. At a public meeting at the First Colored American Congregational Church, the same church to which Jennings belonged and where she played the organ each Sunday, Reverend James Vickes delivered a rousing condemnation of Jennings's treatment. Elizabeth herself was still in bed recovering from her injuries, but she drafted a statement that was read at the meeting, recounting the details of how she was "brutally outraged and insulted" by the conductor. As a victim of what later generations would call Jim Crow segregation, Jennings had experienced the darker side of racial tensions in New York, but the fact that the judge awarded her compensation suggests that public opinion was perhaps changing in favor of civil rights.[4]

To be sure, the pro-Union Wall Street political machine remained vigorous through the 1850s, as Democrats and businessmen maintained that northerners should abide by their constitutional duty to enforce the compromise measures. Prominent voices, like that of lawyer and Democrat Charles O'Conor, reminded anyone who would listen about the North's obligation to placate slaveholders. The problem was that by the 1850s O'Conor and other defenders of the Constitution and the Union were beginning to drift into defenses of slavery, not just defenders of fugitive slave renditions. This shift was dramatic and telling. No longer did Wall Street bankers and their legal allies merely support the Union. By the 1850s they were actively alleging that abolitionism was treason, that slavery was not nearly as vile or corrupt a system as politicians

like William Henry Seward maintained, and that northerners had no reason to interfere with an institution that had generated such startling and unprecedented wealth. Strongly pro-South advocates like O'Conor hardened their positions as abolitionists had heightened their rhetoric opposing slavery, believing that they had to provide a counternarrative to strident Republican claims.

The political cover O'Conor and other pro-South New Yorkers provided soon allowed shocking and newly emboldened reactionary forces to unleash a wave of terror on Black residents unseen since the dark days of the kidnapping club. Nowhere was this fact more evident than in the alarming and almost completely forgotten tales of a group of infamous captains, ship owners, lawyers, and slave traders known as the Portuguese Company. They spent much of the 1850s kidnapping African peoples from their native villages and transporting them across the Atlantic to the Americas. New York City played a central role in the lucrative international kidnapping system that turned West African peoples into valuable commodities.

ALONG THE 100 BLOCK of Pearl Street, deep in the crisscrossing thoroughfares of Lower Manhattan, one of the most infamous gangs in American history used its diplomatic connections to run an illegal trade in African slaves that made a mockery of Gotham's claims to liberty. As alarming and daring as it might appear, New York harbor became the focal point of a trade that had been rendered illegal a half century before. And it all unfolded with Portuguese and Spanish merchants and politicians using their offices on Pearl Street and Broadway to control the elaborate scheme.[5]

Whether it was growing sugarcane in South America and the Caribbean, or cotton in the southern United States, Portuguese slave traders were able to form networks with African slave dealers in which men, women, and children could be purchased for sometimes as little as twenty-five dollars each and then sold on the other side of the Atlantic, often for fifty times the price paid. The slave

trade was immensely lucrative, which helps to explain the chances men like C.H.S. Figaniere took in organizing their businesses.

Figaniere could not have been better positioned to use New York as the key to his slave-trading empire. As the consul general for Portugal and the son of the Portuguese ambassador, Figaniere had access to diplomatic approvals needed to engage secretly in the slave trade. Right above Figaniere's storefront at 81 Front Street sat the office of a notorious slave trader named Cunha Reis, and their redoubts were just a few blocks away from the offices of Lima Viana and John Alberto Machado. Together, Figaniere, Reis, Viana, and Machado became what others termed the Portuguese Company, a group that used a legitimate business in Madeira wine as a cover for an immensely profitable trade in African slaves. Machado in particular left a long record of legal cases, and he was in and out of jail. Throughout much of the 1850s, the Portuguese Company (not all of whom were of Portuguese descent), with the help of white lawyers and investors like John Weeks and Benjamin Wenberg, ran a slave-trading business in the very heart of Manhattan.[6]

The official penalties for slave trading could be severe, including punishment by execution, and many in the business community of New York were appalled to learn that slave ships used their harbors. Even conservative Wall Street editors like Hallock were deeply disturbed by the continued illegal trade, though they might simultaneously wish to protect the cotton trade with the South. It was one thing for white southerners to sustain an institution that had endured for centuries, but even racially conservative New Yorkers drew a line at the slave trade. Hallock publicly denounced the practice in the *Journal of Commerce* and called on city officials to end the embarrassing practice.

The reality, though, was that slave traders in the Empire City had little to fear from public opinion or official sanctions. A single voyage could net tens of thousands of dollars. Balanced against the significant potential to make vast sums of money, the probability of conviction for piracy or slave trading was quite low, thanks

to the efforts of judges like Samuel Betts and John Betts. As in the 1830s, Samuel Betts used his position on the bench of the Southern District of New York to render it almost impossible to prosecute members of the New York Kidnapping Club or to convict captains clearly engaged in the slave trade. Unfortunately for people of color, Samuel Betts had been appointed as district judge in 1826 and three decades later was still making it difficult for juries to convict anyone for slave trading in New York. The case of the slave ship *Julia Moulton* is a prime example.

Like many slavers, the *Julia Moulton* began her career as an unassuming merchant ship in the early 1850s, making repeated runs among Wilmington, North Carolina, Caribbean islands like St. Thomas and Cuba, and New York City. For years it operated in a legal trade of ordinary dry goods. But in early 1854, lawyers and ship owners conspired to make an all-too-common change to the ship's purpose.[7]

To accomplish the transformation of the *Julia Moulton*, C.H.S. Figaniere and his secretaries Cunha Reis, John Machado, and Rodolph Lasala turned to members of the Portuguese Company. William C. Valentine, a prominent Manhattan merchant, was charged with provisioning the slaver. Machado traveled with Captain James Smith to Boston to oversee the purchasing of wood and iron that would facilitate the ship's rebuilding once it was on the way to Africa. In fact, Machado used merchants in New York, Boston, and Philadelphia to outfit his ships for slaving. Smith was contracted to pilot the vessel to Africa and then Cuba. Attorneys Benjamin Wenberg and John Weeks would oversee the official document filings to shroud the ship's true destiny. Bribes would be needed to make sure the customs house officers looked the other way.[8]

In fact, thanks to corrupt officers and customs officials, slavers operated with little fear of reprisal. Slavers often talked about "waiting for the weather to clear," a reference to the need to await a complicit Customs House official to appear on duty. One day Deputy Constable Theodore Rynders, the nephew of the notorious marshal and Tammany Hall thug Isaiah Rynders, was put in

charge of investigating a suspected slaver named the *Storm King*. Anchored in the "Narrows," the ship was clearly outfitted for the illegal trade, and Rynders hopped on a tug and boarded the *Storm King*. When he returned to shore, Rynders reported that he had been offered a bribe of $1,000 to look the other way. But, Rynders proudly declared to his boss, he did not even think of accepting the offer. He countered with $1,500! The bribe was accepted and another slaver left the port for Africa.[9]

By the early fall of 1854, the transformation of the ninety-foot-long *Julia Moulton* was complete, and, using the coordinates Figaniere had provided, Captain Smith had arrived near the Congo River and given the agreed-upon signal to the coastal traders. More than six hundred men, women, and children were forced aboard and the ship hurried for one of the cays along Cuba, where the human cargo was unloaded and the ship and all its evidence burned. Tragically, more than one hundred Africans had perished on the Middle Passage between Africa and Cuba.[10]

Not all of the crew had been aware that they had signed up to serve on a slaver, but after several days at sea Captain Smith revealed their true destination. James Wills, for one, was angered. As soon as the captain and crew returned to New York, Wills went to see District Attorney John McKeon, who issued a warrant for Smith. The captain had been hiding in the back of a business on Water Street, and he and his conspirators were now arrested for slave trading.

To defend themselves in the Southern District of New York, Captain Smith and the members of the Portuguese Company turned to prominent Manhattan lawyer Charles O'Conor, a man notorious within the city's Black leadership for his tireless defense of southern slavery, of Wall Street financiers, and a booster for Unionism within the Democratic Party. Though he had long served the New York Bar and had become one of the most prominent lawyers in the city by the 1850s, the deeply religious O'Conor had just gained notoriety by representing Catherine Forrest in her salacious divorce from actor Edwin Forrest. White ladies were so appreciative of his legal efforts that they presented him

with a silver vase as a gift. O'Conor was well liked and respected by the New York Bar, even though he avoided social gatherings, refrained from joining colleagues at the local pub, and was often found walking deep in thought in the evenings. He oddly passed friends on the streets without acknowledging them, and his social awkwardness and unfamiliarity with commonplace niceties rendered him unapproachable in the eyes of his attorney colleagues. He was a man with a varied temper, who could be agreeable one moment and then aloof and chilling the next. Many fellow lawyers disagreed with him sharply when it came to his Democratic Party loyalty. Yet his sharp memory, his ability to break down the arguments of legal and political foes into tiny and unmeaning pieces, and his willingness to take on unpopular causes and cases had thrust the unassuming O'Conor into the very highest echelons of the New York Bar.[11]

But O'Conor was known among the city's Black leaders for a different reason. In fact, O'Conor could be counted on to discount Black lives whenever the opportunity arose. He had been one of the key organizers of rallies to support implementation of the Fugitive Slave Law, and standing on the stage at Castle Garden he had wondered aloud how abolitionists could even think about jeopardizing the Union for the sake of a few "darkies."[12]

The trial of Captain James Smith in the Southern District of New York for the capital crime of slave trading created a national sensation. As seaman Wills's testimony made clear, Smith was an active and eager participant in turning the ship into a slaver and stood to garner large profits from the sale of human beings. In fact, the business was so profitable, and customs officers so easily bought off, that the *New York Times* declared that one or more slavers a month passed through New York harbors. Another city paper declared solemnly that the trial of the *Julia Moulton* "established beyond denial that the slave-trade with Africa is a branch of the mercantile profits of this City." Who was to blame for letting this wicked traffic continue? The *New York Tribune* blamed Wall Street's "merchant princes," obscenely rich men "wallowing in wealth, living in sumptuous palaces."[13]

Together, judges on the district bench and Wall Street law firms like Beebe, Dean, and Donohue or lawyers like O'Conor made prosecutions difficult even when juries were disposed to deliver convictions. Brooklyn attorney Charles N. Black was also notorious for profiting from slave sales in Cuba. True to form, Captain Smith was declared not guilty, and the hopes for punishing slave trading through the Port of New York evaporated as quickly as water on the streets of Lower Manhattan on a summer day.[14]

Still, many city leaders considered the trade deeply embarrassing. Even Isaiah Rynders, the pugilistic Democrat at the head of the Empire Club who had cheered and vigorously defended the South, denounced the slave trade. Thanks to his support for President James Buchanan in the 1856 election, Rynders was rewarded with an appointment as US marshal for the Southern District of New York. One paper accused wealthy Wall Street Unionist Auguste Belmont of paying for Rynders's trip to the Democratic Convention in Cincinnati. To critics it seemed like the Democrats, Wall Street, and protection of the South went hand in hand.[15]

Although known for his racism and indifference to Black lives in Gotham, Rynders arrested a number of suspected slave traders in New York harbor as the marshal, including the captain of the slave brig *Helen* just after he had been appointed. As the ship sailed down the East River in May 1857, Rynders and several armed men intercepted the *Helen* and found all of the necessary preparations intended for the African slave trade: gunpowder, whiskey, and lumber for building the slave holds. On board the brig, Rynders took the captain by the shoulder and loudly exclaimed: "By the authority vested in every Federal officer to arrest any man engaged in an unlawful traffic—by this authority, I arrest you!" Despite a long-held antipathy toward people of color, Rynders, like many on Wall Street and on the police force, could not countenance the illegal slave trade.[16]

Despite his strong ties to the Democratic Party, District Attorney John McKeon was determined to hold Figaniere, Lasala, Machado, and others in the Portuguese Company accountable, and he brought another case in mid-1856, against the slaver

Horatio, less than two years after the collapse of the Smith case. This time, McKeon wanted to go after the registered owner of the slaver, Rodolph Lasala. Not only was this secretary to the Portuguese consul the owner, but he had also helped to provision the vessel for a slaving voyage. Lasala claimed no knowledge of the ship's history and blamed a Spaniard named Don José Egea for outfitting the ship for slave trading when Egea had traveled to Cuba. The jurors did not believe Lasala's defense and seemed ready to convict him, but Judge Betts gave the jury a shockingly strict charge that virtually made a guilty verdict impossible.[17]

The 1819 law under which McKeon sought Lasala's prosecution made it clear that any person aiding in the outfitting of a ship for the slave trade should be found guilty. But Betts applied, some might even say invented, an interpretation that required active, full, and knowing participation to uphold a guilty verdict. Betts told a confused jury that aiding and abetting the trade was not sufficient for conviction; only if Lasala had controlled the entire process could he be deemed culpable. Lasala was found not guilty. Perhaps even more ominously, Betts had limited the potential fines levied on a slave-trading operation to about $6,000, a mere fraction of the estimated $100,000 in profits that a single voyage could bring.

Predictably, the illegal slave trade continued unabated, with Portuguese consul Figaniere and lawyers like Weeks and Wenberg purchasing and outfitting slave ships throughout the 1850s. Thanks to Betts, a man history has often called "the Father of American Admiralty Law," not a single one of these men was ever convicted. After Betts charged the jury in one case involving the *Julia Moulton*, the jurors acquitted the accused in just three minutes![18]

After the *Julia Moulton* and *Horatio* cases, the slave trade escalated to a major part of Gotham's business. Joining the Portuguese, a new and even more sophisticated group labeled the Spanish Company added to the chaos. By jumping from port to port around the Caribbean, the Spanish Company evaded prosecution until the Civil War. Like the Portuguese Company, the Spanish Company comprised people from different nationalities collaborating

to kidnap African peoples. As the leading voice in the SDNY, Judge Betts had helped to make the wicked machinations of the Portuguese Company and the Spanish Company possible.[19]

Betts quickly garnered an international reputation as soft on slave trading. When Captain Cornelius E. Driscoll was arrested for transporting more than six hundred Africans, he was relieved to find out that Betts was the presiding judge. Betts allowed Driscoll to leave New York City, purportedly so that he could gather evidence in South America for his defense. Once back in Rio de Janeiro, Driscoll boasted in a bar about the SDNY's nonchalance when it came to prosecuting slavers. "Well boys," Driscoll bragged, "you don't have to worry about facing trial in New York City. Let the cruisers take you if they will. I can get any man off in New York for $1,000."[20]

As we have seen, Judge Betts was hardly alone in his willingness to accommodate slave traders; New York City attorneys were widely available to defend slave ship captains, owners, merchants, and ship chandlers whenever they faced arrest. The prominent firm of Beebe, Dean, and Donohue could often be found in the 1850s defending clients who were well-known slavers, including prominent members of the Portuguese Company like Lasala, Machado, and Figaniere. Gilbert Dean graduated from Yale in 1841 and became a prominent Democratic congressman in the early 1850s, and then became a justice of the New York Supreme Court in 1854. Welcome R. Beebe's office stood at 76 Wall Street, and he was so well connected that he even served a term as district attorney. His firm not only aggressively defended accused slavers, but also sued accusers for libel. In the 1857 case of the slaver *Panchita*, Beebe, Dean, and Donahue sued officers of the British navy for $15,000 for having the temerity to charge the captain and owners with being slave traders.[21]

The New York Bar included Benjamin Wenberg, who played a recurring and active role in the transatlantic slave trade among Africa, Cuba, and New York. Wenberg and his brother Louis were natives of Portland, Maine, which is telling because that town was infamous for helping to outfit ships for slave trade. In fact,

throughout the 1830s and 1840s, notorious slave trader Nathaniel Gordon Sr., whose son would soon be executed for piracy, sailed from Portland often on slaving trips to New York, Cuba, and the West African coast. Continuing in the shipping business established by their father, Ben and Louis Wenberg moved to Brooklyn but maintained their main offices on Water Street in Lower Manhattan. They quickly became wealthy and prominent members of the Maritime Exchange. At least for Ben, the slave-trading business proved highly lucrative. The classic dish Lobster Newburg, according to legend, was actually developed by Wenberg, a frequent guest at Delmonico's steakhouse. Considering that wealthy lawyers and merchants like Wenberg had little to fear from the police or from Betts or other members of the Southern District of New York, it is hardly surprising that the slave trade reached its height in the late 1850s, with ships designed to carry hundreds of enslaved people sailing in and out of New York harbor each month.[22]

The *Echo*, a ship that began its career as the *Putnam*, had been built in Baltimore in the 1840s, transporting sugar between Cuba and New York for Everett and Brown, merchants who sold the ship to members of the Portuguese Company in 1857, who transformed the ship into a slave ship and renamed her the *Echo*.[23]

Under the cover of a legitimate trade in West African palm oil, New York merchant Antonio Almeida, a member of the ever-expanding Portuguese Company, began organizing slaving expeditions as soon as he and other investors bought the vessel in 1857. In November of that year, Almeida hired Edward Townsend to register the brig as an American ship. Like many slave-trading captains, Townsend was a New Englander, a Rhode Island native who had made his career in the legal maneuverings required to turn a legitimate ship into a slaver. Bristol and other coastal towns had long been key ports in the transatlantic slave trade, from the colonial era and into the 1850s. Townsend, whose father had purportedly also spent a long career as a slave trader, ventured to New Orleans, where he registered the ship thanks to a proslavery federal customs house. Townsend also left behind falsified

records that indicated he was conducting legal trade with ports in the Dutch West Indies. Instead, Townsend and his crew of Portuguese and American seamen set sail for Havana, where Almeida employed the Portuguese Company's well-established connections to outfit the *Putnam* for its illegal business. Almeida agreed with traders in Cuba that once the enslaved people were boarded in Africa, he would sail to a secretive cove on the northern coast of Cuba, raise a white flag with a black stripe, and await a signal from the shore. The voyage to Africa and back would require massive casks of water, food, medicines, and bribes for local officials. More than a dozen crewmen would be rewarded with $900 each for the planned trip of four months. The expense was borne by shareholders, each of whom invested in a journey that promised to make them rich.[24]

A few days out on the journey from Cuba to Africa, the crew used black paint to cover the name of the *Putnam*. On a wooden plank they emblazoned the ship's new name and nailed it to the bow. With the name change, a well-paid crew, and the promise of rich futures, the *Echo* set its sights on Cabinda on the western coast of Africa.

After three months at sea, the *Echo* reached Angola in late June 1858, and Almeida sought out a place to buy human beings. It

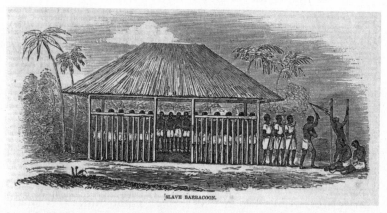

An early illustration of Africans in a barracoon. *(Slavery Images)*

was not an arduous task. The Atlantic coast of Africa was dotted with impressive fortresses engaged in the trade as well as smaller "barracoons," essentially jails that imprisoned people destined for sale. Brazilian traders like Guilherme Correa maintained an active business among Africa, Cuba, and New York City and were well acquainted with the key members of Gotham's Portuguese Company. Within a short period, Almeida had purchased 450 West Africans and loaded them on the *Echo*. The northern coast of Cuba was next.

Though we still don't know as much about the hundreds of individuals loaded into the cargo holds of the *Echo* as we would like, we do know that they ranged from the tender age of just five years old to the mid-twenties. The vast majority were boys and young men, though some one quarter were young women. As scholars have determined, all of the captives were Bantu and likely fishermen, impoverished laborers, and small traders who most likely could communicate using languages and dialects from their villages near the Congo River. As the lives of millions of kidnapped Africans attest, the slave trade was carried out with well-practiced and brutal efficiency. The men were placed in the front of the hold, and the women and young children in a small space in the back of the ship. One hundred thirty-seven died on the six-week sail from Africa to Cuba.[25]

Captain Townsend, Antonio Almeida, and the crew had little reason to fear arrest. Though the British navy actively patrolled the western coast of Africa in search of slavers, the sea was vast and capture unlikely once the *Echo* had cleared Angola. The US Navy maintained a pathetically small number of patrol ships, really a mere show of pretended interest in suppressing the slave trade rather than any kind of commitment to enforcement. The odds were good that the Portuguese Company and the crew of the *Echo* would live to see their risks richly rewarded.

Though the vast majority of slavers made their voyages unimpeded, the US Navy managed to spot the *Echo* as it approached Cuba. On board the frigate USS *Dolphin*, commander J. N. Maffit pursued the *Echo* for two hours as the slaver tried to outrun the navy

vessel, but ultimately the frigate was too fast and Maffit arrested the *Echo*'s crew on a charge of piracy and sailed for Charleston so that the seamen could be tried in federal court for slave trading. In a twist of cruel historical irony, the African captives were quarantined in the newly built Fort Sumter in Charleston harbor, which would soon see the firing of cannons to start the Civil War.

The whole nation watched as the trial of the *Echo*'s crew unfolded in April 1859. The federal judges in the case seemed more disposed to see a successful prosecution than Judge Samuel Betts had been in the Southern District of New York, but the legal hurdles were still substantial. The jury to consider the bills of indictment would be composed of more than twenty men, all of whom were Charleston natives and likely proslavery. As they bought and sold human beings with as much concern as one might trade in horses, why would they view the transatlantic slave trade with any other emotion other than nonchalance? In fact, prominent South Carolinians had already called publicly for the reopening of the international slave trade, including L. W. Spratt, who defended the seamen during the trial. The circuit court judges endeavored in earnest to try the case, even commissioning a scale model (1:48 size) of the *Echo* to aid the jury's determinations. But the jury was easily convinced that Captain Townsend, Almeida, and the rest of the prisoners should not be found guilty, and in the deliberations, which lasted an hour or so, all of the accused were acquitted. The Portuguese Company and its vast international connections had escaped prosecution once again.[26]

While Almeida, Townsend, and the other members of the Portuguese Company continued their illicit business over the next few years, the three hundred or so African captives did not fare nearly as well. President James Buchanan, a Pennsylvania Democrat supported by Tammany Hall and New York's pro-South business community, ordered that the refugees be sent to Liberia, the West African colony established by the American Colonization Society to send enslaved Americans back to Africa. Unfortunately for the captives, they were resettled thousands of miles from their original homes near the Congo River, provided with a spoon and

blanket, and essentially farmed out to landowners to work on large plantations. The American government had added another layer of injustice and callousness to the lives of people who had experienced the misfortune aboard the *Echo*.

As THE *ECHO*'S FORMER captives scratched out a meager existence three thousand miles away from home, courtesy of the federal government, New York's political and financial leaders were working to make sure that slavery continued to be defended and protected. As Christmas 1859 approached, pro-Union forces rallied at the imposing stone façade of the Academy of Music on 14th Street, just blocks away from Union Square. Among the speakers that evening was leading attorney Charles O'Conor, who rose to deliver a speech titled "Negro Slavery not Unjust," which indicated how far Gotham's interests in cotton had clouded its judgment. O'Conor's speech was so powerful and representative that Wall Street merchants requested the printing of hundreds of copies that were distributed across the city.

At the beginning of his speech, O'Conor argued that the racial inferiority of African Americans meant that emancipation was impossible. If liberated, he wrote, the former slaves "would relapse into barbarism." "The negro is a man," O'Conor admitted, "but an inferior *species* of man" who could never be permitted to vote, enter Congress, or serve in the presidency. O'Conor then went on to quote from the writings of New Orleans pseudoscientist Samuel Cartwright, who pointed to the thick lips and flat nose and other supposed physical characteristics of African people to emphasize that they were ill-suited for equality with whites. A New York lawyer quoting from the most racist "scientist" of the South might have been surprising without knowledge of the past decades of the city's history.[27]

To the thousands of New Yorkers gathered at the Academy of Music, O'Conor stressed the need to return any suspected runaways immediately, lest they "wound the feelings" of southern slaveholders. If northerners persisted in questioning the legitimacy

of bondage or of their obligation to return runaways, O'Conor proclaimed, then southerners had every right to secede from the Union and form their own government. As he shouted these words from the podium, someone in the audience yelled, "Three cheers for the Fugitive Slave Law!" Though they needed no reminder, O'Conor told his listeners that the great wealth and prosperity that the city enjoyed were due to their union with slaveholders.[28]

As O'Conor reached his crescendo, he boldly and unabashedly asserted his belief that slavery benefited both whites and Blacks, that it was not an unjust system, that (as the slavers themselves had argued) bondage was "just, wise, and beneficent." Some in the audience were stunned by such a declaration, and some disapproving hissing could be heard amongst the crowd, which was soon replaced by applause. Three cheers went up for O'Conor and for Virginia governor Henry Wise, who had just two weeks before witnessed the hanging of abolitionist John Brown. Brown himself earned three groans from the gathering. "As a white nation" founded by the Caucasian race, the United States benefited from the subjugation of Africans into bondage. And Black people also benefited from a system that took advantage of their lack of "intellect to govern, or willingness to work." God and nature, O'Conor concluded, had made dark peoples inferior, and slavery protected them from themselves and allowed "the wiser white man" to maintain control.[29]

O'Conor delivered a persistent strong voice in favor of any compromises with southern slaveholders needed to keep the Union and its prosperity intact, but the repeated reports of slave traders using New York harbor were too much to endure even for prominent Wall Street interests. It was one thing to back the new Fugitive Slave Law, which it might be argued merely reinforced the constitutional clause established at the nation's founding. But allowing the international slave trade to make a mockery of New York represented another level of conciliation with slave masters that proved too extreme for Hallock. In an editorial Hallock complained that many of Gotham's residents remained unaware "of the extent to which this infamous traffic is carried on." Exhibiting

an almost Ruggles-like frustration, Hallock declared that through "the cunning of well-fed lawyers . . . downtown merchants of wealth and respectability are extensively engaged in buying and selling African negroes," and they have engaged in this illegal business "with comparatively little interruption, for an indefinite number of years." Ruggles would have named specific individuals culpable, but short of that, one of the leading journalistic voices of the Manhattan business community urgently called attention to a trade so commonplace by the late 1850s that slavers leaving New York harbor seemed like a weekly occurrence.[30]

UNFORTUNATELY, NEITHER HALLOCK NOR anyone else disgusted by Gotham's role in the kidnapping of West African peoples could count on legal authorities for help. By the congressional midterm elections, the Whig Party, which had been the main opposition to the Democrats since the days of Andrew Jackson and the beginning of the New York Kidnapping Club, had all but collapsed. The Whig Party of the South, of course, remained strongly and unquestionably supportive of slavery; even broaching the idea publicly that there was something wrong with slavery or that the region should rethink its devotion to cotton and bondage would have resulted in immediate social ostracization and possibly criminal prosecution. The First Amendment declaring press freedoms and freedom of speech was a dead letter in the slave states. So both Democrats and Whigs in the southern states championed and defended slavery.

By the early 1850s, the same could not be said in the free states. In fact, the Whig Party had become bitterly and hopelessly split between "cotton" and "conscience" Whigs in New York. Cotton Whigs dominated the party in New York City and believed that though northern states had abolished slavery, they remained bound by the Constitution's Fugitive Slave Clause reaffirmed and strengthened in the Compromise of 1850. Many, and perhaps most, of the merchants and bankers on Wall Street belonged to the Cotton Whig faction, committed to maintaining the Union

and the economic prosperity it helped to foster. Businessmen in the Chamber of Commerce knew that disunion would jeopardize trade with the South; equally frightening was the possibility that southerners would default on the tens of millions in debt owed to New York firms. Conscience Whigs, on the other hand, began to question whether the free states had surrendered too much of their state sovereignty in bending to the demands of slaveholders. The new Fugitive Slave Law and its federal apparatus seemed to tread mightily on the rights of free states to keep bondage out of their own communities. With pockets of support in Gotham, the Conscience Whigs really counted the small towns and rural areas upstate as their base of support. Under the weight of this sharp division between Cotton and Conscience Whigs, not just in New York but in free states throughout the Union, the Whig Party had essentially ceased to exist by 1854.

Black New Yorkers watched to see whether the new Republican Party, now emerging from political turmoil in states like Michigan and Wisconsin, would gain enough national support to battle the power of Tammany Hall and the Democrats. The new party would quickly grow in popularity, overcoming the temporary power of competing political organizations like the Know-Nothing Party. In Gotham, the Republican Party took root among those who believed slave owners had garnered too much power in all three branches of the federal government. As the Compromise of 1850 had demonstrated, Congress and the White House seemed all too eager to acquiesce to cotton and slavery, and the Supreme Court's decision in the forthcoming *Dred Scott* case would soon provide evidence of the co-opting of the judicial branch. It seemed to many in New York and other free states that a "slave power" had corrupted the parties and every part of the federal government.

For some New Yorkers, the time had arrived to create a branch of the Democratic Party that was antislavery. In 1853 and 1854, several New Yorkers, including abolitionist lawyer John Jay, organized what they called the Free Democratic League, a party that would adhere to the principle that America as a nation operated under the basic idea that freedom was the fundamental assumption,

and that slavery could only exist under local laws. Such a distinction was important, because western territories would remain
free under the assumption that freedom was national and slavery
was sectional. In its original declaration of principles, the Free
Democratic League complained that "the slaver of the South has
obtained the control of the Federal Government," a takeover "aided and
abetted" by the major political parties. In addition to declaring
itself antislavery, the league advocated the construction of a railroad to the Pacific, the establishment of cheap overseas postage,
the welcoming of immigrants, the reduction of taxes and crime,
and a host of other measures. The league would only last a short
while, apparently dissolving in 1854 as many of its prospective
members joined the new Republican Party.[31]

Like New York's political parties, municipal authorities like the
New York Police Department were equally in disarray. By the 1850s
the New York police force was in the midst of unprecedented
chaos and division, in large part because of growing divisions
between the state legislature in Albany and political leadership in
the city. Many upstate residents had come to question the constitutional compromise between the North and South over slavery,
especially the new Fugitive Slave Law. Those who questioned the
new law and who held more sympathetic views regarding people
of color tended to belong to the Whig Party, and then, when it collapsed in 1853, to the new Republican Party. Abraham Lincoln,
for example, had been a Whig congressman and then a leader
of the Republicans. Their strength lay in rural areas in upstate
New York, and politicians like William Henry Seward and Thurlow
Weed led them in Albany. Their somewhat more progressive views
on the injustice of slavery clashed with those in city politics, where
the interests of Wall Street and the cotton trade prevailed in the
Democratic Party. Conservative Gotham was the reactionary coun-
terweight to upstate liberalism, and the leader of Tammany Hall,
Fernando Wood, sat in the mayor's seat.

Fernando Wood, elected mayor in 1854, dominated city
politics during that decade and well into the Civil War. Wood possessed a broad face and a wide mouth, his hair parted neatly on

the left, and his unusual first name came from a novel his mother was reading while pregnant. Though born in Pennsylvania, his Quaker parents had moved to the city to enter the growing merchant community in Lower Manhattan. In the 1830s and 1840s, while Boudinot and Riker and the rest of the New York Kidnapping Club fought with Ruggles for the soul of the city, Wood was rapidly building a shady career as a businessman, mostly in real estate and groceries. While Lincoln served as a Whig in the Illinois House of Representatives, Wood garnered a seat in the US House as a Democrat. And by the time the new Fugitive Slave Law rocked national and local politics, Wood was already a leader of the Tammany Democrats.[32]

As mayor, the divisive and corrupt Wood battled what he believed was the meddling of state Whig leaders like Seward in the city's politics, especially its police department. Wood's Democratic Party–controlled police department relied heavily on Irish immigrants and was resented by nativists within the city and also in the Republican state legislature. By the 1850s, anti-immigrant politicians were trying to establish a new police force, soon to be called the Metropolitans, that would replace Tammany's corrupt police, nicknamed the Municipals. The clash erupted in 1857 when Wood refused to back down, and for months Gotham actually faced two competing police departments that battled each other as much as they combatted crime.

To make matters worse, by the fall of 1857 the city and much of the nation was gripped by an economic downturn that had inflicted considerable suffering among the working and middle classes. Railroads, insurance companies, banks, and other businesses were ruined by high debts, risky investments, and a shortage of gold reserves to back paper currencies. The failure of prominent firms like the Ohio Life Insurance Company shook investor confidence, particularly in the railroad and land speculation sectors of the economy. The Upper Midwest was hard hit, but the panic struck New York City hard as well. As Harriet Morse wrote to her son away at college, the family was experiencing what she called "hard times" like everyone else. The recession shaped

her daily habits: "There is little else talked of in New York, and retrenchments, economy, and the wearing of old things is the order of the day." So while Harriet Morse and others made sacrifices to their family economies, the city police were locked in a costly and distracting civil war.[33]

Both Wood's Municipals and the state's Metropolitans were guilty of malfeasance and dereliction of duty. In fact, the Municipals, led by Police Chief George Matsell, had been called "slave catchers" by the city's Black community and its allies in the Republican press. After all, they had helped to capture and arrest George Kirk, James Hamlet, and other supposed runaways throughout the last twenty years, and Matsell had put the full weight of the NYPD in support of rounding up as many Black New Yorkers as he could.

Matsell himself was suspected of corruption, and rumors spread that he extorted money from criminals, seized stolen property for his own use, and skimmed the profits of illegal activities like those of abortionist Madame Restell. Matsell had been a member of the NYPD since 1840, and daguerreotypes show him with a long face anchored by heavy jowls and a bushy beard. By the time the Municipals and Metropolitans vied for control of the New York police, Matsell had managed to build a sprawling summer mansion within a vast vineyard in Iowa, where local landmarks still bear his name. Anti–Tammany Hall politician Mike Walsh labeled the heavyset Matsell a "walking mass of moral and physical putrefaction."[34]

Nativists and Republicans, frustrated by the Democrats' ability to appoint Irish police to the force in a Tammany Hall patronage ploy, demanded that Chief Matsell report the birthplace and ethnic identity of every officer. Matsell reported that just over a quarter of his eight hundred officers were Irish-born, but the board of aldermen accused him of grossly underestimating the total. Alderman John Briggs declared that the city was being controlled by a "foreign standing army" as the split between Irish Catholic immigrants and the nativist Protestants who resented the diversification of their city erupted into chaos. The police were divided, but so,

too, were fire departments, which, like the crime-fighting police, battled each other as much as they did conflagrations. Gangs like the Dead Rabbits and the Bowery B'hoys added to the rampant crime and violence pervading the city during the period.[35]

A new wrinkle developed when Matsell's origins came under investigation in the original "birther controversy." The board of aldermen began to question the chief's birthplace, which they claimed was not America but England. The aldermen sent a very odd character named Stephen Branch to England to investigate the claim, and he indeed returned with what he termed proof of Matsell's foreign birth. Matsell was charged with "alienage" by the police commission, and the case then fell into the all-too-eager hands of Mayor Wood and his close ally in the recorder's office. Matsell was declared an American citizen.[36]

Though Matsell was safe for now, the NYPD remained divided between the Municipals and the Metropolitans in the summer of 1857. Riots and personal disputes between the two forces meant that they did little to check the activities of the Portuguese Company, the efforts of the remnants of the New York Kidnapping Club, and the constant terrorizing of the Black neighborhoods in the name of upholding the Fugitive Slave Law. The state called out its Seventh Regiment, which would soon be deployed to support the Union in the Civil War, to arrest Wood for helping to incite riots against the Metropolitans, and Wood responded by questioning the legality of the state's authority within the city. The crisis was only resolved when Wood and the Municipals finally backed down and the Metropolitans emerged as the city's only legitimate police force.[37]

While the city police officers fought among themselves in their own little civil war, kidnappers took full advantage of the chaos. Illegal kidnappings without trials or hearings continued to rock the Black community in the 1850s, and the city's determination to enforce the Fugitive Slave Law blurred the lines between arresting those who had been born free and those who were runaways under the law. The truth is that those lines had been blurred from

the nation's very founding, with abolitionists eagerly slapping the label "kidnapper" on any officers capturing a suspected fugitive, whether or not that individual was in fact a runaway, and officers in turn arresting accused runaways whether they were legally free or enslaved. The fuzzy lines between kidnapping and legal fugitive slave renditions mirrored the indistinct borders between the free states and the slave states, creating confusion and chaos that only added to the disquiet felt by Black New Yorkers.

Wall Street and its defenders did little to ease that disquiet. In the case of accused runaway Benjamin Bradley, the closest Wall Street would come to helping the self-emancipated was to purchase their freedom, as if it was just another transaction intended to keep the Union intact. Of mixed race, Bradley apparently had been enslaved in Annapolis, Maryland, and had demonstrated considerable engineering skill. As a teenager under slavery working in a printer's office, Bradley had created a working model of a steam engine from spare parts, much to the marvel of those around him. Using some pieces of pewter and steel, a piece of a gun barrel, and other items, he built his working engine. Bradley's owner, impressed by the teenager's abilities, landed him a job as a helper at the Natural and Experimental Philosophy Department at the Naval Academy, and Bradley quickly became adept at focusing steam heat, manipulating gasses, understanding how to calculate resistance, and other engineering matters. A Professor Hopkins appreciated Bradley's developing skills and particularly the young man's desire to understand the physical laws behind his experiments, and soon Hopkins's family was teaching Bradley math and literacy. Hopkins and other professors at the Naval Academy were soon raising funds to help Benjamin purchase his freedom. Gerard Hallock, one of the most prominent press voices on Wall Street, contributed enough money to reach the $1,000 cost of purchasing Ben's freedom.[38]

Though Ben's story ended well, subsequent cases proved more troubling. In Brooklyn in late 1857, Captain Crowell guided the steamship *Florida* into New York harbor concealing a fugitive named John Steers. Steers had been enslaved in Charleston

where he worked in a saloon, but his light skin color allowed him to pass as white as he slipped into Savannah in November 1857. For a few days Steers stayed at the home of a friend, trying to gin up the courage to leave the South. On November 25, he walked up to the ticket counter, bought passage to New York aboard the *Florida*, and sat among the steamer's guests and crew.

Steers's "owner" quickly realized the escape and somehow found out that his property had passed as a white man aboard the steamer. Fearful of losing his investment, he telegraphed Mayor Fernando Wood and the New York police that they should search the ship as soon as it docked in the city. The proslavery Wood was all too eager to honor the request. Four police officers boarded the *Florida* and began questioning every passenger. Certain that they had their man, the officers seized one man, but his friends on board testified that he was not Steers and the officers released him. This fiasco continued for hours until the officers finally arrested Steers. The officers had already questioned Steers, who could read and write, three or four times and then had moved on, and lodged him in the Brooklyn home of Thomas McNulty, who operated a grocery store and boardinghouse near the East River.[39]

The captain, worried that his southern friends would think he knowingly abetted the escape from bondage, immediately notified the New York police that Steers was aboard. Four officers, Thomas Lawler, Timothy K. Mason, John Jackson, and John Cowen, smelled a rich reward and took the self-emancipated Steers to a safe house at Red Hook Point in Brooklyn. The four special police officers took turns standing guard over Steers day and night, worried that Black activists might hear of Steers's arrest and stage a rescue. The four officers and McNulty split the thousand-dollar reward.[40]

If David Ruggles had still been alive and keeping watch on the NYPD, there is little doubt that the tireless dissenter would have rung the alarm bells and roused the community to action. But with Ruggles gone, his go-it-alone approach had been replaced by a better-funded and more elaborate warning system that began with the Vigilance Committee, which in turn had notified wealthy

abolitionist Lewis Tappan of Steers's illegal detention in Brooklyn. Tappan hurried to secure a writ of habeas corpus, and a judge ordered court officials across the East River, where they arrested the four officers for kidnapping and illegal detention and held them on bail of thousands of dollars.

John Steers, meanwhile, escaped across the border into Canada and out of the reach of New York's complicity in the Fugitive Slave Law. The officers stood trial, and in a telling development that suggested the city was indeed shifting in its willingness to sacrifice Black lives in the name of Wall Street's prosperity, the officers were fired for their role in imprisoning Steers without charging him. Even more surprising, a grand jury handed down indictments for McNulty and the four officers for false imprisonment and kidnapping. Were New York's political and legal authorities finally rethinking their willingness to appease the South and acquiesce to every demand of slaveholders? Was the city starting to question whether the sacrifices made to keep the Union intact were proving too costly? And could African Americans dare to hope that their homes and communities were going to be defended rather than attacked by the NYPD?[41]

Time would tell, and the future was by no means assured, but at least now abolitionists could point to the fact that police officers claiming to be acting on behalf of the Fugitive Slave Law had been relieved of duty for failing to follow due process procedures. And that was a major improvement over the days of Boudinot, Riker, Nash, and others who flaunted Black civil rights when the New York Kidnapping Club was at its height a generation prior.[42]

As THE PRESIDENTIAL ELECTION of 1860 approached, Democrats like Charles O'Conor and Fernando Wood pledged to keep the Union and its compromises over slavery intact. In fact, Wood himself planned to head to the convention to seek the presidential or vice presidential nomination, pledging that only he knew how to defeat liberal New York politicians like Seward, a leading

candidate on the Republican side. In state elections in 1858, the Republicans had gained majorities in both houses of New York's legislature, which, together with the strong Democratic hold over Gotham, promised epic political battles as the nation lurched inevitably toward civil war. But while white politicians jostled for office, the Portuguese Company operated in and out of the city's harbor with near-impunity, even as New Yorkers headed to the polls.

New York and Secession

I<small>N THE FALL OF</small> 1859, <small>A FEW HUNDRED MILES SOUTHWEST OF</small> M<small>ANHAT</small>-tan, a religious zealot named John Brown ignited an ambitious attempt to seize federal weapons at an armory in Harpers Ferry, Virginia. His objective: to spark an uprising among southern slaves. The plan failed, and ten of his men were killed, including Brown's own son, when Lieutenant Colonel Robert E. Lee was sent to subdue the attempted revolt. Brown himself was captured and hanged weeks later in a Virginia execution witnessed by the actor John Wilkes Booth. Thanks to the lightning speed of the telegraph, the entire nation quickly became aware of the ill-conceived raid, and shocked Americans realized that Brown's actions represented a new level of violence and disruption that might one day soon lead to outright civil war.

In the weeks after Brown's raid, Americans alternately praised the abolitionist as an antislavery martyr and a crazed madman bent on overthrowing the government. Massachusetts writers Ralph Waldo Emerson and Henry David Thoreau celebrated Brown's antislavery courage, and Frederick Douglass hailed Brown's bravery if not his violence. White southerners decried Brown as a

lunatic and radical, the natural outcome of incendiary abolitionist rhetoric that had been building for decades.

Like all other Americans, New Yorkers divided over whether Brown was madman or martyr. Black residents of Gotham saw in him a tragic hero willing to die for the defeat of slavery. But New York City's white community was far less certain that Brown's raid was courageous and much less convinced that his actions deserved praise.[1]

Wall Street financiers and Democratic Party leaders rushed to convince slaveholders that they unanimously and vigorously opposed Brown's violent attempted revolution, and they were quick to draw direct lines between John Brown and the Republican Party's desire to limit slavery's westward expansion and the "atrocious disunion doctrines" of party leaders like William Henry Seward. Groups like the Democratic Vigilance Association were not above telling voters that merchants had warned that the violence perpetrated by Brown was the natural outcome of Republican rhetoric. Wall Street and its press allies loudly denounced Brown as an evil and crazed radical and reminded slaveholders that Gotham's business community had been on their side while the Republicans harbored the champions of a "higher conscience" like Seward.[2]

As had been true in previous national controversies, Wall Street's response to John Brown's raid had been rooted in fears of alienating white southerners and in losing the cotton trade. Slaveholders and their southern allies made sure that Wall Street was reminded of the stakes. In the most widely circulated southern economic magazine, the editor pointed out that more than 80 percent of southern cotton made its way through New York, at least on paper, and the consequences of civil war would decimate that city's economy: "What would become of the great metropolis, New-York? The ships would rot at her docks; grass would grow at Wall Street and Broadway; and the glory of New-York, like that of Babylon and Rome, would be numbered with the things that are past!" Wall Street did not need reminding. Bankers, cotton brokers, shippers, and merchants knew exactly where their wealth originated.[3]

By late December 1859, with John Brown having already hung from the gallows outside Harpers Ferry, New York's firms and financiers fell over themselves in rushing to demonstrate and publicize their pro-South bona fides. Sycophantic merchants rushed to convince slaveholders of their loyalty. Shop owners drafted letters to southern newspapers declaring their eagerness to defend the Union and the rights of southerners to own slaves. One merchant was "ready to go as far as any Southern men" in defending the right of masters to own slaves.[4]

Atlanta's daily newspaper had published its infamous "black and white list," which publicly named forty firms in Gotham suspected of abolitionist sympathies. "We have true southern born men in New York," the paper warned, "who will keep us posted as to the status of each firm or concern who are attempting to do business with the South." Firms like George Opdyke & Co., B. P. Shaw, the Fifth Avenue Hotel, and Rushmore, Cone, and Co. were all named in blacklists that were reprinted in city papers like the *New York Times*. In response, keeping careful tally of those sympathetic to slavery, many plantation owners kept their cotton bales from going north, sending waves of fear throughout Lower Manhattan.[5]

Much to the city's horror, southerners were reportedly turning away from Manhattan businesses in favor of western or European firms. Slaveholders were coming to believe that perhaps they were too dependent on New York banks to lend them lines of credit or too reliant on the city's firms to outfit their plantations. "Why does the South allow itself to be tattered and torn by the dissensions and death struggles of New York money changers?" asked one Charleston paper. Wall Street feared that if southerners really began to shy away from doing business with its firms, then prosperity would quickly become imperiled. How could the free states allow themselves to put the interests of a few thousand Black people above those of maintaining the economic health of the Union? It was way past the time, they argued, that economic concerns subsume the national controversy over slavery.

Writing in the *Journal of Commerce*, Gerard Hallock blamed Republicans like Seward for creating a political environment in

which abolitionist anarchists could dream of a raid like the one on Harpers Ferry. Hallock tried to reassure southerners that the vast majority of city businessmen were "sound" on the question of defending slavery. He wanted New York readers to know that the South was serious about secession, particularly after "the atrocious Abolitionist outrages" at Harpers Ferry. As soon as the slave states left the Union, Hallock reminded Wall Street by reprinting a southern editorial, they would enter into a treaty with Britain for direct trade with low tariffs, raise tariffs on northern goods, and leave Gotham "to live on fanaticism and philanthropy."[6]

In the midst of such strongly pro-South sentiments, both the kidnapping of African Americans and the illegal transatlantic slave trade continued to find New York fertile ground. New York mayor Fernando Wood and Brooklyn mayor Samuel Powell both believed adamantly that northern cities had a duty under the Fugitive Slave Law to return accused runaways, but as we have seen, courts were often unable to determine whether a person of color had been born free or enslaved, and even more troubling, officials frequently cared little about the distinction. Defenders of Black residents angrily questioned the role of the NYPD in enforcing the 1850 law. "It is not the business of a New York policeman," the *New York Evening Post* declared, "to carry out a federal fugitive slave law. . . . Liberty is not a crime in this state." But in spite of such protests, fugitive slave renditions continued, and in the broad net cast by the police, outright kidnappings were bound to occur. In fact, a proposal before the police board of commissioners to make officers liable for punishment if they participated in the arrest of accused runaways failed, in no small part because of Mayor Wood's opposition.[7]

As New York officials debated their precise responsibilities under the Fugitive Slave Law, Black New Yorkers like John Thomas suffered. Thomas was kidnapped from the streets and whisked away to bondage in Kentucky. Claimed by a slave owner from Louisville, Thomas supposedly fled slavery along the Ohio River, then traveled through Canada, and ultimately found a job as a porter in Manhattan. In late 1860, Thomas was arrested as a fugitive and

taken to a grand jury room on Chambers Street. While in prison, Thomas hastily drafted a note, dropped it out his cell window, and asked a passing boy to give the note to his employer, who submitted a writ of habeas corpus. Unfortunately, the officer on duty was none other than Tammany attack dog Isaiah Rynders, fresh from his attendance at the Democratic convention in Charleston, who produced a completely different man of color in response to the writ. No doubt Rynders knew exactly what he was doing by bringing a substitute to court, but the judge, likely assuming that Black men were interchangeable anyway, declared the writ satisfied. In the meantime, the police had sent the real John Thomas to enslavement. His employer and his friends learned that one of Rynders's deputies took Thomas to Richmond, awaiting transportation to Kentucky.[8]

At the same time, the transatlantic slave trade persisted as well. According to one estimate, about one hundred slavers set sail from New York between early 1859 and the summer of 1860. Initially engaged in legal business in commodities like ivory and palm oil, ship owners and captains were lured by the tremendous profits to be gained in slaving. Investors were drawn from all quarters of New York and Brooklyn; two female investors netted astonishing profits of nearly $40,000 on their initial outlay. With a cost of only about $35,000, successful slavers could garner a half million dollars' profit. And by paying only about one hundred dollars each for African men, women, and children who could be sold across the Atlantic for as much as $2,000 each, there is little wonder that the trade continued unabated even as the nation began preparing for the 1860 presidential election.[9]

Leaders of the Portuguese Company, such as C.H.S. Figaniere and John Machado, along with their allies John Weeks and Benjamin Wenberg, bought slavers, hired ship chandlers, and bribed captains throughout late 1859 and early 1860. Just after Christmas Day in 1859, Lima Viana purchased the bark *William G. Lewis*, which left for the Congo River delta the following January before it was captured off the coast of Cuba in the summer of 1860 with three hundred African people aboard. The *Buckeye* landed at Cuba

with five hundred purchased Africans in May 1860. Some ships had nearly nine hundred people packed on board. Several were captured by European or US Navy patrols, which burned slavers and tried to find places for those people recovered. But investors and ship owners simply shrugged off the financial loss and began preparations for the next illegal voyage that might well escape official patrols. There was simply too much money to be made to stop.

Weeks, Wenberg, Viana, and others were joined in the fiendish enterprise by newcomers like Mary Jane Watson, who bought a whaler in June 1860 and reportedly profited from landing enslaved people in Cuba later that year. Born Mary Jane Lackey in Lower Manhattan near Gold Street, Watson had divorced her husband, a move that embarrassed her brother, who was an important city official. Apparently, she had lost her two-year-old daughter to illness in 1850 before turning to a life in piracy. Watson had been attracted to the highly profitable slave trade, probably through John Alberto Machado of the Portuguese Company, with whom she was having an affair. Thanks to the likes of Watson and Machado, in just the years 1859 and 1860, some fifty-three thousand African people were forcibly taken from West Africa to Cuba.[10]

Political and legal authorities tried to tackle the problem, and even committed Democrats like US Marshal Rynders took their legal responsibilities to end the illicit commerce seriously. But it seemed that only the most glaring and obvious slavers were at risk of seizure by officials. In June 1860, as the schooner *Mariquita* was loading supplies along the wharves of New York harbor, one of the boxes broke open and out tumbled iron shackles that could only be intended to confine African bodies. Hardworking stevedores and other dockworkers, many of them people of color, could not help but notice, and soon Rynders had boarded the ship and arrested the crew.[11]

Rynders's true feelings toward people of color could not be concealed, however, in an unusual case that developed just weeks before Lincoln's election as president. After boarding a suspected slaver lying in the harbor, Rynders and his men discovered three very young boys who had been kidnapped from Africa. Marshal

Rynders intended to take the children to Baltimore, where they would be handed over to the Colonization Society and sent to Liberia. White abolitionist Lewis Tappan and his grandson William Barney visited Rynders at his office and pleaded with the marshal to let the children remain in Gotham. Tappan and Barney had arranged for them to be housed and educated at the city's Colored Orphan Asylum, but Rynders responded angrily to the benign request. The marshal rose from his desk and before a room full of people shouted:

> I have been annoyed enough about these damned infernal n——. Educate them! Why do you not ed-e-cate poor white boys? You don't care a damn for them, but have a mighty love for the damned n——. It is all a pretense. I don't believe a word of it.... I would like to know what you Goddamned abolitionists come around here to bother me for. I hate your damned hypocritical philanthropy; why don't you look after poor white people; but no, it is the n——.... I would like to hang every damned n—— so high that God Almighty could not cut him down. I would like to hang you.

TAPPAN RESPONDED CALMLY THAT he had not intended to trouble the marshal, replying, "I have no doubt, if the time comes, you will hang me in your best style." The furious Rynders jumped from behind his desk and continued to berate Tappan and Barney, shaking his fist in their faces while the deputy marshals and other officers and clerks in the room stomped their feet in approval. But the calm demeanor of Tappan and his grandson only made Rynders angrier. "I hate your damned calmness and moderation, it makes me mad; I hate you; I want you to hate me." The elder abolitionist responded, "I hate no one, not even the devil! I do not hate you, Marshal Rynders, and I wish you well." Whipped up into greater fury, Rynders went to strike Tappan, but his grandson stood between them and declared that he would not allow Tappan to be punched, whereupon Rynders grabbed Barney by his hair and threw both men out of the office.[12]

Rynders's fierce hatred for African Americans and their abolitionist allies reflected the feeling not just of the federal marshals,
but of many officials in Manhattan. Republican state leaders like
Senator Seward had tried to gain support in the Northeast for
more stringent enforcement of laws banning the trade, but, as he
lamented, "the root of the evil is in the great commercial cities, and
I frankly admit, in the City of New York." Particularly disturbing to
Seward was the fact that opposition to curtailing the trade "came
not so much from the Slave States as from the commercial interest
of New York." But legal authorities like Judge Samuel Betts, who
by 1860 still ruled in many federal maritime cases, continued to
make it almost impossible to prosecute anyone for slave trading.
And represented by the firm of Beebe, Dean, and Donohue, the
venerable defenders of slave trading who were responsible for letting countless slavers escape justice, successful prosecutions were
almost nonexistent.[13]

Such claims became even more plausible as fugitive slave renditions and outright kidnappings of freeborn people of color
persisted. Courts ruled that two accused fugitives be returned to
bondage in the spring of 1860, while authorities shied away from
prosecuting what abolitionists termed kidnapping. Tobias Boudinot remained in the police force, together with scores of other
officers who remained, at best, aloof from the welfare of Black
Gothamites, and at worst actively complicit in arresting supposed
runaway slaves with little to no proof of their true status. In the
face of such intransigence, Black New Yorkers had already begun
to heed David Ruggles's call to meet violence with violence. As
the editor of the *Weekly Anglo-African* reminded readers, "until
slave-catching is made dangerous—yea, fatal—to those engaged
in it, we may look for the recurrence of such transactions."[14]

For optimistic antislavery protesters, there were signs perhaps
of positive change: the firing of four officers for illegally detaining
John Smith, the indignation expressed by Wall Street leaders like
Hallock over the continuance of the illegal slave trade, and the
emergence of a new Republican Party that expressed skepticism

about the Democrats' unbridled defense of the South and slavery all provided grounds for thinking the New York of 1860 had
become more sympathetic to the claims of Black folks, especially
compared with the heyday of the New York Kidnapping Club in
the 1830s.

Republican Party leader Abraham Lincoln's widely read speech
at the nine-hundred-seat Great Hall in New York's Cooper Institute
in February, months before he would secure the party's nomination for president, gave African Americans and their allies further
hope for change. Attended by a large audience and reported by all
of the major city newspapers, Lincoln's speech elevated him into
one of the leading candidates for the nomination. The Illinois
Republican was already nationally known, in no small part due to
his famous debates with Democratic incumbent Stephen A. Douglas in the 1858 Illinois campaign for Senate. New Yorkers looking
for an alternative to the Democrats' constant genuflection to the
South and slavery, on the one hand, and to the incendiary radicalism of Seward, on the other, found much to admire in Lincoln's
Cooper Union speech.[15]

Lincoln began by telling New Yorkers that the Republican
Party was the true conservative party, opposed to the new and dangerous Democratic Party supposition that all federal policies had
to protect and defend bondage, even in the new western territories then opening up for settlement. He argued forcefully that
Republicans adhered to the Constitution and the intentions of the
Founding Fathers when it came to limiting slavery's expansion,
and he chided white southerners for childishly asserting that their
every demand must be met lest they leave the Union. Lincoln also
distanced himself from John Brown and his raid on Harpers Ferry,
reminding listeners that Brown was not a Republican nor did he
receive aid from anyone in the party.

The day after Lincoln's Cooper Union speech, New Yorkers
divided over its meaning. The Republican press lauded Lincoln's
speech as an articulate defense of the party and its basic conservative principles. Horace Greeley, editor of the *New York Tribune*,

praised the talk as one of the best recent political speeches the city had witnessed. Democratic papers barely noted the lecture, and those that did took issue with Lincoln's claim that the federal government was constitutionally empowered to keep slavery from spreading into the western territories. Democrats would also use the Cooper Institute to deliver their own speeches providing counterweights to Lincoln's address. In September and again in October, the city's wealthiest bankers and merchants gathered at the Cooper Union to join all of the anti-Republican groups into a "fusion ticket" that might carry the city. Republicans complained that New York's fusion ticket was further evidence of the Democrats' eagerness to kowtow to southern slaveholders and of Wall Street's blatant willingness to place the cotton trade above the city's dignity and political independence.[16]

Lincoln's Cooper Union speech may have helped launch his successful bid for the Republican nomination in the 1860 presidential election, but it did not help him garner enough votes to win over the overwhelmingly Democratic vote in New York City. Rural upstate voters aligned with Seward, and the Republican Party's antislavery sentiments provided the basis for Lincoln's ability to garner the state's electoral votes. But New York City went for the Democratic candidate Stephen Douglas by nearly a two-to-one margin over Lincoln. The rest of the state proved far more friendly to Lincoln and helped him capture the presidency, but the city remained true to its conservative politics. As one upstate newspaper put it, Gothamites "would do well to bear in mind, that Manhattan Island does not comprise *quite* all there is of the State of New York." But Lincoln ran up against a powerful Tammany Hall Democratic Party political machine, and the anti-Black pols like Mayor Fernando Wood constantly reminded voters that only his party could keep the Union intact. Hallock wrote several editorials in the *Journal of Commerce* denouncing abolitionism, the Republican Party, and Lincoln. Like many in the pro-business press, Hallock thought southern secession was illegal and unwise, but he also thought that the free states had

Abraham Lincoln, circa 1860.
(Library of Congress)

antagonized slaveholders with personal liberty laws and a general flouting of the Fugitive Slave Law. As angry as Wall Street leaders were over South Carolina's threats of secession, they thought that abolitionists and Republicans bore much of the blame.[17]

Not all merchants opposed Lincoln, of course. Many simply wanted to end the constant bickering over slavery, the Fugitive Slave Law, and the western territories and thought a Republican president might end once and for all these deeply divisive controversies. Others saw Lincoln as capable, uncorrupted, and conservative and believed he would limit slavery's expansion without doing anything too radical to anger the South. Though political opinions within the business community were diverse, it was clear to most merchants and bankers that a Lincoln administration would prove ruinous to their trade with the South. Apparently, Wall Street financiers even staged a fake economic panic in October, just before the election, to provide voters with a taste of the disasters that might befall the city if Lincoln was elected![18]

As the manufactured crisis on Wall Street suggested, tensions were so high that small events and issues could erupt into major conflagrations. In late July, a group of Savannah residents had traveled to New York, when a tourist's enslaved man was rescued by abolitionists. Democrats and businessmen reacted furiously to the "stealing" of such property, and the anti-Black newspaper the *New York Day Book* decried the "negro thieves here who insult our guests" and, just as troublesome, "do incalculable damage to the business interests of the city" by angering white visitors. As the November election approached, Tammany Hall and Democrats employed racist rhetoric and appeals to the fears of Irish voters as they cast Lincoln and the "Black Republicans" as "amalgamationists."[19]

Under the leadership of Isaiah Rynders, the Democrats gathered at Tammany Hall to crow about the city's apparent vote against Lincoln and the Republicans. On the night after the vote, Rynders took the podium before thousands of Democratic Party faithful, who lapped up his appearance like "a crowd of Spaniels around a good natured mastiff." It was already apparent that Lincoln was likely elected president, and Rynders dolefully announced that the "Black Republicans" could probably claim a national victory. But those gathered in the cigar smoke–filled hall took solace in the local returns, which showed a healthy majority against Lincoln. "It shows," Rynders said of the local results, "that the wards of New York are all right for the Union." He reminded his listeners that Black people and their friends in the antislavery community were the enemy of all Manhattan. "I hate the whole Abolition party. . . . I despise the dirty rascals. . . . I'd like to hang 'em all up, by God! Wouldn't you?" The crowd responded with shouts of "Yes! Yes!" and considerable laughter. New York had shown itself to be, in Rynders's words, "eminently conservative" and willing to uphold the constitutional compromise with the South over slavery. "If there are men," he told the crowd, "who are willing to trample on such interests for the love they bear the n——," at least New York City had stood firm against Lincoln and

abolition. "As for me, I would as soon as fight the fanatics of the North as the fire-eaters of the South."[20]

THANKS TO MAYOR FERNANDO Wood, Isaiah Rynders, the Wall Street press, and the Democrats' appeals, Gotham's voters delivered a humiliating defeat for Lincoln and his party, proving that whatever inroads the abolitionists had made into city politics were still mere towpaths. When the results were tallied, Lincoln lost the city as Wall Street remained committed to pro-Union and generally Democratic Party rhetoric. In Brooklyn the Democrats also won, though by a narrower margin. Lincoln won the state by about 7 percent and went on to win the Electoral College vote by a fairly wide margin, garnering almost twice as many electoral votes as he needed to capture the presidency. All of Lincoln's votes came from the Northeast, Pacific West, and Midwest as he did not even appear on the ballot in southern states. To the dismay of New York City's Black community, Manhattan and Brooklyn had again cast their lots with the Democrats and their anti-Black, pro-South platform.[21]

Equally distressing for Black residents of Gotham, the election resulted in a major defeat for Black suffrage. Republicans in the state legislature had managed to get a referendum on the ballot that would have granted African American men the right to vote. Veteran leaders like James McCune Smith worked hard to drum up support for the proposal, and even helped to create the New York City Suffrage Committee to build support. The committee wrote letters to newspapers, published essays, and delivered speeches, and a large convention held in the city in May set up more than sixty local clubs and distributed thousands of pamphlets to promote the right to vote. Smith argued that approval of the referendum would aid "the cause of Justice and Right, so long denied to the colored man in this State." Together with fellow Black city leaders John J. Zuille and James P. Miller, Smith urged people to meet with and persuade white friends to vote as proxies for the ballot that they themselves were not allowed to cast.[22]

The New York Hotel, always the preferred residence for white southerners visiting the city for business or pleasure, was the site of considerable frustration over the Black suffrage referendum. Southern men at the hotel declared that they would prefer the Devil as president rather than Lincoln or allow Blacks to vote. After a young southern man loudly expressed his opinions on Lincoln, a Republican took exception and a fistfight broke out on the sidewalk in front of the hotel. One Virginian claimed disgustedly that Black workers seemed unusually disrespectful at the hotel, a perceived change that he attributed to the suffrage referendum. Black intellectuals and political observers like Smith had reason to be at least a bit optimistic, given the popularity of the Republicans across the free states. Unfortunately for Smith and Zuille, neither the southern patrons at the New York Hotel nor the pro-Union Democrats around Wall Street had reason to fear. The referendum proved unpopular across the state, in rural and urban areas alike. The vote to give Black men the right to vote was defeated within Gotham by almost seven to one. The stinging defeat was only partially ameliorated by Lincoln's victory.[23]

While New York Democrats and most of Wall Street's business community lamented Lincoln's election, white southerners were preparing much more drastic actions. Leading southern politicians, known as "fire-eaters" for their disunionist and proslavery rhetoric, had been questioning the value of remaining in the Union for decades, even though virtually every president had been friendly to their interests and even though the rest of the federal government, including Congress and the Supreme Court, had almost always given in to the demands of slaveholders, so much so that many Republicans had complained that a "slave power" ruled all three branches of government. The Fugitive Slave Law and the *Dred Scott* court decision were just two glaring examples of Washington's bowing to slaveholding concerns.[24]

In fact, as they themselves often acknowledged, white southerners did not have much room to complain when it came to the federal government. Georgia senator Robert Toombs stood up in the Senate and maintained that "we do not charge these

wrongs against the Federal Government. . . . There has been no time, since its establishment, when it has been truer to its obligations" regarding slavery. The states' rights arguments that we usually associate with the white South were actually mirrored in the free states, as Massachusetts, Pennsylvania, Michigan, and others argued that the Fugitive Slave Law unconstitutionally required states opposed to slavery to participate actively and directly in the recapture of supposed runaways.[25]

That calculation altered dramatically with Lincoln's election. From the viewpoint of white southerners, they had long depended upon proslavery presidents to lead the federal government, but the election of the "Black Republican" Lincoln placed a man in the Executive Mansion much more skeptical of bondage. Lincoln had never been a radical abolitionist, a strident activist along the lines of Garrison or Douglass, both of whom toiled for immediate emancipation. Even in his famous Cooper Union speech, Lincoln pledged to leave the South alone, to let slavery exist under local laws without interference by the North or the federal government. Lincoln's moderate position, the main thrust of Republican Party philosophy, was to keep slavery out of the new states that would emerge from the western territories.

But moderation would not suffice for the southern fire-eaters, who declared that they should be allowed to take their enslaved property anywhere they chose, and to deny that right was to deny white southerners equal protection under the law. No matter how much Lincoln told white southerners that he had no intention of interfering with existing bondage in the South, a position he repeated in his inaugural speech in March 1861, the most extreme proslavery southerners refused to live under a federal government headed by a man who even expressed moderate misgivings about slavery. White southerners were used to genuflection from their presidents, and Lincoln refused to bow.

One month after Lincoln's election, South Carolina, that constant thorn in the side of the Union, voted to withdraw from the United States. No one was sure secession was possible or legal or constitutional. Slavery's political mouthpieces had been arguing

for decades that states had individually ratified the Constitution agreeing to join the United States, and those same states had the right to leave when they deemed it necessary. Not all white southerners supported the idea of secession; in some states like North Carolina and Virginia, a majority of whites appeared to oppose secession as a dangerous and rash move. But by the time Lincoln stood on the steps of the US Capitol, raised his right hand, and took the oath of office, he already had a rebellion on his hands. Between December 1860 and March 1861 seven Deep South states had seceded from the Union and established their new confederacy in Montgomery, Alabama.

How would New York respond to the secession crisis led by the slave states? Remarkably, the city responded at first by considering its own secession from the Union.

Never ones to miss the chance for a massive rally to demonstrate their power, Wall Street interests, including *Journal of Commerce* editor Hallock, staged a meeting of thousands of New York businessmen not long after Lincoln's election. In what would soon become infamously known as the Pine Street Meeting, Hallock and others gathered to support South Carolina's complaints. Not all defended secession or agreed with that state's decision to secede from the Union. Some merchants saw secession as a rash and radical move that would soon backfire. But those gathered at the Pine Street Meeting were quick to lay the fault of the national crisis not on South Carolina, but on Massachusetts. Republicans in New England were guilty of disobeying the Fugitive Slave Law, passing so-called personal liberty laws that thwarted the enforcement of the Constitution's Fugitive Slave Clause, and drumming up antislavery passions against the South. It was no wonder, Wall Street declared, that South Carolina wanted to withdraw from a pact with such philanthropists and fanatics. Two venerable New York Democrats, Charles O'Conor and John McKeon, claimed that slaveholders had every right to secede and blamed Republicans

Prominent New York
lawyer Charles O'Conor.
*(Library of Congress Prints and
Photographs Division, Brady-
Handy Photograph Collection)*

and abolitionists for leaving the South no choice but to form its own government.[26]

O'Conor and McKeon were two of the more extreme speakers that cold evening in December 1860, but the overriding sentiment expressed at the Pine Street Meeting was an attempt to convince slaveholders that Wall Street wanted a peaceful compromise. In a resolution directed toward the South, the merchants and bankers reminded slaveholders that "we have stood by you" and "we have asserted your rights as earnestly as though they had been our own." They pointed to Wall Street's overwhelming support for the Fugitive Slave Law in 1850 as evidence for the protection of southern interests. If the slave states would only pause in their rush to secede and come to the table for negotiations, the whole calamity caused by disagreements over slavery could be swiftly resolved.[27]

The Pine Street Meeting represented Wall Street's continued intention to appeal to the South for compromise. Manhattan was a physical island, but business leaders like Moses Taylor and

Auguste Belmont, Democratic mayor Wood, and their allies in the press like Hallock felt like they were marooned on a political island as well, surrounded by free states that had voted for Lincoln, and engulfed by a state government that had delivered a powerful majority for Lincoln, the hated Seward, and the Republican Party. If the southern states could secede from the Union, why couldn't Gotham? New York mayor Wood asked precisely that question.

It was a treasonous inquiry, and Republicans were stunned that Wood would even consider taking the city out of New York State. But as the mayor viewed the matter, the city and state had been at odds over the police force, Unionism, the Fugitive Slave Law, municipal governance, and a host of other issues for years. Just four years prior, Wood had been arrested by state-sanctioned officers for refusing to acknowledge the authority of the Metropolitan police. In his opinion, while New England and upstate New York clung to puritanical ideas about reforming the world and fanatical notions of abolitionism, the city remained aloof from such "isms" and the finger-wagging philanthropists who promoted them. Perhaps a bold step like seceding from the United States would at once free New York from an overweening state government and a Republican presidency. Most important, if it could somehow become an independent city, New York could continue trading in cotton with the slave states.[28]

As southern states held votes and referendums on secession in early 1861, Mayor Wood pitched independence to the city council as a cure-all for New York's ills. In a major speech before the Common Council, Wood sided with "our aggrieved brethren of the Slave States" with whom New York had "a common sympathy." To be sure, many New York businessmen were angered by South Carolina's secession. A frustrated Hallock denounced the political maneuverings, as Gotham's business community had been working so hard to find a national compromise. But Wall Street's feeling of brotherhood and commiseration with slaveholders was undeniable, enduring, and robust. From the moment police officer Tobias Boudinot and Marshal Daniel Nash had used their blanket

writ to haul supposed runaways before Richard Riker in the 1830s, to debates over the Fugitive Slave Law in the 1850s, Wall Street had stood with slavers and cotton and against Black civil rights. From the darkest days of the New York Kidnapping Club to John Brown's raid and Lincoln's election, the business community had almost always sided with any decision that appeased the South and protected the lucrative cotton trade. New York had every right, Wood thought, to expect that vital business relationship with the slave states to continue.

Now Wood was simply asking the city council to take one more step. Secession would allow New York to keep tariff revenues, to trade with the South without interference from the federal government, and to shed the yoke of the governor and state legislature. Wood presented a convincing argument, and the corrupt city council, labeled "The Forty Thieves" in the press, voted in favor of creating an independent free city. Called the Free City of Tri-Insula, the new entity would link Manhattan, Staten Island, and Long Island into an autonomous republic. Less than two months after Lincoln's election, and long before southern states like North Carolina withdrew from the Union, New York City had voted to secede. It was a shocking turn, even in a city known for southern sympathies.

Even this step was not enough for some. James Kerrigan, a New York congressman newly elected, decided that an independent city would need an independent army. He called for a new "military organization to protect the municipal rights of the city" that would be proslavery and aligned with the southern states. On the evening of January 21, 1861, several hundred men began to gather outside the Brooklyn Navy Yard, though no one seemed quite sure what they were doing there. Rumors had spread over the past few days that if the men heard the bell at City Hall ring ten times, then the Fifth Brigade was supposed to gather at the armory. More rumors spread that none other than the ubiquitous Marshal Isaiah Rynders, angry at the notion that northerners would try to force the South back into the Union, had called for an attack on the yard.[29]

Not wanting to take any chances, the navy called out troops to prevent the mob from entering the yard. No one seemed to know whether the threat was legitimate or imagined. Confederate politician John Forsyth, one of Savannah's wealthiest slaveholders, traveled to New York to find out more about Kerrigan's plans, and he was heartened to learn that a major plot was under way to seize the federal armory in Brooklyn and to use the weapons to defend the city in case of war. The "double tyranny" from which Gotham had long suffered under the state government in Albany and the federal government in Washington, Forsyth believed, would lead the city to join with the South. Republican threats to punish New York for its Democratic support by raising the tariffs, combined with the Confederacy's plan to lower its tariffs, might mean a dramatic shift in foreign trade from New York to New Orleans. Kerrigan and political and financial leaders believed that they could not let this happen, and they plotted to seize the federal armory in Brooklyn just as John Brown had tried to capture the one at Harpers Ferry for a very different purpose.[30]

Nothing came of Kerrigan's plot, but while the city council voted to form an independent republic, Wall Street was busily and relentlessly trying to find a compromise that might reel the Deep South states back into the Union and end the prospects of any more southern states withdrawing. Two delegations organized along party lines departed the city for Washington in January, both armed with proposals for appeasing the South. Increasingly alarmed at the prospect of a horrific civil war, even Seward and his Republican allies declared their intentions to forge a settlement if possible. And there was no shortage of compromise plans. Some Wall Street representatives supported a plan that would extend the original 1820 compromise line at the 36°30' latitude through the western territories to permit slavery below the line and only free soil above it. Other proposals offered further commitment from the free states to enforce the Fugitive Slave Law, repealing state laws that rendered that enforcement more difficult, and the prohibition of any future constitutional amendments that might jeopardize bondage.[31]

Wall Street cared less about the particulars than about finding a resolution to the crisis. With southern firms unwilling or unable to pay their debts, northern bankers, insurance companies, and merchants were bleeding money. For example, the Charleston firm of Spencer and Teague enclosed a small down payment on its debt to a New York merchant: "It is the best we can do at present. . . . We of the South have done all we could to avert this calamity and our efforts have availed us nothing. The Republicans have achieved the victory and brought it upon us, both south and north, a financial crisis and stagnation of trade . . . we want to pay our debts and will do it as soon as possible." Thousands of businesses in both sections were in similar predicaments, and the fear of Wall Street that secession and war would mean economic torpor and unpaid debts was coming to fruition.[32]

Just as the Common Council voted to form an independent republic, leading businessmen, including many New Yorkers, descended on the nation's capital wielding a massive petition signed by forty thousand merchants and bankers urging a settlement of the slavery issue, whatever concessions had to be made. But Republican leaders like Massachusetts senator Charles Sumner and Pennsylvania's Thaddeus Stephens, well aware that "cotton loving" businessmen in Gotham had long defended slavery, were not impressed. Wall Street, one city paper admitted, could always be counted on to "eat a little dirt for the sake of slavery." And indeed the main complaint from leading merchants like A. T. Stewart seemed to be the decline of trade and the loss of business, not whether the nation would become a haven for slavery's western expansion. As the nation lay in political turmoil, Wall Street's chief concern was the economy. The Stock Exchange fluctuated wildly, responding favorably with even the slightest hint of a national compromise, and falling precipitously as hopes were dashed. The turmoil was real. The uncertainty over secession and the possibility of a civil war suspended trade between the South and New York, leading countless merchants to close their businesses. Clerks, usually busy writing letters, sending out bills, and reconciling accounts, were left idle or let go. It seems that the prediction of

southern economist James D. B. De Bow that "grass would grow" in the streets of Manhattan if the cotton trade dried up was not very far from the truth.[33]

In fact, the metaphor for weeds sprouting from the sidewalks along Wall Street became a powerful theme in the city's politics. President-elect Lincoln visited New York in February 1861 and sat down for breakfast with many of the city's most prominent Republicans, who came away dubious about his ability to solve the national crisis, and unconvinced that he even wanted to avoid a clash with the South. At one meeting, William E. Dodge, one of the few leading Wall Street businessmen who had joined the Republicans, implored Lincoln to find a compromise no matter what had to be sacrificed. Standing before the wealthy men gathered, Dodge turned boldly to Lincoln and asserted that "it is for you, sir, to say whether the whole nation shall be plunged into bankruptcy, whether the grass shall grow in the streets of our commercial cities." Lincoln responded politely, but Dodge continued to press him. Dodge and Wall Street wanted the new president to "yield to the just demands of the South." If you are determined to avoid ruin, Dodge declared, "you will not go to war on account of slavery." Now clearly being publicly pushed, Lincoln grew angry and replied:

> I do not know that I understand your meaning, Mr. Dodge . . . nor do I know what my acts or opinions may be in the future beyond this. I shall take an oath that I will to the best of my ability, preserve, protect and defend the Constitution of the United States. . . . The Constitution will not be preserved and defended until it is enforced and obeyed in every part of every one of the United States. It must be so respected, obeyed, and enforced, and defended, let the grass grow where it may.

DODGE AND THE REST of Wall Street had their answer from the president-elect. They had wanted Lincoln to bend to southern demands and to avoid a war over something as "inconsequential" as slavery or Black civil rights. Lincoln made clear to their faces

that he would neither give in to slaveholders' demands nor let the cotton trade subsume the need to end the southern rebellion. Wall Street was stunned that Lincoln would place the interests of "some vagabond negroes" above the preservation of the Union.[34]

The reaction to Lincoln's unequivocal statements to Wall Street drew swift reaction. It was now clear to financiers and merchants that the nation would soon be plunged into immediate and permanent division, two countries where once there stood a single republic. Some thought that they could still do business with the new Confederate South, perhaps the same way that they had traded with other foreign governments around the world. Tariffs would have to be set, new trade agreements and contracts drawn up, and a diplomatic corps would have to guide the separation. But old trade routes might still be used; railroad networks and shipping lanes could be policed and reorganized. An optimism and entrepreneurial spirit prevailed among many merchants, the same outlook that had made Gotham one of the world's foremost financial capitals. Some even moved to the South to start new branches of their businesses.

For most of Wall Street, though, Lincoln's steely determination to end the rebellion was an ominous and dangerous warning signal, one that helped plunge the city into financial crisis. Grass was not yet emerging from Broadway, but the seeds had become lodged in the cracks of sidewalks and germination had begun. How long before seedlings sprang up was anyone's guess. But the stock exchange dropped fast and clerks were once again idle. Business slowed to a crawl, stunted by the suspension of credit, and the once mighty flow of cotton through Gotham's ledgers had dwindled to a mere trickle. As Lincoln delivered a conciliatory inaugural address on March 4, New York merchants cared less about the new president's stirring words than about the bleak numbers listed in their account books.

Civil War

T HE FIRST REAL BATTLE OF THE CIVIL WAR STRUCK NEW YORK
City like an earthquake, upending deeply entrenched
interests and causing a revolution in Wall Street's thinking.
Lincoln had pledged a cautious and conciliatory approach to the
rebellious states, but when South Carolinians fired shots at Fort
Sumter in Charleston harbor just a month into his presidency,
he had little choice but to respond. The federal government surrendered Fort Sumter to the Confederacy, but Lincoln called for
seventy-five thousand volunteers to subdue the rebellion. The
Civil War generated a nationalist fervor that swept across Manhattan and threatened to drown the proslavery and pro-South voices
that had long prevailed on Wall Street. The wave did not completely devour the likes of Charles O'Conor and his Democratic
allies, and they would continue throughout the Civil War to criti-
cize Lincoln and the Republicans. During the fighting, the city's
formidable white supremacist views would surface to espouse
opposition to Lincoln's prosecution of the war and to attack especially the Emancipation Proclamation and the assertion of Black
civil rights. But during the war years the most extreme voices were
relegated to islands of discontent, and though they remained a

visible presence, still the constant beating of Unionist breakers battered their shores.

Such a dramatic change in public opinion in favor of the Union and the Republican prosecution of the war had caught Wall Street and its Democratic allies by surprise. How could Manhattan, which only weeks before with Mayor Wood's vigorous backing had voted to abandon the Union, now just as rapidly and enthusiastically line up behind Lincoln in his attempt to subdue the Confederacy? How could Wall Street bankers and businessmen, who had devoted much of the last thirty years to protecting slavery and defending the interests of southern slaveholders, now so completely forsake those efforts to back the Union? To be sure, conservative voices, most powerfully heard among Democrats, remained amplified within city politics, and many supporters in the Irish working class would continue to question the war. But in the late spring of 1861, the swing in political and popular feeling was undeniable, swift, and profound.[1]

One Wall Street magnate's change of heart illustrates the broader shift in thinking. Alexander T. Stewart had been born in Ireland in the early years of the nineteenth century and arrived in Gotham barely out of his teens. As he crossed the Atlantic, Stewart carried with him a parcel of linens, Irish-made lace, and other goods he intended to sell in New York. By the late 1840s, just after David Ruggles had left the city for Massachusetts, A. T. Stewart & Company's marble multistory department store attracted customers to Broadway.

Although generally apolitical, Stewart had joined the chorus of voices on Wall Street that supported a compromise with the South no matter what had to be sacrificed. Just after South Carolina's secession, Stewart had seen that the prosperity and the republic itself lay in great danger, which, he insisted, necessitated "a kind and conciliatory spirit towards our Southern brothers." Stewart argued that the Constitution would never have been ratified unless northerners had compromised over slavery, and that same feeling of cooperation should prevail in quelling the anger of slaveholders over their right to recapture runaway slaves. "The

refusal at Washington to concede costs us millions daily," Stewart complained bitterly in early 1861. Within a few months, however, the dry goods millionaire had completely changed his mind, motivated by the outbreak of fighting at Fort Sumter. Southern rebels had fired upon the federal garrison mercilessly and in doing so had made war on the United States itself. Such a brazen attack had to be countered.[2]

Stewart himself acknowledged that the time for compromise had passed, and he no longer felt comfortable sitting on the political fence. One southern businessman wrote to him to ascertain if the rumors were true: Was Stewart now siding with Lincoln and the Republicans after having worked so hard for conciliation? The answer, Stewart wrote in a reply, was yes. "All that I have of position and wealth," he openly acknowledged, "I owe to the free institutions of the United States. . . . The government to which these blessings are due, calls on her citizens to protect the capitol from the threatened assault." Feeling an overwhelming sense of duty to respond to Lincoln's call to defend the Union and defeat the Confederacy, Stewart pledged his fortune and his life.

Stewart's loyalty to the Union was echoed by businessmen both great and small in April 1861, and they joined the Republican Party en masse in an alliance between Wall Street and the GOP that still stands today. Richard Cary Morse, who hailed from a conservative New York religious family, was unequivocal in his changed opinion: "The seceding states [have] acted as mere children frightened by imaginary future evils, products of their own distorted fancies and brains . . . they need to have a little of their childish folly and prejudice <u>whipped</u> out of them."[3]

Like the super wealthy A. T. Stewart, everyday broker Samuel Raisbeck, who kept an office at 70 Wall Street, had come to believe that southerners acted foolishly in withdrawing from the Union and that the time had come to stop appeasing slaveholders. After Lincoln's victory and South Carolina's secession, Raisbeck was content to just let the South go its own way. "Secession troubles keep Wall St. quiet," he wrote in one of the many business letters he sent each week. "We are feeling quite indifferent to the

Cotton States being out of the Union and rather think it may be the best for both sections of the country to separate. . . . If the peace congress can keep in the Border States, the South may go and be blessed." Business on Wall Street had slowed dramatically, and if the slaveholders wanted their own government, then so be it. It was time for business to resume.[4]

After the brief battle at Fort Sumter, Raisbeck's opinions of secession and war turned significantly. In another business letter, Raisbeck expressed his hopes that the mustering of Union troops "will cause the Jeff Davis Army to back down, if not the war will be one of extermination of the rebels and slavery will get its death blow." Raisbeck's pride in his home state contrasted in his mind with the treachery of South Carolina. "If Washington is attacked," he wrote to a fellow broker, "or demonstration made that way, you may expect a good 50,000 from the Empire State." The changing views of wealthy merchants like Stewart and ordinary brokers like Raisbeck show that as long as compromise was viable, Manhattan's business community wanted peace if possible. But once the fighting commenced in earnest, and compromise between North and South seemed impossible, they cast their lot with the Union cause.[5]

Hallock and other members of the conservative press came in for heavy criticism for the pro-South editorials they had penned over the years, and by the summer of 1861 they were charged with sending treasonous materials through the mail. The *Journal of Commerce*, the *New York Day Book*, the *Brooklyn Daily Eagle*, and other papers were indicted by a grand jury in the Southern District of New York, charged with "encouraging rebels now in arms against the Federal Government." Rather than embarrass the *Journal of Commerce* further, Hallock elected to retire from journalism, a career in which he had spent the last three decades. The editor declared to readers that he had devoted his "best efforts as a public journalist" to preserving the Union, a cause that required more compromise with the South and slavery than his fellow northerners were willing to forbear.[6]

While Lincoln's call for troops to defend the Union generated a powerful sense of duty among white New Yorkers across the social and political spectrum, and the city's Black residents rejoiced that a battle had commenced that might ultimately lead to the end of slavery, the stirring sights of soldiers in uniform helped to sway the feelings of white Manhattanites who had remained neutral.

New York became a staging area for Union troops, and by May 1861 some twenty-five hundred men crowded into the Battery awaiting orders. In City Hall Park, the same space that had witnessed so many African American protests against the actions of the New York Kidnapping Club in the 1830s and 1840s, stood temporary barracks for six thousand soldiers ready to take on the southern rebels. The fervor and excitement caused by the presence of soldiers in Manhattan could not be quashed. On April 19, just a week after the outbreak of fighting at Fort Sumter, New York's Seventh Regiment, made up of many young men who hailed from elite families, armed with their prized twelve-pound howitzer, marched as an enormous crowd of men and women of all ages cheered. Theodore Winthrop, a wealthy writer in the making, was charged with guarding the cannon, and, together with his fellow New Yorkers, he marveled at the crowd. As he marched, he looked up at the Astor Library and spotted the waving handkerchief of a woman who had made sandwiches for the soldiers. As Winthrop and his comrades paraded down Broadway through two miles of cheering crowds lined up along the street, he passed A. T. Stewart's famous department store and the shops and banks of businessmen who just weeks before had been so eager for compromise with slaveholders. Winthrop and his comrades were applauded and slapped on the back. Handkerchiefs, he later recalled, showered down on the marchers like snow. Men handed pocketknives, soap, combs, cigars, and matches to the troops. "We knew now," Winthrop proudly declared, "that our great city was with us as one man, utterly united in the great cause we were marching to sustain."

Though the war had begun as a battle to end the southern rebellion, it was soon to morph into a war that would also end

New York celebrating the Seventh Regiment in early 1861. *(Harper's Weekly)*

slavery. In the much more prolonged campaign toward Black civil rights, racial equality, and the end of bondage, New York had traveled perhaps further than any other free city. From the early 1830s, when the New York Kidnapping Club reigned, through the worst trials over the Fugitive Slave Law in the 1850s, the city had proved a devoted ally of slaveholding interests. But those dark days were now obscured by the huzzahs and cheers that rained down on the Union troops soon to leave New York for the battles of Virginia.[7]

THE CITY WAS RALLYING around the Union war effort, and Republicans would soon throw their support behind Lincoln's Emancipation Proclamation and the Thirteenth Amendment ending slavery. But perhaps no single event indicated the unexpected changes in New York politics more than the hanging of Nathaniel Gordon Jr. for slave trading. For the past thirty years, the city had become one of the most important ports in the illegal transatlantic slave trade.

Now New York became home to the only execution for slave trading the nation had ever witnessed.

Nathaniel Gordon, of slender build and medium height, with a sharp nose and small, dark eyes, had been born in 1826 into a long line of ship captains in Portland, Maine. His grandfather had fought the British in the Revolutionary War, while his father, as we have seen, had entered the business of slave trading around the time Nathaniel was born. Nathaniel himself was eager to engage in the business, given how much money could be made, and he was repeatedly caught and arrested in the 1850s but never convicted by the southern-friendly juries of Manhattan. Just over thirty-five years old, Gordon lived in Williamsburg outside of Manhattan with his young wife and four-year-old son and over the years had already made quite a lot of money in legal and illegal trade. His luck changed, though, when he was arrested aboard the slaver *Erie* in the fall of 1860, just as Lincoln approached victory in the campaign.[8]

Gordon's trial for piracy and slave trading was covered eagerly across the nation just before the First Battle of Bull Run garnered headlines in the summer of 1861. That Gordon was arrested and charged was significant in itself; so many New York district attorneys had refused to prosecute slavers, and even when they had been charged, judges like Samuel Betts rendered conviction almost impossible. But now the district attorney and the courts were determined to make an example of Gordon.

District Attorney E. Delafield Smith laid out the arguments to the grand jury, and they were indeed shocking. Gordon had picked up nearly a thousand Africans near the mouth of the Congo River, a number of captives high even for seasoned slavers. But even more disturbing was the fact that the vast majority were children, whose young age made them more pliable and less likely to revolt. Not long after all were aboard, a US Navy ship patrolling the West African coast spotted the *Erie* and began a pursuit. Gordon was arrested and confined on board as the navy vessel escorted the *Erie* to the African colony of Liberia, where several hundred people

were forced into Monrovia, far from their original homes. Despite the facts of the case and the testimony of both naval officers and Gordon's own first mate, the first trial resulted in a hung jury. At first it seemed that perhaps New York had not changed that much after all.[9]

Previous prosecutors would have thrown up their hands, but District Attorney Smith was determined to make an example of Gordon, and the case was tried again the following summer before the US Circuit Court. Though Betts was still on the bench, Gordon's case would be heard by Judge William Shipman. Shipman had been appointed by the Democratic president James Buchanan, but Shipman was horrified by Gordon's callousness, especially in the treatment of children. With a determined district attorney and a judge less willing to exonerate slavers, the prosecution had a better chance for a conviction. It was far from guaranteed, however, because Gordon's defense was headed by the notorious firm of Beebe, Dean, and Donohue, the same outfit that had defended countless other slavers and abductors since the days of the New York Kidnapping Club.

At the second trial, the prosecution pushed harder to make its case. This time new witnesses were found to testify that the *Erie* had landed in Havana and took on additional stores and crew, before crossing the Atlantic to Africa. Some members of the crew claimed not to be aware that they were on board a slaver until it was too late, and they proved eager witnesses against Gordon. They claimed that Spanish slave traders in Cuba and off the coast of Africa near Shark Point had aided Gordon in forcing the children on board. The evidence was clear and not even Beebe, Dean, and Donohue could get Gordon off this time. The jury convicted Gordon of piracy almost a year to the day after Lincoln had been elected president.[10]

The following month Gordon received a sentence of death, another shocking twist in the long history of New York as a slave port. Before he was to be hanged at the Tombs on February 7, 1862, Beebe, Dean, and Donohue appealed to President Lincoln to commute the sentence. The criminal defense firm presented

Lincoln with a petition signed by many influential citizens of Maine and leading politicians, and soon New Yorkers added their weight to the plea to turn Gordon's death sentence into life in prison. The pressure on Lincoln to commute the sentence was powerful and persistent. Two of Gordon's lawyers traveled down to the capital to implore Lincoln to convert his punishment to life in prison. His lawyers tried every legal maneuver they could think of, including making an unconvincing claim that Gordon had actually been born aboard a ship in the Mediterranean, and therefore was not an American citizen, to save his life. The lawyers and some members of the public pointed to the plight of Gordon's wife and son. Gordon himself complained that no one had ever been sentenced so severely for piracy and slave trading since the law against piracy had been enacted decades before, so he had no reason to suspect such a harsh sentence. Why not commute Gordon's death sentence and then make clear to future slavers that convictions would result in execution?[11]

With all of the pleas for mercy toward Gordon emanating from New York, few white commenters pointed to the horrific plight of the hundreds of children and adults he had forced aboard the *Erie*. The Africans who had been imprisoned on his ship and then summarily deposited in Liberia with barely enough to eat and drink had fallen away from the discussion of clemency. And as the details of the case emerged, Gordon's unrelenting cruelty was laid bare. More than a third—some three hundred men, women, and children—had died between the time the *Erie* was caught and the time it took to sail to Liberia. Gordon would later blame the US Navy, which took charge of the Africans and did not know how to feed and take care of so many captives. But, of course, the fault lay with Gordon, who had kidnapped them in the first place. No one doubted Gordon's guilt, even his lawyers. But his friends in the shipping trade hoped that by placing placards around the city and writing letters to Lincoln and other political leaders, they might yet save his life.[12]

Concerned that the president might actually pardon Gordon, District Attorney Smith went to Washington to plead with the

president and the administration to stick with the lethal punishment. Smith argued that New York and the nation needed to see the execution carried out so that Gordon could be made an example for the many other slavers engaged in piracy. Nearly everyone—from Wall Street ship chandlers to ship owners to captains—was betting that once again slave trading would go unpunished, Smith warned Lincoln. Following through with the hanging would signal to anyone else engaged in slave trading that the penalty would be the severest possible. If Lincoln gave in to requests for mercy, Smith feared, "this revolting, sickening traffic may grow bold again."[13]

As it turned out, Lincoln's resolve to make an example out of Gordon would not waver. Well aware of Manhattan's long-standing reputation for harboring slavers and the difficulty of obtaining arrests and convictions, Lincoln clearly intended to set a standard, particularly for all those watching in New York. With a resolute determination that would characterize his approach to emancipation and the prosecution of the war, Lincoln believed it his duty to refuse to pardon or reduce Gordon's sentence. The president did, however, decide to delay the execution for two weeks so that Gordon could say goodbye to his family and to make plans, as Lincoln wrote, "for the awful change which awaits him." On February 21, 1862, the hanging would be carried out.[14]

The *New York Times*, then just about a decade old but firmly aligned with Lincoln and the Republicans, agreed with the president that the city had to set an example in carrying out Gordon's execution. Yes, mercy toward an individual was often justified, the *Times* argued in an editorial, but there remained in Gordon's case "a debt of long standing due to society, to justice, to public morality, which should at last be paid." That Gotham had to sacrifice the life of one its own citizens was only fitting, given the ease with which New York harbor had ignored the slave trade for most of the last half century. In fact, the paper concluded, the city *needed* to have the sentence fulfilled as a kind of exorcism for having participated in kidnapping over the past forty years.[15]

Although New York shipping interests continued their efforts to save one of their own, Gordon resolved to face his execution

as February 21 approached. The night before his hanging, he visited with his wife and mother, and then sat down to write several letters, including one to his young son to be opened when he was older. He asked the guards for whiskey and cigars, and stayed up well past midnight drafting letters and smoking.

In the early morning hours, the guards were alarmed to hear Gordon moaning and convulsing. In an attempt to commit suicide, he had asked one of the guards to lace the cigars with strychnine. Now he was in great pain and semiconscious, but the guards used a stomach pump to remove the poison. Unable to stand on his own, and only partially alive, he would meet his maker in the newly constructed scaffold outside of the Tombs just after noon. The hanging was quick, with only a small crowd, surrounded by some forty marines guarding the event, there to witness it. District Attorney Smith, though still convinced that Gordon needed to be made an example, could not stomach the execution and left the prison early.

As the *New York Times* had argued, Wall Street perhaps had finally helped to pay a bill long past due. The "cursed greed of gain," the *Times* declared, had blinded everyone from Wall Street ship owners to shops along Broadway that supplied the trade, to the longshoremen and stevedores who loaded those supplies on board. "New York," argued the paper, "has been most deeply engaged in the traffic" and "her merchants have largely profited by its blood-stained gains." Though the *Times* acknowledged sympathy for Gordon's friends and family, it could not "but rejoice that the Slave-trade has received so heavy a blow." "Our city," the paper concluded, "has been disgraced by it long enough."[16]

Word of Gordon's hanging spread across America and indeed across the globe. As one writer put it, "All up and down little African rivers that you never heard the names of, it was known that an American slave-trader had been hanged."[17]

THE DISTURBING EPISODE OF Gordon's execution was soon subsumed by a deadly civil war that would stretch on for another three bloody

years and cost the lives of three quarters of a million more. Wall Street and much of the city had thrown its considerable political and financial might behind Lincoln and the Union cause, but Civil War New York City would remain a complicated place to live for African Americans. The hanging of Nathaniel Gordon for piracy was intended to send a signal to intransigent forces of racial conservatism that blatant flouting of laws against kidnapping and slave trading would no longer be tolerated. But though Mayor Fernando Wood's dream of an independent New York died and with it Wall Street's hopes of maintaining its hold on slave-grown cotton, the start of the war did not mean that the kind of pain inflicted by the New York Kidnapping Club was forever overcome. Unfortunately, the Manhattan of the 1860s would bear many of the hallmarks of racism and discrimination that had so angered David Ruggles in the 1830s. In the 1864 presidential election, the city stayed true to its conservative politics and voted against Lincoln by the same two-to-one margin as it had four years earlier.

And Wall Street, forgetting that Lincoln was trying to save the Union, sometimes appeared more concerned with recovering southern debts than in the defeat of the rebellion or the end of slavery. The New York Chamber of Commerce petitioned the president in a lengthy letter, reminding him that "citizens of states, now in rebellion, owe to citizens of loyal states a commercial debt" of about two hundred million dollars. "At present there are no means of collecting any portion of these debts," the chamber whined, and "the unfortunate creditors" requested Lincoln's help. Specifically, the businessmen implored Lincoln to use his authority wherever the Union forces were victorious in seizing rebel territory to force debtors to pay up. Without a hint of irony, the chamber even suggested to the president that he use military tribunals to extract money to pay back those who had supported the Union cause "with such patriotic zeal and liberality." It is true that after decades of defending the city's economic ties to southern slavery, the chamber offered strong support to the Union, but the plea to Lincoln neglected to mention that two members of the chamber had actually left New York to join the rebels.[18]

WHILE THE CHAMBER OF Commerce complained about money owed to city bankers and merchants, the New York Kidnapping Club and its successors in the police, the courts, and Wall Street might have considered the Civil War little more than an inconvenience. Tobias Boudinot, still ensconced in the city's Third Ward, had become a captain in the police force, moved into the conservative wing of the Republican Party after the demise of the Whigs, and garnered party appointments during and after the war. While the Seventh Regiment marched to fight in Virginia, Boudinot moved to Washington, DC, and worked for the House of Representatives and then took a patronage job as the supervisor of roads. After the war, Boudinot became a tax collector in the capital and served until his death in 1873. As the war ended, Boudinot appeared to be doing quite well; tax records show a decent income of about $250 a year and an expensive watch and carriage among his possessions.

His kidnapping club colleagues also continued to thrive during and after the war. The notorious city marshal, Daniel D. Nash, had become an auctioneer and lived comfortably in a brick Brooklyn home with a servant. Judge Samuel Betts served on the bench until his death in 1868. The Wall Street legal team of Beebe, Dean, and Donohue, which had defended so many accused slave traders before the war, now took up the defense of blockade runners. Fontaine H. Pettis, the New York lawyer who had placed ads in southern papers promising to round up runaways for money, supplemented his slave-hunting law practice by selling waterproof clothing. He died in Gotham just before the Civil War at the age of fifty-nine.[19]

The local and federal officers who had been charged by the Southern District of New York with enforcing the fugitive slave laws lived long after the war concluded. William Coventry Waddell, who had served as a marshal during the tumultuous 1830s, earned and then lost fortunes as an investor. His son served bravely at the Battles of Fort Donelson, Pittsburgh Landing, and Vicksburg, and after the war Waddell would become one of the founders of the Society for the Prevention of Cruelty to Animals. Isaiah Rynders, who had threatened to hang abolitionist Lewis Tappan "and every

damned n——" in New York, resigned as US marshal for the Southern District of New York just after Lincoln's election. Rynders
remained, however, a prominent New York Democrat during and
after the war, despite the fact that his days as a fighter and brawler
were long over. At least officials at the New York Customs House
had received a reprimand for the corrupt ways in which they had
conducted their business for so long.[20]

As one of the successors of the New York Kidnapping Club, the
Portuguese Company seemed hardly chastened at all by Nathaniel
Gordon's execution at the gallows. John Alberto Machado also
made Brooklyn his home and continued to use his legal business
as a cover for slave trading even as the Civil War raged, operating
an especially successful trade in and out of Havana. Remarkably,
Machado was arrested numerous times throughout the war for
slave trading. In September 1862, as the Battle of Antietam witnessed the bloodiest day of the entire war, and as President Lincoln
signed the Emancipation Proclamation, Machado sat in court,
accused of organizing the slaving voyage of the bark *Mary Francis*
with his mistress Mary Jane Watson. Watson oversaw the loading of
supplies onto the *Mary Francis* in New York harbor, including 160
casks of water, 200 barrels of bread, 500 boxes of fish, timber for
building the slave decks, and medicine. Stunningly, Mary Watson
then joined the ship's captain on the dangerous trip through the
blockade and into Wilmington, North Carolina, where the ship
was intercepted by the Union Navy. Mary Jane soon fled to Cadiz,
Spain, to outfit three more ships for the slave trade before officials
there discovered her plan and canceled the ships' registrations.
Mary Jane Watson, the most infamous female slave trader in New
York's history, died of "delirium tremens" in Spain, drunk and
impoverished, in early 1862.[21]

Machado was convicted of slaving and served a short sentence
at Fort Lafayette in New York harbor, but then was arrested again
in 1863. Meanwhile, C.H.S. Figaniere remained in New York
during the war and then became Portugal's ambassador to Washington until he was transferred to Russia. He died back in New

York in 1871 and received a heroic funeral at St. Peter's Catholic Church. Cunha Reis and Lima Viana, two other main members of the Portuguese Company, lurked in Gotham throughout the 1860s, while Francisco da Cunha e Silva made California his base of operations.[22]

Former mayor Fernando Wood had won election to the House of Representatives, and he continued to undermine the case for Black civil rights. During Reconstruction after the war, Wood questioned the value of the Freedmen's Bureau because he claimed the freed people lacked the capacity for improvement or self-government. Wood even joined with another pro-peace Democrat in 1862 to embark on an informal diplomatic mission to Richmond to try to find an end to the war.[23]

The machinations of Machado and others lingered because New York itself was fraught with tensions over race and abolitionism during the Civil War. Though now firmly in the Union column, the city would not surrender its long legacy of racism and proslavery sentiments that easily. The same prewar forces that had made the New York Kidnapping Club and the Portuguese Company possible remained nearly as powerful as the war unfolded. Not long after Lincoln's ascension to the presidency, the editors of one city paper changed its name to reflect the strong anti-Black and pro-Democratic ideology that still pervaded Manhattan and Wall Street. The *New York Weekly Caucasian* gave racism a potent and persistent voice throughout the 1860s and into Reconstruction, publishing article after article that promulgated white supremacy. In fact, editors Rushmore Horton and John Van Evrie established their own white supremacist publishing house, which printed hundreds of pamphlets and books that proclaimed Black inferiority and constantly attacked Lincoln's prosecution of the war. With support of the merchants and bankers of Wall Street who had been strong Democrats all along, Horton and Van Evrie gave voice to white supremacy, especially after Lincoln's Emancipation Proclamation had inserted the end of slavery into the Union cause. Anti-Black political and legal authorities, including former

district attorney for the Southern District of New York John Mc-
Keon, helped to fill the *Weekly Caucasian*'s pages with speeches
and essays that purported to demonstrate European superiority
over African lowliness.

The work of Horton and Van Evrie had its intended effect,
especially among an Irish working class already resentful of Black
progress. When the Union Army announced that whites would
be drafted into the fight, a struggle that by 1863 included the
possibility of slavery's demise, Irish workers rebelled. They had
vigorous encouragement from the *Weekly Caucasian*, which fanned
the flames of working-class despair by printing articles specifically designed to appeal to white labor. Their publishing house
churned out a series titled "Anti-Abolition Tracts" that were sponsored by a group calling itself the Democratic Anti-Abolition State
Rights Association.[24]

The frustration spilled into the streets with the so-called Draft
Riots, a series of murderous eruptions that crippled Manhattan in mid-July 1863, just after Union forces repelled Robert E.
Lee's foray at the Battle of Gettysburg. What began as a protest
against the draft quickly escalated into an all-out deadly assault
on the Black community. More than one hundred people were
killed, and the Colored Orphan Asylum, such a real and symbolic
example of the best of the Black community, was burned to the
ground. In the midst of the turmoil, Elizabeth Jennings, the same
woman who had just a few years before emerged victorious in a
case against streetcar segregation, faced her own personal crisis.
Her only child, a small boy prone to seizures, passed away. With
the help of a white undertaker, Jennings and her husband, carrying their deceased son, frantically weaved their way through the
rioting to bury him.

Still, New York's Black community, especially those whose lives
had covered much of the century, could point to important signs
of progress. The Emancipation Proclamation now centered abolition as a key goal of the war, and Black Americans across the
country recognized how important that document was in the long
and tortured history of American slavery.

The deadly Draft Riots in New York City, July 1863. (*The Miriam and Ira D. Wallach Division of Art, Prints and Photographs: Picture Collection, The New York Public Library*)

While they cheered the symbolic but monumental importance of the proclamation, African Americans also rejoiced in small victories wherever they could find them. African American children welcomed the famous Robert Small to New York's schools, not long after he had craftily commandeered a Confederate ship out of Charleston harbor and into freedom, together with several other escapees. The children cheered Small along with several city leaders, such as Henry H. Garnet, who hailed Small as a hero of the war for using such cunning to fool the rebels and reach freedom. Charles B. Ray, who had given so much of his life to the cause of human rights, proudly noted that his daughter Charlotte had become a lawyer in Washington in the same city where Black people had been bought and sold just a generation before.[25]

The assassination of Abraham Lincoln shocked and saddened New York's communities of color. Though they had been wary of his commitment to ending slavery at the start of the war, they had come to see his sacrifices on behalf of abolition as vital and would soon venerate him as the Great Emancipator, even before white northerners had begun to appreciate his martyrdom for liberty.

Much had changed since Ben and the other enslaved men and women had left the shores of Norfolk in 1832 to find freedom in the North. Jacob Francis, visiting the city in 1865, wrote, "Railroad cars and stages now accommodate colored people on all their routes without molestation—the lion and the lamb now set down together. All that is wanted is the franchise [i.e., the right to vote], and New York will be worth living in." Soon Francis and other Black men would win the right to vote when the Fifteenth Amendment passed in 1870.[26]

Yet Gotham's officials had proved true to the long and painful legacy of the city's protection of slavery and racism. A week after Lincoln's murder, the city was planning to honor the slain president with a massive funeral procession from which Black residents were pointedly excluded. Three different delegations of Black leaders had waited upon the city's political and financial leaders to appeal, but to no avail. African American leader Sella Martin complained bitterly to anyone who would listen, but the Common Council announced its decision to allow "positively no Black people in our procession." Such a disrespectful move by city leaders, of course, hardly surprised Black New Yorkers.

But as the Draft Riots demonstrate, and as the virulent racism of *The New York Weekly Caucasian* suggests, New York still had a long way to go to become a modern metropolis that saw its Black residents as citizens with equal rights. New York, like the nation more broadly, entered the postwar era with nearly as many questions about race, equality, and justice as it had before the war. In the late nineteenth century much work remained, and still remains in the early twenty-first century, to reach the ideals for which David Ruggles and countless others had given their lives.

The Hidden Past
and Reparations Due

⋆⇥⊐ ⊏⇤⋆

T HOUGH EVEN THE CITY'S MOST ARDENT BOOSTERS WOULD ACKNOWL-
edge that it is far from perfect, modern New York City is a
remarkable and wonderful metropolis that includes people
from all kinds of ethnic backgrounds, class standings, gender pref-
erences, and racial identities. Older enclaves of brick and stone
buildings sit sometimes uneasily with the teeming crowds and dizzying glitz of Times Square. A city of neighborhoods, where only a
few adjacent blocks can seem distinctive from streets just a quarter
mile away, New York also boasts great universities like Columbia,
some of the world's finest restaurants, and world-famous museums and historic sites. The imposing New York Stock Exchange
wows visitors from around the globe, and billions of dollars' worth
of goods are managed and traded each workday.

The glamour of modern Gotham hides a much more somber
history on which its impressive affluence and cosmopolitanism
are founded. Like any city, New York would rather distance itself
from this history of racism, slave trading, and kidnapping, but
the evidence is there all the same, pervading the paved streets

and steel skyscrapers and the very soil of Central Park. As with America itself, the richness and stature New York enjoys today were generated in no small part on the backs of southern slaves laboring under inhumane conditions to grow cotton. Contemporaries knew exactly where their fortunes came from, which is why they worked so hard to keep the country from dissolving into civil war. Vital institutions like the New-York Historical Society and the Schomburg Center for Research in Black Culture strive to keep these memories alive, but they are easy to forget amid the everyday jostling of modern New York.

Not all have forgotten, of course. A plaque today marks David Ruggles's home and office on Lispenard Street, and another marker reminds us that the African Burial Ground had been covered over by callous generations and then forgotten. The beautiful Weeksville Visitors Center in Brooklyn protects the remaining Hunterfly Street homes, educating tourists about the once proud and independent community of hundreds of African Americans who cherished their own neighborhood. The New York Public Library and other vital city institutions have helped generations of visitors from around the world understand the city's complicated racial past. Dedicated staff members and volunteers across Manhattan and the surrounding boroughs, professionally trained historians, public scholars, and activists have all contributed to our appreciation for the nuances of New York's history. Still, there remains much to be retold.

The fight David Ruggles and other abolitionists led against the New York Kidnapping Club is redolent of today's Black Lives Matter movement. Since their earliest arrival in the city, Black New Yorkers have long struggled against slavery and Jim Crow. Even the battle against racial segregation in public transportation, a struggle that we often associate with Rosa Parks and mid-twentieth-century Alabama, was initiated by Ruggles, George Downing, and Elizabeth Jennings before the Civil War. As they quarreled with white Americans over the morality of southern slavery, these New Yorkers had to combat the daily insults and injuries of living in a society that believed their basic human rights were far less

important than the Constitution's Fugitive Slave Clause or the cotton trade.

While we can appreciate the intellectual and activist links between the antebellum abolitionist campaign and the Black Lives Matter movement, we can also understand the long history of animosity between the African American community and the officials appointed to keep law and order. Part of the story we learn from the New York Kidnapping Club is that the relationships between the Black community and the police have long been fraught. We have watched in horror in recent years as Eric Garner uttered the phrase "I can't breathe," as thousands of people of color had their basic civil rights violated with "stop and frisk," and as police shootings sparked riots and unrest. Yet as Ruggles and his community learned every time they stepped out of their homes, the legacy of racism in the broader society was all too frequently manifested in police harassment and abuse. The criminalization of blackness in the nineteenth-century North, which Kali Gross, Cheryl Hicks, and Khalil Gibran Muhammad have so clearly shown, entrapped untold numbers of African Americans in a system that would later be called mass incarceration. The abuses inflicted on the Black community by Boudinot, Nash, and Riker remind us that, while there were always African Americans willing to challenge slavery and segregation, the police were used as a tool to control a substantial part of the community whose only crime was that they wanted to work and live and raise their own families without dominance and interference.[1]

This is why the study of history, so often neglected in favor of more lucrative fields of inquiry, is so fundamental, because without knowing the daily trials of ordinary individuals, it becomes easy to pretend that the past represents an idyllic world. Within the Black community there were many joys and celebrations, but there was also much suffering, often at the hands of officials acting with the authority of the wider community. And just as important, we can celebrate and memorialize those who bravely fought injustice, often surrendering their very lives to build a better world for future generations.

As I was finishing this book, author Ta-Nehisi Coates was testifying before Congress about reparations to compensate African Americans for the thieving legacy of slavery and racism, and I hope that this book adds to the call for justice. During the nineteenth century, Black New Yorkers were arrested and jailed without cause, were abused by the police and other authorities, had vast amounts of property confiscated, and were themselves sold and resold. The question of reparations is fraught, and the details will no doubt take a long while to figure out, but surely with the input of historians and many others we can find a solution that will in some significant way attempt to compensate generations of African Americans north and south who have endured the theft of rights and belongings and lives. The descendants of David Ruggles, Thomas Van Rensselaer, George Downing, Hester Carr, Elizabeth Jennings, William Dixon, along with Ben and the other fugitives who left Norfolk under the cover of night in the summer of 1832, surely deserve justice and recompense.

ACKNOWLEDGMENTS

During the many years it took to research and write this book, I accrued many debts to a number of people and institutions, and it is a pleasure to thank them here: archivists at the New-York Historical Society, the Museum of the City of New York, the Schomburg Center for Research in Black Culture, the American Antiquarian Society (especially Kimberly Toney and Vincent Golden), the Municipal Archives in New York (especially Geof Huth, Joseph Van Nostrand, Jane Chin, Rossy Mendez, and Dwight Johnson), the New York Law Institute (especially Lucy Curci-Gonzalez), and the New York Public Library. I could not have written this book without the valuable help and deep knowledge of the many librarians and archivists at these vitally important institutions.

Many individuals have helped me greatly through conversations about race, slavery, New York City, and other subjects as I wrote this book. I want to thank especially Eric Foner, Martha S. Jones, Shane White, Leslie M. Harris, Manisha Sinha, and Graham Russell Hodges. My editor, Katy O'Donnell, together with Geri Thoma of Writers House, have been unflagging supporters and meticulous readers as well as givers of great advice.

My wife, historian Heather Ann Thompson, and our children Dillon, Wilder, Ava, and Shawn, my niece Isabel, as well as my supportive parents Daniel and Elizabeth Wells and always encouraging in-laws Frank and Ann Thompson, are constant sources of joy and inspiration. I want also to thank Carrie, Brynne, and Saskia. As always, Heather listened and gave unfailing encouragement. She is at once my best friend and the love of my life.

NOTES

PROLOGUE: SUMMER 1832: NORFOLK, VIRGINIA

1. *Proceedings of the Board of Aldermen* vol. III (June 27, 1832), 127.

2. Edwin G. Burrows and Mike Wallace, *Gotham: A History of New York City to 1898* (New York: Oxford University Press, 1998), 109, 176–177.

3. "Slave Case No. 3," *The Colored American* (May 9 and 16, 1840), 1; "Police— The Slave Case," *Courier and New-York Enquirer* (April 3, 1837), 2; "Riot," *Journal of Commerce* (November 13, 1832), 1; "Kidnapping by Authority," *The Emancipator* (April 8, 1841), 197; Eric Homberger, *The Historical Atlas of New York City*, 3rd ed. (New York: St. Martin's Griffin, 2016), 59; Eric Foner, *Gateway to Freedom: The Hidden History of the Underground Railroad* (New York: W. W. Norton, 2015), 63–66.

4. Though largely forgotten today, Philip S. Foner's pathbreaking *Business and Slavery* (Chapel Hill: University of North Carolina Press, 1941) is still an insightful and useful examination of the ties between Wall Street and slavery in the 1850s. Foner's book informed much of my thinking about the ties between merchants and bankers in New York and southern slaveholders before the Civil War.

5. One of the most important books I examined for this study is Graham Russell Gao Hodges's remarkably thorough and thoughtful *David Ruggles: A Radical Black Abolitionist and the Underground Railroad* (Chapel Hill: University of North Carolina Press, 2012). I learned a great deal about Ruggles from Hodges's biography, including my first introduction to what Ruggles labeled "The New York Kidnapping Club." Equally important, two masterful books on African Americans in antebellum New York were vital to my understanding of both the rich communities Black people had built in the city and the forces they were up against: Leslie M. Harris, *In the Shadow of Slavery: African Americans in New York City, 1626–1863* (Chicago: University of Chicago Press, 2003); and Leslie M. Alexander's *African or American?: Black Identity and Political Activism in New York City, 1784–1861* (Champaign: University of Illinois Press, 2008). Eric Foner's *Gateway to Freedom: The Hidden History of the Underground Railroad* (New York: W. W. Norton & Co., 2016) evinces the meticulous research that readers have come to appreciate in all of his works. Also vitally important are Judith Wellman,

Brooklyn's Promised Land: The Free Black Community of Weeksville, New York (New York: New York University Press, 2014); Carla L. Peterson, *Black Gotham: A Family History of African-Americans in Nineteenth-Century New York City* (New Haven: Yale University Press, 2011); Ira Berlin and Leslie M. Harris, eds., *Slavery in New York* (New York: The New Press, 2005).

6. "Isaiah Rynders, President of the Empire Club," *New York Herald* (February 2, 1845), 2; "Friend Brown," *Cayuga Chief* [Auburn, New York] (July 30, 1850), 3.

7. Outright kidnapping, as opposed to legal recaptures of escaped slaves, has received limited but nonetheless vital attention in a handful of works. See Richard Bell, *Stolen: Five Free Boys Kidnapped into Slavery and Their Astonishing Odyssey* (New York: Simon & Schuster, 2019); W. Caleb McDaniel, *Sweet Taste of Liberty: A True Story of Slavery and Restitution in America* (New York: Oxford University Press, 2019); David Fiske, *Solomon Northup's Kindred: The Kidnapping of Free Citizens Before the Civil War* (Santa Barbara: ABC-CLIO, 2016); Lucy Maddox, *The Parker Sisters: A Border Kidnapping* (Philadelphia: Temple University Press, 2016); Milt Diggins, *Stealing Freedom Along the Mason-Dixon Line: Thomas McCreary, the Notorious Slave Catcher from Maryland* (Baltimore: Maryland Historical Society, 2015). Carol Wilson's pioneering *Freedom at Risk: The Kidnapping of Free Blacks in America, 1780–1865* (Lexington: The University Press of Kentucky, 1994) was one of the first books on this topic. On the mayor's ability to use marshals, see the act in Gideon Lee Papers, March 4, 1833, Box 1, Clements Library, University of Michigan.

8. On African Americans and abolitionism, see Kellie Carter Jackson, *Force and Freedom: Black Abolitionists and the Politics of Violence* (Philadelphia: University of Pennsylvania Press, 2019); Erica Armstrong Dunbar, *She Came to Slay: The Life and Times of Harriet Tubman* (New York: Simon & Schuster, 2019); Martha S. Jones, *Birthright Citizens: A History of Race and Rights in Antebellum America* (Cambridge: Cambridge University Press, 2018); David W. Blight, *Frederick Douglass: Prophet of Freedom* (New York: Simon & Schuster, 2018); R.J.M. Blackett, *The Captive's Quest for Freedom: Fugitive Slaves, the 1850 Fugitive Slave Law, and the Politics of Slavery* (Cambridge: Cambridge University Press, 2018); Andrew Delbanco, *The War Before the War: Fugitive Slaves and the Struggle for America's Soul from the Revolution to the Civil War* (New York: Penguin Press, 2018); Sean Wilentz, *No Property in Man: Slavery and Antislavery at the Nation's Founding* (Cambridge: Harvard University Press, 2018); Manisha Sinha, *The Slave's Cause: A History of Abolition* (New Haven: Yale University Press, 2016); Catherine Clinton, *Harriet Tubman: The Road to Freedom* (Boston: Little, Brown, and Co., 2004).

9. Foner, *Gateway to Freedom*, 52; Burrows and Wallace, *Gotham*, 491–492.

CHAPTER ONE: THE BATTLE ENGAGED

1. For an eye-opening examination of the North's general complicity in southern slavery, see Anne Farrow, Joel Lang, and Jenifer Frank, *Complicity: How the North Promoted, Prolonged, and Profited from Slavery* (New York: Ballantine Books, 2006). The new history of capitalism as it developed in America has also revealed the extent to which financial capitals like New York and London profited

from slavery. See Stephanie E. Jones-Rogers, *They Were Her Property: White Women as Slave Owners in the American South* (New Haven: Yale University Press, 2019); Caitlin Rosenthal, *Accounting for Slavery: Masters and Management* (Cambridge: Harvard University Press, 2018); Daina Ramey Berry, *The Price for Their Pound of Flesh: The Value of the Enslaved, from Womb to Grave, in the Building of a Nation* (Boston: Beacon Press, 2017); Sven Beckert and Seth Rockman, eds., *Slavery's Capitalism: A New History of American Economic Development* (Philadelphia: University of Pennsylvania Press, 2016); Ibram X. Kendi, *Stamped from the Beginning: The Definitive History of Racist Ideas in America* (New York: Bold Type Books, 2016); Calvin Schermerhorn, *The Business of Slavery and the Rise of American Capitalism, 1815–1860* (New Haven: Yale University Press, 2015); Edward E. Baptist, *The Half Has Never Been Told: Slavery and the Making of American Capitalism* (New York: Basic Books, 2014); Sven Beckert, *Empire of Cotton: A Global History* (New York: Knopf, 2014).

2. Ruggles relays the details of this trip in the footnotes of his pamphlet "The 'Extinguisher' Extinguished! Or, David M. Reese, M.D., 'Used Up'" (New York, 1834), 45–46. I first learned of this story from Hodges's biography *David Ruggles*, 56–57.

3. Hodges's remarkable and thorough biography provides rich and long-forgotten details about Ruggles's early life. See especially chapters 1 and 2 in Hodges, *David Ruggles*.

4. For evidence of the NYPD dealing with lost children, see the records from the Twentieth Ward in New York Police Department Records, 1862–1864, Clements Library, University of Michigan. On the plea from the American Anti-Slavery Society, see *Proceedings of the Board of Aldermen*, vol. VII (New York, 1834), 130.

5. Pope's circular, John H. Pope & Co. Broadside, New-York Historical Society.

6. New York City records provide ample evidence of Boudinot's eagerness to fight: The People vs. John Kendall, December 15, 1832, Court of General Sessions Minutes, 365; The People vs. Tobias Boudinot (1835), 147; The People vs. Tobias Boudinot (1836), 298; John Scott vs. Tobias Boudinot, October 5, 1837, New York Court of Common Pleas Records, Municipal Archives, New York.

7. Jabez Hayes vs. Tobias Boudinot, October 8, 1836, Court of Common Pleas; Jabez Hayes vs. Tobias Boudinot, July 3, 1837, Superior Court Records; Henry Garner vs. Tobias Boudinot, July 6, 1837, Court of Common Pleas; Robert Cunning vs. Tobias Boudinot, July 5, 1838, Court of Common Pleas; David R. Manning vs. Tobias Boudinot, June 22, 1837, Court of Common Pleas; Tobias Boudinot vs. Moses Payson, July 15, 1839, Court of Common Pleas, Municipal Archives, New York.

8. Organization and Minutes of the Society for the Prevention of the Absconding and Abduction of Slaves, Richmond, 1833, New-York Historical Society.

9. Homberger, *The Historical Atlas of New York City*, 87.

10. Homberger, *The Historical Atlas of New York City*, 65.

11. Bennett quoted in Shane White, *Prince of Darkness: The Story of Jeremiah G. Hamilton, Wall Street's First Black Millionaire* (New York: Picador, 2015), 131.

12. Foner, *Gateway to Freedom*, 29.

13. Homberger, *The Historical Atlas of New York City*, 31.

14. Harris, *In the Shadow of Slavery*, 11–15.

15. Harris, *In the Shadow of Slavery*, 20–29.

16. Jill Lepore, *New York Burning: Liberty, Slavery, and Conspiracy in Eighteenth-Century Manhattan* (New York: Knopf, 2005).

17. Harris, *In the Shadow of Slavery*, 50–51.

18. Shane White's groundbreaking biography of Hamilton reveals much about race and Wall Street, in addition to offering new insights into an unusual and controversial personality. See White, *Prince of Darkness*.

19. Leonard P. Curry, *The Free Black in Urban America, 1800-1850* (Chicago: University of Chicago Press, 1981), 73–74.

20. Theodore S. Wright, "Prejudice," *The Colored American* (July 8, 1837).

21. Harris, *In the Shadow of Slavery*, 96–97.

22. Curry, *The Free Black in Urban America*, 218, 222–223; Foner, *Gateway to Freedom*, 86–87.

23. Howard Dodson, *The Black New Yorkers: The Schomburg Illustrated Chronology: 400 Years of African American History* (New York: Wiley, 1999), 60; Harris, *In the Shadow of Slavery*, 72–75; Alexander, *African or American?*, Chapter 7; Diana diZerega Wall, Nan A. Rothschild, and Cynthia Copeland, "Seneca Village and Little Africa: Two African American Communities in Antebellum New York City," *Historical Archaeology* 42 (2008), 97–107.

24. Harris, *In the Shadow of Slavery*, 128.

25. Alexander, *African or American?*, 68; "Notice," *Freedom's Journal* (February 1, 1828), 3; "New-York African Free Schools," *New York Commercial Advertiser* (March 1, 1828), 2; Sinha, *The Slave's Cause*, 116–117.

26. On Reason and Smith, see C. Peter Ripley, ed., *The Black Abolitionist Papers*, vol. 2 (Chapel Hill: University of North Carolina Press, 1985), 186, 189.

27. Harris, *In the Shadow of Slavery*, 135–137, 163, 180; Jane E. Dabel, *A Respectable Woman: The Public Roles of African American Women in 19th-Century New York* (New York: New York University Press, 2008); Elizabeth McHenry, *Forgotten Readers: Recovering the Lost History of African American Literary Societies* (Durham: Duke University Press, 2002), 108–111; "Celebration," *Freedom's Journal* (March 28, 1829), 8; "First Annual Report of the Governors of the Alms House" (New York, 1859).

CHAPTER TWO: THE BIRTH OF THE KIDNAPPING CLUB AND THE REBIRTH OF MANHATTAN

1. Elizur Wright, "A Child Kidnapped from School!" *The Emancipator* (April 1, 1834), 3. On Haxall, see "The Stockholders," *Richmond Whig* (June 8, 1847), 2; "Notes," *News and Observer* [Raleigh, NC] (December 19, 1882), 3; "Late News," *Harrisburg* [PA] *Telegraph* (December 2, 1881), 1.

2. "Boy Stealing!" *The Liberator* 4 (April 5, 1834), 14.

3. Benson J. Lossing, *History of New York City* (New York, 1884), 78, 241. Daniel M. Tredwell, *Personal Reminiscences of Men and Things on Long Island* (New York, 1917), 24. Ruggles had appeared in court before Riker in 1833: James M.

Patterson vs. David Ruggles, January 28, 1833, Court of Common Pleas, Municipal Archives, New York.

4. Riker quoted in Ruggles, "Editorial Notice of Our Enterprise," *Mirror of Liberty* 1 (January 1839), 17.

5. Wright, "A Child Kidnapped," 3.

6. Wright, "A Child Kidnapped," 3; Wright, "Chronicles of Kidnapping in New York," *The Emancipator* 3 (April 22, 1834), 2; "Monday Evening Concert," *The Liberator* 4 (May 3, 1834), 18; "Notice," *The Emancipator* (March 25, 1834), 2.

7. Two years after Henry Scott's arrest, his story was remembered in "Henry Scott," *The Slave's Friend* (New York, 1836), 34–35.

8. "The Pardoning Power," *New York Spectator* 34 (December 23, 1831), 2; Foner, *Gateway to Freedom*, 49–50.

9. Pettis, "Important to the South" advertisement reprinted in *The First Annual Report of the New York Committee of Vigilance* (New York, 1837), 53. See also Allen Johnson vs. Fontaine H. Pettis, November 5, 1845, Court of Common Pleas, Municipal Archives, New York City.

10. According to historian Stephen Kantrowitz, Boston escapee Lewis Hayden had booby-trapped his front porch. Kantrowitz's important and beautifully crafted book reveals a great deal about African American abolitionism in Massachusetts: *More Than Freedom: Fighting for Black Citizenship in a White Republic* (New York: Penguin Press, 2012).

11. Though Riker clearly favored white slaveholders when they appeared in his courtroom, there is evidence that he was more nuanced than simply the dark villain depicted in abolitionist literature. According to one contemporary lawyer, Riker could exhibit humane feelings when the mood struck him. Every night Riker visited his elderly mother, and one evening he was walking on Broadway, near Worth Street, when he saw a crowd of white men throwing rocks at a home. He quickly learned that a young white woman had married a Black man, and the rioters drove the couple out of the house and had cornered them outside. Riker embraced the trembling couple, shouted down the rioters, and walked the victims to City Hall. Charles Edwards, *Pleasantries About Courts and Lawyers of the State of New York* (New York, 1867), 393.

12. William L. Marcy to John Gayle, December 1835, Marcy Papers, New-York Historical Society.

13. Speech by Douglas on the Fugitive Slave Law, "Minutes of the State Convention of the Colored Citizens of Ohio" (Columbus, 1851), 7.

14. "Commotions," *New York American* (July 18, 1834), 2; Wright, "Trial by Jury," *New York Evangelist* 5 (May 3, 1834), 71.

15. "Circuit Court," *New York American* (November 27, 1833), 2.

16. "The Hon. Richard Riker," *The Emancipator* (November 4, 1834), 3; Wright, "Horrible Transaction: Kidnapping of Stephen Downing," *The Emancipator* (May 20, 1834), 2.

17. Wright, "Chronicles of Kidnapping in New York, No. III," *The Emancipator* 2; Wright, "Chronicles of Kidnapping, No. 1," *The Emancipator* 2 (April 1, 1834), 4.

18. Ruggles, "Kidnapping in the City of New York," *The Emancipator* (November 1, 1835), 3; Harris, *In the Shadow of Slavery*, 124–125. On the city's efforts to improve the life of poor and elderly African Americans, see *Proceedings of the Board of Aldermen*, vol. XXVII (New York, 1842), 588–590.

19. Charles Graham to Gideon Lee, December 16, 1835, Gideon Lee Papers, Clements Library, University of Michigan.

20. January 5, 1836, Minutes of the New York Chamber of Commerce, volume III, Commerce Papers, Columbia University. For eyewitness accounts of the fire and requests to Congress to aid banks and insurance companies, see David Lyon to Gideon Lee, December 17, 1835; John W. Richardson to Lee, December 17, 1835; and John J. Palmer to Lee, December 19 and 21, 1835, Gideon Lee Papers, Box 2, Clements Library, University of Michigan.

21. See the notice in *New York Evening Post* (December 31, 1835), 3. Downing had provided refreshments to the police and firefighters during the conflagration and later appealed for reimbursements. *Proceedings of the Board of Aldermen*, vol. XXIII (New York, 1842), 356, 407.

22. White, *Prince of Darkness*, 74–75.

23. Gerard Hallock, "The New Year," *Journal of Commerce* (January 2, 1836), 2.

24. Samuel R. Betts to Gideon Lee, February 2, 1836, and J. J. Coddington to Lee, December 30, 1836, Gideon Lee Papers, Box 2, Clements Library, University of Michigan.

25. Philip Hone quoted in Bayrd Still, *Mirror for Gotham: New York as Seen by Contemporaries from Dutch Days to the Present* (New York: Fordham University Press, 1994), 85.

26. Philip Hone quoted in Homberger, *Historical Atlas of New York City*, 219.

27. William Lee to Gideon Lee, January 20, 1837, Gideon Lee Papers, Box 3, Clements Library, University of Michigan.

CHAPTER THREE: NEW YORK DIVIDED

1. Lydia Maria Child to Anna Loring, September 22, 1844, Box 1, Folder 27, and Child to Loring, October 13, 1844, Box 1, Folder 28, Lydia Maria Child Papers, Clements Library, University of Michigan.

2. Richard Cary Morse to Richard Cary Morse Jr., May 6, 1856, Box 2, Richard Cary Morse Papers, Clements Library, University of Michigan.

3. Edwards, *Pleasantries About Courts and Lawyers*, 392.

4. On working-class New York, see Mark A. Lause, *Free Labor: The Civil War and the Making of an American Working Class* (Champaign: University of Illinois Press, 2015); and Sean Wilentz, *Chants Democratic: New York City & the Rise of the American Working Class, 1788–1850* (New York: Oxford University Press, 1984).

5. For a thorough and insightful view of the riots, see Paul A. Gilje, *The Road to Mobocracy: Popular Disorder in New York City, 1763–1834* (Chapel Hill: University of North Carolina Press, 1987), 162–170. See also Lawrence B. Goodheart, *Abolitionist, Actuary, Atheist: Elizur Wright and the Reform Impulse* (Kent: Kent State University Press, 1990), 68–71.

6. George Coles to James Harper, June 4, 1844, Harper Papers, New-York Historical Society.

7. Gilje, *The Road to Mobocracy*, 169.

8. Webb, "The Fanatics," *Morning Courier and New York Enquirer* (September 23, 1834), 2; "Police," *MCNYE* (November 12, 1834), 2; "Fanaticism," *MCNYE* (November 19, 1834), 2. See also "The Fanatics," *MCNYE* (December 27, 1834), 2.

9. Sidney Morse, "Is This Right?" *New-York Observer* (August 9, 1834), 2.

10. Wright, "Chronicles of Kidnapping in New York," *The Emancipator* 2 (September 16, 1834), 3.

11. "Kidnapping—Slavery," *The Emancipator* 2 (November 4, 1834), 3.

12. Ruggles, "Southern Chivalry," *The Liberator* (September 26, 1835), 3.

13. "Contemplated Assassination of Arthur Tappan," *New York Evangelist* (September 26, 1835), 245.

14. Ruggles, et al., *First Annual Report of the New York Committee of Vigilance* (New York, 1837).

15. Harris, *In the Shadow of Slavery*, 191.

16. Alexander, *African or American?*, 72–73.

17. *The First Annual Report of the New York Committee of Vigilance* (New York, 1837).

18. Sinha, *The Slave's Cause*, 383–388.

19. Graham Russell Gao Hodges retells this story with great sympathy in *David Ruggles*, 57–58.

20. "A Runaway Slave," *New York Commercial Advertiser* (June 23, 1834), 2. See also Wright, "Chronicles of Kidnapping in New York, No. 7," *The Emancipator* (July 7, 1834).

21. "A Runaway Slave," *New York Commercial Advertiser* (June 23, 1834), 2. See also "Slavery," *The Liberator* (July 5, 1834), 105.

22. Elizur Wright, "Chronicles of Kidnapping, No. 4," *The American Anti-Slavery Reporter* (June 1, 1834), 92. New York City attorneys Theodore and Robert Sedgwick, soon to earn fame in the *Amistad* case, valiantly tried to request that the court release Martin, but attorney Thomas L. Wells, who often served clients who claimed slaves in the city, successfully quashed the writ. See the deliberations on October 31, 1834, US Circuit Court Minutes, Southern District of New York, National Archives, Washington, DC.

23. S. A., "Legal Kidnapping," *The Emancipator* 3 (February 7, 1839), 165; "Slave Case," *Alexandria Gazette* (January 30, 1839), 3.

CHAPTER FOUR: NEW YORK, A PORT IN THE SLAVE TRADE

1. "For the Journal of Commerce," *Journal of Commerce* (February 13, 1836), 2.

2. "Governor Marcy's Address," *Journal of Commerce* (January 9, 1836), 3.

3. William J. Wilson to Frederick Douglass, March 5, 1853, in Ripley, ed., *Black Abolitionist Papers*, vol. 4, 140–143.

4. "Speech by William Wells Brown Delivered at the City Assembly Rooms, May 8, 1856," reprinted in Ripley, ed., *Black Abolitionist Papers*, vol. 4, 342.

5. Bruce Chadwick, *Law & Disorder: The Chaotic Birth of the NYPD* (New York: St. Martin's, 2017), 58.

6. Roquinaldo Ferreira, *Cross-Cultural Exchange in the Atlantic World: Angola and Brazil During the Era of the Slave Trade* (Cambridge: Cambridge University Press, 2012), 7, 9. Many thanks to historian Greg Childs for bringing this book to my attention.

7. On the transatlantic slave trade, see Jeffery R. Kerr-Ritchie, *Rebellious Passage: The Creole Revolt and America's Coastal Slave Trade* (Cambridge: Cambridge University Press, 2019); Sowande M. Mustakeem, *Slavery at Sea: Terror, Sex, and Sickness in the Middle Passage* (Champaign: University of Illinois Press, 2016); John K. Thornton, *A Cultural History of the Atlantic World, 1250–1820* (Cambridge: Cambridge University Press, 2012); David Eltis and David Richardson, *Atlas of the Transatlantic Slave Trade* (New Haven: Yale University Press, 2010); Marcus Rediker, *The Slave Ship: A Human History* (New York: Viking, 2007); Stephanie E. Smallwood, *Saltwater Slavery: A Middle Passage from Africa to American Diaspora* (Cambridge: Harvard University Press, 2007); Hugh Thomas, *The Slave Trade: The Story of the Atlantic Slave Trade, 1440–1870* (New York: Simon & Schuster, 1999); John Thornton, *Africa and Africans in the Making of the Atlantic World, 1400–1800* (Cambridge: Cambridge University Press, 1992).

8. For an important history of the later slave trade, see Sylviane A. Diouf, *Dreams of Africa in Alabama: The Slave Ship Clotilda and the Story of the Last Africans Brought to America* (New York: Oxford University Press, 2007).

9. For an insightful expose on insurance companies profiting from slavery, see Rachel L. Swarns, "Insurance Policies on Slaves: New York Life's Complicated Past," *New York Times* (December 18, 2016).

10. On Weeks and Wenberg and other investors in the slave trade, see Warren S. Howard, *American Slavers and the Federal Law, 1837–1862* (Berkeley: University of California Press, 1963); and Gerald Horne, *The Deepest South: The United States, Brazil, and the African Slave Trade* (New York: New York University Press, 2007).

11. See Gordon's advertisement in *Burlington Weekly Free Press* (August 3, 1838), 3.

12. On the importance of Cuba and slave ship designs, see "The Slave Trade," *Journal of Commerce* (November 12, 1836), 2.

13. Georgina Betts Wells, *Life and Career of Samuel Rossiter Betts* (New York, 1834).

14. "The Alleged Slave Ship," *Journal of Commerce* (February 12, 1836), 2; "Slaving from the Port of New York," *The Liberator* (February 13, 1836), "Seizure of a Slave Vessel," *Journal of Commerce* (February 13, 1836), 4.

15. "The Alleged Slave Ship," *Journal of Commerce* (March 5, 1836), 1.

16. Untitled editorial, *Journal of Commerce* (March 26, 1836), 1. See also the untitled article in *New York Mercury* (March 31, 1836), 2.

17. "Abolition," *Journal of Commerce* (January 9, 1836), 1.

18. *The First Annual Report of the New York Committee of Vigilance* (New York, 1837), 34–35. See also untitled article in *MCNYE* (December 27, 1836), 2; and

untitled article in *Journal of Commerce* (December 17, 1836), 4; and "United States District Court," *Journal of Commerce* (December 21, 1836), 1.

19. *The First Annual Report of the New York Committee of Vigilance*, 40, 47.

20. "Slave Trade," *Newport* [RI] *Mercury* (June 27, 1835), 2.

21. US vs. Caleb Miller, October 1835, US Circuit Court Minutes, Southern District of New York, National Archives, Washington, DC. George Barker testified that he had seen "two colored girls on board, 9 or 10 years old," and that Captain Miller claimed that he was taking the girls to be paid servants in his home. The two girls were taken from Miller and placed under the guardianship of US Marshal William Coventry Waddell until the president could provide guidance on what to do with the girls. See "Captain Caleb Miller," *Pittsburgh Gazette* (September 8, 1835), 2.

22. The story and details about Miller and the brig *America* can be found in "United States Court," *New York Evening Post* (August 3, 1835), 2.

CHAPTER FIVE:
POLICING AND CRIMINALIZING THE BLACK COMMUNITY

1. James F. Richardson, *The New York Police: Colonial Times to 1901* (New York: Oxford University Press, 1970), 17–18.

2. Richardson, *The New York Police*, 19.

3. Hallock, "Fruits of Trades Unions," *Journal of Commerce* (February 27, 1836), 4; untitled letter to the editor, *Journal of Commerce* (March 5, 1836), 1.

4. Gideon Lee, "Message," reprinted in *Proceedings of the Board of Aldermen*, vol. V (New York, 1834), 13.

5. Richardson, *The New York Police*, 27; Whitman quoted in Bruce Chadwick, *Law & Disorder: The Chaotic Birth of the NYPD* (New York: St. Martin's, 2017), 56.

6. See A. B. to Gideon Lee, January 25, 1833, and "An Inhabitant of the First Ward" to Lee, January 29, 1833, Gideon Lee Papers, Box 1, Clements Library, University of Michigan.

7. "Message of His Honor the Mayor, Transmitting the Report of the Chief of Police" (New York, 1849), 1100–1101; "Board of Aldermen" (New York, 1850), 158–163.

8. William W. Fisher to Gideon Lee, December 8, 1834, Gideon Lee Papers, Box 1, Clements Library, University of Michigan.

9. See the reports of absenteeism in "Complaints Against Policemen," New York City Municipal Archives. In just one month in October 1852, suspensions for missing roll call happened at least every few days. On October 2, 1852, Henry Peters was suspended for being late. Peters admitted that "I was very much fatigued." Two days later officers John McCluskey and John Mitchell also missed roll call, reporting that they were fatigued and fell asleep. A couple of weeks later, Officer Hugh Martin went AWOL all day, much to the consternation of Police Chief Matsell.

10. Information from the logbook of the Twentieth Ward, New York Police Department Records, 1862–1864, Clements Library, University of Michigan; see Mayor

Gideon Lee's message to the aldermen in *Proceedings of the Board of Aldermen* vol. V (New York, 1834), 63, 229. The District Attorney Indictment Papers at the Municipal Archives in New York City offer ample evidence that many of those charged with crimes were illiterate and were members of the working class. See, for example, the entry for Tighe Davie in microfilm roll 145 (Sept. 6–Dec. 6, 1832). Davie was indicted for offering his vote for sale in the Eleventh Ward. Officer James Scott suspension, October 30, 1852, "Complaints Against Policemen," Municipal Archives, New York.

11. Chadwick, *Law & Disorder*, 15, 62, 69.

12. Timothy J. Gilfoyle, "'America's Greatest Criminal Barracks': The Tombs and the Experience of Criminal Justice in New York City, 1838–1897," *Journal of Urban History* 29 (July 2003), 528.

13. On Nash's involvement in court cases, see Thomas Scales vs. Daniel Nash, November 2, 1841, Superior Court Records, Municipal Archives, New York City; Daniel Nash vs. John D. Kellogg, June 29, 1842, Court of Common Pleas, Municipal Archives, New York City; Caroline A. Wood vs. Daniel Nash, May 21, 1845, Court of Common Pleas, Municipal Archives, New York City.

14. "Early Impressions," *New York Mirror* 7 (February 20, 1830), 260–261; Richardson, *The New York Police*, 16–17. See also *Proceedings of the Board of Aldermen*, vol. XVI (New York, 1839), 3, 282, 309.

15. Lossing, *History of New York City*, 12.

16. Ruggles, "Beware of Kidnappers," *New York Weekly Advocate* (January 14, 1837), 1.

17. Ruggles, "Beware of Kidnappers," *New York Weekly Advocate* 1 (January 14, 1837), 3.

18. "Arrest and Alarm," *MCNYE* (December 29, 1836), 2.

19. Ruggles, "Beware of Kidnappers," *New York Weekly Advocate* (January 14, 1837), 3.

20. "Negro Riots," *MCNYE* (December 30, 1836), 2.

21. Ruggles, "Kidnapping in the City of New York," *The Liberator* (August 6, 1836).

22. Ruggles, "Kidnapping in the City of New York," *The Liberator* (August 6, 1836). See also Ruggles, "Look Out for Kidnappers!!" *New York Zion's Watchman* (August 3, 1836).

23. Foner, *Gateway to Freedom*, 70.

24. "The Slave Case," *Journal of Commerce* (September 3, 1836), 2; and (September 10, 1836), 1; *The First Annual Report of the New York Committee of Vigilance* (New York, 1837), 21. See also documents related to the case in The Law Office of Robert and Theodore Sedgwick Records, Harvard University Library.

25. "The Slave Case," *Journal of Commerce* (September 3, 1836), 2; and (September 10, 1836), 1. "The Slave Case Decided," *Alexandria* [VA] *Gazette* (September 19, 1836), 2.

26. "The Slave Case," *Journal of Commerce* (September 3, 1836), 2. See also the case of Seymour Cunningham in Wells, *Blind No More: African Americans*

Resistance, Free-Soil Politics, and the Coming of the Civil War (Athens: University of Georgia Press, 2018).

27. "Attempt to Rescue the Alleged Slave," *Journal of Commerce* (September 14, 1836), 1. David Ruggles to Robert and Theodore Sedgwick, June 6, 1836, in The Law Office of Robert and Theodore Sedgwick Records, Harvard University Library.

28. "Special Sessions," *New York Commercial Advertiser* (October 26, 1836), 1.

29. "For the Evening Post," *New York Evening Post* (October 26, 1836), 2; Thomas Van Rensselaer, "City Recorder and People of Color," *Pennsylvania Freeman* (November 26, 1836), 45. Meanwhile, despite Van Rensselaer's pleas for basic respect and civil rights protections, New York's Black children continued to fall prey to kidnapping. Children began to vanish again in late 1836. A Mr. Reveloid (or Reveliad) somehow drew young Jane away from her parents' home in Upper Manhattan. For two months, suspicious neighbors of the Reveloid family kept a watchful eye out for Jane, but she never appeared. Jane's parents planned to travel to the South in search of their daughter, an incredibly risky and desperate plan since they might also be abducted as slaves. Just a few days before they were to leave someone caught a glimpse of Jane, probably through a window, and the parents sounded the alarm. Ruggles rushed to the Reveloid home and saw Jane playing in the yard with a child of the Reveloids. Ruggles went around to the front and rang the doorbell, and one of the Reveloid children answered. Ruggles asked directly if Jane was in the home, and the child said she would see and asked Ruggles to wait by the door. The civil rights activist, ever bold and determined, followed the little girl into the house where he was stopped by Reveloid himself, who said that Jane hadn't been there for two months and was working in New Jersey. Ruggles left quickly and ran to City Hall to get a writ of habeas corpus. The home lay in the western part of Lower Manhattan, near today's Washington Market Park. But by the time the writ was issued Reveloid had already left the city with Jane, reportedly on his way to Florida by way of New Orleans. For more details on this sordid incident, see "Kidnapping," *The Long-Island Star* (November 21, 1836), 3; *The First Annual Report of the New York Committee of Vigilance* (New York, 1837), 67–69.

30. "Annals of Kidnapping," *Pennsylvania Freeman* (January 14, 1837), 73; Ruggles, "Important Meeting," *The Colored American* (March 11, 1837); Ruggles, "Look out for Kidnappers," *The Emancipator* (December 1, 1836).

31. On the Phoenix Society, see Dorothy Porter, *Early Negro Writing, 1760–1837* (Baltimore, 1971), 82.

32. "City Recorder," *The Emancipator* (October 6, 1836).

33. *The First Annual Report of the New York Committee of Vigilance* (New York, 1837), 55–57.

34. "'Illegally held in slavery': Hester Jane Carr," online exhibit, Library of Virginia, www.virginiamemory.com/online-exhibitions/exhibits/show/to-be-sold/from-richmond-to-new-orleans/-illegally-held-in-slavery.

35. *The First Annual Report of the New York Committee of Vigilance*, 40–41.

CHAPTER SIX: ECONOMIC PANIC

1. "Editorial," *MCNYE* (December 28, 1836), 2.

2. "Governor's Message," *MCNYE* (January 6, 1837), 1.

3. For excellent studies of the Panic, see Jessica M. Lepler, *The Many Panics of 1837: People, Politics, and the Creation of a Transatlantic Financial Crisis* (Cambridge: Cambridge University Press, 2013); and Scott Reynolds Nelson, *A Nation of Deadbeats: An Uncommon History of America's Financial Disasters* (New York: Knopf, 2012).

4. For the Panic's effects on the plantation South, see Scott P. Marler, *The Merchants' Capital: New Orleans and the Political Economy of the Nineteenth-Century South* (Cambridge: Cambridge University Press, 2013); and Joshua D. Rothman, *Flush Times and Fever Dreams: A Story of Capitalism and Slavery in the Age of Jackson* (Athens: University of Georgia Press, 2012).

5. "Alms House," *MCNYE* (January 22, 1837), 2.

6. "Outrage and Riot," *MCNYE* (February 14, 1837), 2.

7. "Outrage and Riot," *MCNYE* (February 14, 1837), 2; "The Flour Rioters," *MCNYE* (February 15, 1837), 2.

8. "The Sun Newspaper," *New York Herald* (February 20, 1837), 2. See also a poem on the riots: "The Flour Riot," *New York Herald* (February 22, 1837), 1.

9. "The Cotton Market," *MCNYE* (February 21, 1837), 2; see correspondence in *MCNYE* (March 17, 1837), 2; "The Failures in New Orleans," *MCNYE* (March 18, 1837), 2; "The English Money Market," *MCNYE* (March 23, 1837), 2.

10. Ruggles, "Strange Occurrence," *The Emancipator* 2 (March 1, 1838), 170; "A Marvelous Thing," *The Colored American* (February 3, 1838). For an important study of the cadaver trade, see Berry, *The Price for Their Pound of Flesh*.

11. "Beware of Kidnappers," *New York Weekly Advocate* (January 14, 1837); "The Negro Ruggles," *MCNYE* (January 7, 1837), 2.

12. Henry B. Stanton to James G. Birney, August 7, 1837, Box 2, Folder 28, James G. Birney Correspondence, Clements Library, University of Michigan.

13. "Congress," *Journal of Commerce* (February 15, 1837), 1; "Correspondence," *Journal of Commerce* (February 11, 1837), 4; "Editorial," *Journal of Commerce* (February 15, 1837), 4; "Our Country," *Journal of Commerce* (March 25, 1837), 4; "Correspondence," *MCNYE* (February 14, 1837), 2.

14. "Police, Thursday," *MCNYE* (March 31, 1837), 2.

15. Philip A. Bell, "Important Meeting," *New York Weekly Advocate* (February 2, 1837), 1; "Petition for a Jury Trial from Brooklyn," *The Colored American* (March 11, 1837); "Reception of Our Petition," *The Colored American* (March 11, 1837).

16. "Slave Case—No. 4," *The Colored American* (June 13, 1840). See also notice in *The Colored American* (May 27, 1837).

17. Henry C. Wright, "Kidnapping in New-York!!" *The Liberator* (April 21, 1837), 66–67.

18. Marjorie Waters, "Before Solomon Northup: Fighting Slave Catchers in New York," History News Network, historynewsnetwork.org/article/153653.

19. Henry C. Wright, "Kidnapping in New-York!!" *The Liberator* (April 21, 1837), 66–67.

20. David Ruggles, "Second Anniversary of the New York Committee of Vigilance," *The Emancipator* 3 (May 24, 1838), 15. On Morrill's role as a prominent attorney and member of Tammany Hall, see "Eleventh Ward," *New York Evening Post* (December 30, 1830), 2; "Tammany Society," *New York Evening Post* (March 2, 1832), 3. Wright, "Dear Brother," *The Liberator* (April 13, 1837), 65, 67.

21. "Case of William Dixon," *Brandon* [VA] *Telegraph* (May 17, 1837), 1.

22. "The Slave Case," *Gloucester* [MA] *Telegraph* 11 (April 26, 1837), 2. Wright, "Dear Brother," *The Liberator* (April 13, 1837), 67; "The Slave Case—Riot," *Journal of Commerce* (April 15, 1837), 4; "Another Black Riot," *New York Evening Post* (April 21, 1837), 2.

23. "Cornish Correspondence," *Journal of Commerce* (April 19, 1837), 1.

24. See the notice in *The Liberator* (April 21, 1837).

25. "Dixon's Case," *The Liberator* (June 30, 1837), 105; "Dixon Meeting," *The Colored American* (July 15, 1837); Marjorie Waters, "Before Solomon Northup: Fighting Slave Catchers in New York," History News Network, historynewsnetwork.org/article/153653.

26. Malcolm Bell Jr., "Ease and Elegance, Madeira and Murder: The Social Life of Savannah's City Hotel," *Georgia Historical Quarterly* (Fall 1992).

27. Hopper's story was reprinted in many northern newspapers when he returned home. The version recounted here appears in "Outrage upon a Freeman," *Centinel of Freedom* (May 2, 1837), 4.

28. "Communications," *The Liberator* (May 19, 1837).

29. "Slave Case," *Journal of Commerce* (April 15, 1837), 4; "The Slave Case," *Journal of Commerce* (April 26, 1837), 2; "Slave Case No. 3," *The Colored American* (May 9, 1840).

30. "Police Office," *Journal of Commerce* (April 1, 1837), 1.

31. "Fugitive Slave," *Southern Patriot* (April 1, 1837), 2.

32. "The Case of 'Ben,'" *New York Evangelist* (April 15, 1837), 63; "Kidnapping," *Boston Recorder* (April 28, 1837), 68; "Slave Case No. 3 Concluded," *Colored American* (May 16, 1837); "Police Office," *Journal of Commerce* (April 1, 1837), 1; "Fugitive Slave," *Southern Patriot* [Charleston] (April 1, 1837), 2.

33. "Northern Distress Produced by Southern Slavery," *The Colored American* (May 13, 1837). Twenty-two-year-old George Natt went missing in April, and twelve-year-old Francis Maria Shields disappeared in early May. Nash and Boudinot apprehended John Davis in late May, and Riker sent a suspected fugitive named Charles Fearn back to slavery in Mobile, Alabama, in late June. "To the Country," *Journal of Commerce* (May 20, 1837), 2; "Missing," *The Colored American* (May 13, 1837); Ruggles, "Child Lost," *The Colored American* (May 20, 1837); Notice, *The Colored American* (May 27, 1837); "Another Slave Case," *Journal of Commerce* (June 28, 1837), 1.

34. Ruggles, "A Methodist Slaveholder in Brooklyn," *The Liberator* (October 13, 1837), 1.

35. "Slave Trade," *Journal of Commerce* (March 29, 1837), 2.

36. "Communications," *The Liberator* (May 19, 1837).

37. Ruggles, "A Boy Kidnapped," *The Colored American* (September 16, 1837).

38. "From the Journal of Commerce," *New York Commercial Advertiser* (October 14, 1837), 2.

39. Wright, "The Bitter Fruits of Slavery," *The Liberator* (May 19, 1837), 83.

40. "Public Meeting and Expression of Sentiments," *The Colored American* (December 9, 1837); "What Has the North to Do with Slavery?" *The Colored American* (February 17, 1838).

41. "Public Meeting and Expression of Sentiments," *The Colored American* (December 9, 1837): "Slave Case," *New York Sun* (October 28, 1837), 2.

CHAPTER SEVEN: NO END IN SIGHT

1. Ruggles, "New-York Committee of Vigilance," *The Emancipator* 2 (March 1, 1838), 170; "Kidnapping and Piracy," *Journal of Commerce* (June 13, 1838), 2; "Charge of Kidnapping Africans," *Journal of Commerce* (August 23, 1838), 2.

2. *The First Annual Report of the New York Committee of Vigilance* (New York, 1837), 162; "Outrage and Kidnapping," *The Emancipator* (December 8, 1836), 126. David Ruggles to Theodore Sedgwick, November 30, 1836, and William Johnston to Theodore Sedgwick, April 1, 1837, The Law Office of Robert and Theodore Sedgwick Records, Harvard University Library.

3. Ruggles, "Introductory Remarks," *Mirror of Liberty* 1 (August 1838), 1.

4. For an important history of the African American village, see Judith Wellman, *Brooklyn's Promised Land: The Free Black Community of Weeksville, New York* (New York: New York University Press, 2014).

5. On George Washington's underhanded effort to use Pennsylvania's nine-month law to keep his enslaved property, see Erica Armstrong Dunbar, *Never Caught: The Washingtons' Relentless Pursuit of Their Runaway Slave, Ona Judge* (New York: Simon & Schuster, 2017).

6. Ruggles recounted the details of the Dodge affair in "The N.Y. Gazette and the Brooklyn Affair," *Mirror of Liberty* 1 (August 1838), 2.

7. Ruggles," "The N.Y. Gazette and the Brooklyn Affair," *Mirror of Liberty* 1 (January 1839), 30–32.

8. "Richard Riker," *Hudson River Chronicle* (May 29, 1838), 2; Untitled, *The Madisonian* (March 20, 1838), 2.

9. "The Great Locofoco Meeting in the Park This Afternoon," *New York Morning Herald* (March 27, 1838), 2; "Tremendous Meeting of the Mobocracy," *New York Morning Herald* (March 28, 1838), 2.

10. Ruggles, "Second Anniversary of the New York Committee of Vigilance," *The Emancipator* (May 24, 1838).

11. Ruggles, "Ex-Recorder Riker," *Mirror of Liberty* (July 1838), 4. In fact, in one of the last cases before him, Riker declared Henry Robertson to be a slave even though he claimed to be a free man. In the early hours of March 22, Nash brought Robertson to Riker's house, before Riker even left for work, and on the

spot Riker let Nash take Robertson to the South. See "Postscript," *The Colored American* (March 22, 1838); and Ruggles, "Kidnapping in New York," *The Emancipator* (March 29, 1838).

12. United States vs. Nathaniel Gordon (August 1838), US Circuit Court Criminal Case Files, 1790–1871, 1022.

13. Ruggles, "Case of Bercier and Gordon of the Brig Dunlap," *Mirror of Liberty* 1 (January 1839), 24–25.

14. Ruggles, "Case of Bercier and Gordon," 25.

15. Ruggles, "Case of Bercier and Gordon," 25–26.

16. Ruggles, "Case of Bercier and Gordon," 28–29.

17. Ruggles, "Capt. Jonathan Dayton Wilson," *Mirror of Liberty* 1 (January 1839), 22.

18. Stephen Dickerson Jr., "Narrative of Stephen Dickerson, Jr.," *The Colored American* (December 5, 1840), 1.

19. Stephen Dickerson Jr., "Narrative of Stephen Dickerson, Jr.," *The Colored American* (December 5, 1840), 1.

20. Stephen Dickerson Jr., "Narrative of Stephen Dickerson, Jr.," *The Colored American* (December 5, 1840), 1.

21. Ruggles placed a newspaper ad announcing Wilson's arrest. See *New York Evangelist* 3 (June 23, 1838), 99. See also a notice in *The Colored American* (July 21, 1838).

22. "Arrest of Lewis," *The Colored American* (August 18, 1838). See also Ruggles's report in "What Is to Be Done Must Be Done Quickly," *New York Evangelist* 9 (July 28, 1838), 119, and the short notice in *The Liberator* (August 17, 1838), 2.

23. Ruggles reprinted the quotation from Daniels that had appeared in the *New York Gazette*. See "David Ruggles and the Daily Papers," *Mirror of Liberty* 1 (January 1839), 21. On the Black community's mobilization on behalf of Dickerson and Wright, see "Important Public Meeting," *The Colored American* (October 20, 1838), 1; and "New Year's Present," *The Colored American* (January 2, 1841), 1.

24. Isaac T. Hopper, *Exposition of the Proceedings of John P. Darg, Henry W. Merritt, and Others* (New York, 1840), 7; C. Vann Woodward, ed., *Mary Chesnut's Civil War* (New Haven: Yale University Press, 1981), 27; Foner, *Gateway to Freedom*, 73.

25. Hopper, *Exposition of the Proceedings of John P. Darg*, 7.

26. Hopper, *Exposition of the Proceedings of John P. Darg*, 5, 8.

27. Hopper, *Exposition of the Proceedings of John P. Darg*, 4; "Abolitionism in Practice," *Richmond Enquirer* (September 14, 1838), 2.

28. Hopper, *Exposition of the Proceedings of John P. Darg*, 5–6; "Let Us Have a Little Justice," *New York Evangelist* 9 (September 22, 1838), 150; "Examination of the Black Man, Ruggles," *New York Morning Herald* (September 10, 1838), 2.

29. The People vs. Thomas Hughes, et al., October 16, 1838, Court of General Sessions Minutes, Municipal Archives, New York, 298, 647, 649; March 7, 1839, 651.

30. The People vs. Barney Corse, March 8, 1839, Court of General Sessions Minutes, Municipal Archives, New York, 654, 656. The People vs. Barney Corse et al., September 17, 1839, Court of General Sessions Minutes, 484–485, 559; October 17, 1839, 560; October 18, 1839, 561–562.

31. "New York Committee of Vigilance," *The Liberator* (October 5, 1838); Hopper, *Exposition of the Proceedings of John P. Darg*, 19; "The Journal of Commerce and the Kidnappers," *The Emancipator* 3 (September 6, 1838), 77; Daniels quoted in "David Ruggles and the Daily Papers," *The Emancipator* 3 (August 30, 1838), 71.

32. *Trial of Henry W. Merritt, a Special Justice for Preserving the Peace in the City of New York* (New York, 1840); Hopper, *Exposition of the Proceedings of John P. Darg*, 6. "Court of Sessions," *Journal of Commerce* (October 28, 1839), 2.

33. Lydia Maria Child, *Isaac T. Hopper: A True Life* (Boston, 1854), 355–356.

CHAPTER EIGHT:
NEW YORK AND THE TRANSATLANTIC SLAVE TRADE

1. John Russel vs. David Ruggles, et al., October 23, 1838, Court of Common Pleas, Municipal Archives, New York. See also James R. Hicks vs. David Ruggles, December 21, 1833, Court of Common Pleas, Municipal Archives, New York.

2. Ruggles's letter to Cornish was published in "Agent of the Vigilance Committee," *The Colored American* (January 26, 1839); "AN ABOLITIONIST, David Ruggles," *The Colored American* (February 23, 1839). On the dispute between Cornish and Ruggles, see also Foner, *Gateway to Freedom*, 75–76; and Hodges, *David Ruggles*, 148–151.

3. See Ruggles's letter in *The Colored American* (January 26, 1839). See also The Law Office of Robert and Theodore Sedgwick Records, Harvard University Law Library, Box 84, Files 4 and 5.

4. For an excellent analysis of the controversy, see Jamila Shabazz Brathwaite, "The Black Vigilance Movement in Nineteenth-Century New York City" (M.A. Thesis, CUNY City College, 2014), 36–38. David Ruggles vs. William Johnston, et al., October 19, 1839, Court of Common Pleas Records, Municipal Archives, New York.

5. "David Ruggles's Meeting," *The Colored American* (July 27, 1839). Second Ruggles Letter, printed in *The Colored American* (February 23, 1839). See also Ruggles, "The Suppressed Letter," *Mirror of Liberty* 3 (August 1840), 41–49. Thomas Van Rensselaer, "A National Reform Convention," *The Colored American* (August 1, 1840); "Preamble and Constitution of the Manhattan Anti-Slavery Society," *National Anti-Slavery Standard* (September 24, 1840).

6. Charles L. Reason, "Mr. Van Rensselaer Again," *The Colored American* (July 10, 1841).

7. Charles B. Ray to James G. Birney and Henry B. Stanton, May 20, 1840, in Ripley, ed., *Black Abolitionist Papers*, vol. 3, 335.

8. Cornish, "Journal of Commerce," *The Colored American* (November 17, 1838); "Abolition Victory," *The Colored American* (November 17, 1838); "Letter from Communipaw," *Frederick Douglass' Newspaper* (February 12, 1852), 3.

9. Tyler Anbinder, "Isaiah Rynders and the Ironies of Popular Democracy in Antebellum New York," in Manisha Sinha and Penny Von Eschen, eds., *Contested Democracy: Freedom, Race, and Power in American History* (New York: Columbia University Press, 2007), 31–34.

10. "Fashionable Movements," *New York Weekly Herald* (November 30, 1844), 377; "Fracas at Washington," *New York Weekly Herald* (December 28, 1844), 413; "By the Southern Mail," *New York Herald* (March 7, 1845), 4; "Riot in Waterford," *Schenectady Cabinet* (April 8, 1845), 2.

11. For further information on religion and politics in upstate New York, see John L. Brooke, *Columbia Rising: Civil Life on the Upper Hudson from the Revolution to the Age of Jackson* (Chapel Hill: University of North Carolina Press, 2010); Mary P. Ryan, *Cradle of the Middle Class: The Family in Oneida County, New York, 1790–1865* (Cambridge: Cambridge University Press, 1981); Paul E. Johnson, *A Shopkeeper's Millennium: Society and Revivals in Rochester, New York, 1815–1837* (New York: Hill and Wang, 1978).

12. For Ruggles's views on the two parties, see "Reform's Mirror," *Mirror of Liberty* 3 (August 1840), 38–40. On Nash and Boudinot's alleged involvement in political corruption, see "To the Editors of the Evening Post," *New York Evening Post* (October 30, 1840), 2. Boudinot became commissioner of deeds in March 1840: "Tobias Boudinot," *The Emancipator* 4 (March 12, 1840), 182.

13. "The Slave Ships," *Philadelphia Inquirer* 20 (June 13, 1839), 2; "The Slave Trade—More Developments," *The Colored American* (July 13, 1839).

14. This account of the *Ulysses* is drawn from a detailed report in "Capture of the Ulysses," *The Colored American* (April 4, 1840).

15. "American African Slave Trade," *The Colored American* (June 1, 1839).

16. R. R. Madden, "A Letter to W. E. Channing, D.D. on the Subject of the Abuse of the Flag of the United States in the Island of Cuba" (Boston, 1839). On the negative press Trist received back home, see "The Slave Trade," *The Emancipator* (July 4, 1839), 39; "Mr. Consul Trist Again," *New York Commercial Advertiser* (July 15, 1839), 2; "American Slavers," *New York Commercial Advertiser* (July 26, 1839), 2.

17. "A Meeting of Ship Masters," *New York Evening Post* (September 3, 1839), 2; "Consul Trist," *New York Commercial Advertiser* (August 10, 1839), 2; "Mr. Consul Trist Again," *New York Evening Post* (September 5, 1839), 2; "Consul Trist and the Newspapers," *The Colored American* (November 16, 1839).

18. "LOOK OUT FOR KIDNAPPERS," *The Colored American* (May 1, 1841); "Child Lost," *The Colored American* (October 9, 1841); "Kidnappers Abroad," *The Colored American* (June 12, 1841).

19. "The Case of Mr. Downing," *The Colored American* (February 20, 1841); "The Abuse of Downing," *The Colored American* (January 16, 1841).

20. "Treatment of Mr. Ruggles," *The Liberator* (July 23, 1841), 2; Louis Ruchames, "Jim Crow Railroads in Massachusetts," *American Quarterly* 8 (Spring 1956), 62–63.

21. "Case of David Ruggles" and "Infamous Decision," *The Liberator* (August 6, 1841), 4.

22. Ruchames, "Jim Crow Railroads," 63–66.

23. H. W. H., "An Appeal to Abolitionists in Behalf of David Ruggles," *The Liberator* (June 14, 1844), 4. With the help of friends, Ruggles still penned letters and drafted essays in support of abolitionism. See, for example, David Ruggles to David L. Child, September 4, 1843, Anti-Slavery Collections, Boston Public Library. In 1843 and 1844, Ruggles wrote a few essays that were published in *The Liberator*.

24. "Slave Hunting in New York," *National Anti-Slavery Standard* (January 4, 1849), 2; "Fugitive Slaves," *National Anti-Slavery Standard* (January 25, 1849), 2.

25. "Meeting in Behalf of The Mirror of Liberty," *Mirror of Liberty* supplement (July 1841), 1, 2, 4; Richard Archer, *Jim Crow North: The Struggle for Equal Rights in Antebellum New England* (New York: Oxford University Press, 2017), 97.

26. Hodges, *David Ruggles*, 182–196.

27. "Pillars for the New York Exchange," *The Colored American* (July 24, 1839); "New York Commercial Association," *The Colored American* (December 19, 1840).

28. "Bankrupt Applications," *New York Evening Post* 40 (December 15, 1842), 2. On Riker, see "Death of Richard Riker," *New York Spectator* 45 (September 28, 1842), 3; "Death of Richard Riker," *Southern Patriot* [Charleston] 48 (September 30, 1842), 2; "Death of Richard Riker," *Times-Picayune* [New Orleans] (October 6, 1842), 2.

29. On the Lemmon Case, see Sarah L. H. Gronningsater, "On Behalf of His Race and the Lemmon Slaves: Louis Napoleon, Northern Black Legal Culture, and the Politics of Sectional Crisis," *Journal of the Civil War Era* (June 2017), 206–241; Foner, *Gateway to Freedom*, 140–141; Blackett, *The Captive's Quest for Freedom*, 386; Delbanco, *The War Before the War*, 318–319.

CHAPTER NINE: "BLESSED BE COTTON!": THE FUGITIVE SLAVE LAW AND NEW YORK CITY

1. Dodson, *Black New Yorkers*, 79; Ripley, ed., *Black Abolitionist Papers*, vol. 2, 191.

2. "From the Savannah Republican," *National Anti-Slavery Standard* (November 12, 1846), 1. See also "An Interesting and Important Fugitive Slave Case," *National Anti-Slavery Standard* (October 29, 1846), 3.

3. Samuel Owen, ed., "Supplement to the New-York Legal Observer, Containing the Report of the Case in the Matter of George Kirk" (New York, 1847); "Release of the Slave Boy, George Kirk," *Boston Recorder* (November 12, 1846), 182; "The Slave Case," *New York Tribune* (November 2, 1846), 1. For Child's quotation, see notices in *National Aegis* (December 2, 1846), 3. See also Foner, *Gateway to Freedom*, 112–113.

4. "The Slave, George Kirk," *Richmond Whig* (November 6, 1846), 4.

5. "The Police of New-York on a Slave Hunt," *New York Tribune* (October 30, 1846), 2. "The Slave Case Again," *National Anti-Slavery Standard* (November 5, 1846), 1; "The Recent Slave Case," *New York Tribune* (November 18, 1846), 2; "City Items," *New York Tribune* (November 3, 1846), 1.

6. "The Slave Case—The Fugitive Freed!" *National Anti-Slavery Standard* (November 5, 1846), 2.

7. "New York Supreme Court," *New York Legal Observer* (New York, 1849), 81–83; Foner, *Gateway to Freedom*, 114–115.

8. "City News," *New York Spectator* (December 28, 1848), 2; "The Kidnappers," *New York Evening Post* (December 22, 1848), 3.

9. "Brooklyn," *Commercial Advertiser* (January 18, 1849), 1.

10. "Slave Case in New York and the Colored Meeting," *Pennsylvania Freeman* (January 4, 1849).

11. "The American Anti-Slavery Society," *New York Evening Post* (May 7, 1850), 2; "American Anti-Slavery Society," *Pennsylvania Freeman* (May 16, 1850); Tyler Anbinder, "Isaiah Rynders and the Ironies of Popular Democracy in Antebellum New York," in Sinha and Von Eschen, eds., *Contested Democracy*, 38–40; David W. Blight, *Frederick Douglass: Prophet of Freedom* (New York: Simon & Schuster, 2018), 202–203. On Black abolitionism in New York, see Manisha Sinha, *The Slave's Cause: A History of Abolition* (New Haven: Yale University Press, 2016), 77–85, 141–142, 224–225, 232–237, and 384–387. Importantly, Sinha contextualizes the abolitionist movement in Manhattan within the broader national scene.

12. Anbinder, "Isaiah Rynders and the Ironies of Popular Democracy," in Sinha and Von Eschen, eds., *Contested Democracy*, 39–40, 44; Blight, *Frederick Douglass*, 203–204.

13. Blight, *Frederick Douglass*, 204–205.

14. "Sentiments of the Colored People of New York City," *The North Star* (April 5, 1850).

15. On the anger and chaos caused by the Fugitive Slave Law of 1850, see Andrew Delbanco, *The War Before the War* and Blackett, *The Captive's Quest for Freedom*. On the Compromise of 1850, see Michael E. Woods, *Arguing Until Doomsday: Stephen Douglas, Jefferson Davis, and the Struggle for American Democracy* (Chapel Hill: University of North Carolina Press, 2020); and Stephen E. Maizlish, *A Strife of Tongues: The Compromise of 1850 and the Ideological Foundations of the American Civil War* (Charlottesville: University of Virginia Press, 2018).

16. For a fuller explication of this argument, see Wells, *Blind No More*.

17. "Rev. Charles B. Ray," *National Anti-Slavery Standard* (October 10, 1850); Bibb, "High Handed Kidnapping," *The Voice of the Fugitive* (March 26, 1851), Bibb, "Slave Market at the North," *The Voice of the Fugitive* (April 9, 1851).

18. "Proceedings of the State Convention of Colored People Held at Albany" (Albany, 1851), 72.

19. Dodson, *Black New Yorkers*, 74.

20. "Conscience and Law," *Journal of Commerce* (December 21, 1850), 1; "Rev. Cox's Thanksgiving Sermon," *Journal of Commerce* (December 21, 1850), 4; "Letter to the Editor," *Journal of Commerce* (December 28, 1850), 1; "Duty of Citizens with Respect to the Fugitive Slave Law," *Journal of Commerce* (December 25, 1850), 1; "The Higher Law," *Journal of Commerce* (January 1, 1851), 1.

21. Gerard Hallock, "The Union Movement," *Journal of Commerce* (December 25, 1850), 2; "The New Haven Meeting," *Journal of Commerce* (December 21,

1850), 2; "Great Union Meeting at New Haven," *Journal of Commerce* (December 28, 1850), 1.

22. Hallock, *Life of Gerard Hallock*, 208–219.

23. "The Proceedings of the Union Meeting, Held at Castle Garden, October 30, 1850" (New York, 1850), 3; printed letter from Union Safety Committee in New York, December 2, 1850, Box 6, James G. Birney Papers, Clements Library, University of Michigan.

24. Hallock, "Cotton," *Journal of Commerce* (December 21, 1850), 2.

25. "The Proceedings of the Union Meeting, Held at Castle Garden, October 30, 1850" (New York, 1850), 7.

26. 1852 essay by James G. Birney in Birney Papers, Box 8, Clements Library, University of Michigan.

27. Kyle B. Roberts, *Evangelical Gotham: Religion and the Making of New York City, 1783–1860* (Chicago: University of Chicago Press, 2016), 215, 261.

28. Roberts, *Evangelical Gotham*, 215.

29. Roberts, *Evangelical Gotham*, 272–273.

30. "The First Blood," *National Anti-Slavery Standard* (October 3, 1850), 2; "The Slave Bill in Operation," *Brooklyn Daily Eagle* (September 28, 1850), 2; "The First Victim Under the New Fugitive Slave Bill," *Frederick Douglass' Newspaper* (October 3, 1850), 2; "The Fugitive Slave Law," *New York Evening Post* (October 2, 1850), 2; "Meetings of Colored Citizens of New York," *The North Star* (October 24, 1850), 1.

31. "Mr. William P. Powell," *National Anti-Slavery Standard* (October 10, 1850), 3; "City Intelligence," *New York Evening Post* (October 5, 1850), 2; "A Great Mass Meeting," *New York Daily Tribune* (October 5, 1850), 1; "The Fugitive Slave Agitation," *New York Daily Tribune* (October 14, 1850), 6.

32. James McCune Smith, "Dr. Smith," *National Anti-Slavery Standard* (October 10, 1850). For more on Hamlet's case, see Blackett, *The Captive's Quest for Freedom*, 71–72.

33. Entry for December 28, 1850, Diary of William H. Bell, New-York Historical Society. See also Sean Wilentz, "Crime, Poverty and the Streets of New York City: The Diary of William H. Bell, 1850–51," *History Workshop* 7 (Spring 1979), 136.

34. "The Fugitive Slave Law," *New York Herald* (December 24, 1850), 2; "US Circuit Court," *New York Tribune* (January 1, 1851), 7.

35. "Henry Long's Case," *New York Tribune* (January 8, 1851), 4; "The Fugitive Slave Case," *New York Evening Post* (December 28, 1850), 2; "Meeting at Zion Church," *New York Tribune* (January 3, 1851), 7; "The Fugitive Slave Case," *Brooklyn Evening Star* (January 7, 1851), 2; "The Case of Henry Long," *New York Tribune* (January 3, 1851), 4. The *Tribune*'s editor, Horace Greeley, also publicly collected donations. On African American opposition, see Jamila Shabazz Brathwaite, "The Black Vigilance Movement in Nineteenth-Century New York City" (M.A. Thesis, CUNY City College, 2014). See "To Give Henry Long a Chance for Freedom," *New York Tribune* (January 4, 1851), 4.

36. "Decision of the Case of Long," *New York Evening Post* (January 8, 1851), 2.

37. On the widespread support of the city's merchants for upholding the Fugitive Slave Law, see "Peace and Harmony," *National Era* (October 31, 1850), 174. On Rynders see "City Intelligence," *New York Evening Post* (May 12, 1849), 7; and "Friend Brown," *Cayuga Chief* (Auburn, New York) (July 30, 1850), 3. Matsell had been appointed chief of police in 1846. See *Proceedings of the Board of Aldermen*, vol. XXXI (New York, 1846), 145.

38. Ariel, "Virginia," *New York Tribune* (January 31, 1851), 7.

39. "Departure of Long," *New York Tribune* (January 9, 1851), 5; "Henry Long's Case," *Brooklyn Evening Star* (January 10, 1851), 2; Gerard Hallock, "The Slave Case," *Journal of Commerce* (December 28, 1850), 1; "Henry Long," *Pennsylvania Freeman* (January 16, 1851), 3; "Presentation," *New York Tribune* (March 24, 1851), 5.

40. Frederick Douglass, "Lecture No. VII," *Frederick Douglass' Newspaper* (January 16, 1851), 2.

41. Ariel, "Virginia," *New York Tribune* (January 31, 1851), 7; "The Non-Intercourse Scheme," *New York Evening Post* (November 21, 1850), 2; "Cotton Zeal for the Union," *New York Tribune* (March 25, 1851), 3; "Welcome to the Union Safety Committee," *The Tennessean* (December 16, 1850), 2; "Don't Forget, Freemen!" *New York Tribune* (November 4, 1851), 4.

42. "Gems from Gen. Foote," *New York Tribune* (February 26, 1851), 4; "The Southern Senators," *Poughkeepsie Journal* (December 14, 1850), 2; "The Fugitive from Justice," *New York Evening Post* (April 21, 1851), 2; "Mr. Webster in Town," *New York Evening Post* (November 20, 1850), 2.

43. "Sale of Henry Long, the Fugitive," *Pennsylvania Freeman* (January 23, 1851), 3; "Henry Long at Auction," *New York Tribune* (January 21, 1851), 7.

44. Conservative, "A Slave Sale," *Pennsylvania Freeman* (January 30, 1851), 1.

45. Conservative, "A Slave Sale," *Pennsylvania Freeman* (January 30, 1851), 1.

46. "Varieties," *Pennsylvania Freeman* (August 21, 1851), 3; *Louisville Journal* quoted in *New York Tribune* (August 18, 1851), 6.

47. "The Union Club and Abolitionism," *New York Tribune* (January 8, 1851), 5; "Facts and Reflections on the Late Fugitive Slave Case," *New York Tribune* (January 14, 1851), 6.

48. William Powell, "Fellow Citizens," *National Anti-Slavery Standard* (October 30, 1851), 1.

49. Charles B. Ray, "The New York Vigilance Committee," *The Vigilance Committee* 1 (June 1844), 1.

50. Sinha, *The Slave's Cause*, 225, 264, 304–305, 319–321.

CHAPTER TEN: THE PORTUGUESE COMPANY

1. For more details of this argument, see Wells, *Blind No More*.

2. Harris, *In the Shadow of Slavery*, 270–271; Alexander, *African or American?*, 126. "Testimony of Elizabeth Jennings," reprinted in Ripley, ed., *Black Abolitionist Papers*, vol. 4, 230–232.

3. Alexander, *African or American?*, 126–127.

4. "The Right of Colored Persons to Ride in the Railway Cars," *Pacific Appeal* 1 (May 16, 1863).

5. One of the leaders of the Portuguese Company, John A. Machado, kept an office at 165 Pearl Street, just northeast of City Hall Park. See addressed letter, Benjamin Upton to John A. Machado, August 11, 1854, Jacob Morris Papers, New-York Historical Society.

6. On the members of the so-called Portuguese Company, see Warren S. Howard, *American Slavers and the Federal Law, 1837–1862* (Berkeley: University of California Press, 1963), 49–51. Remarkably, the machinations of the Portuguese Company have received little to no attention from historians. For exceptions, see Robert Trent Vinson, "The Law as Lawbreaker: The Promotion and Encouragement of the Atlantic Slave Trade by the New York Judiciary System," *Afro-Americans in New York Life and History* 20 (July 1996), 35; and Ronald Raymond Mutz, "The Portuguese Company in New York City: Slave Traders to Cuba in the 1850's," M.A. Thesis (University of Oregon, 1979). For brief but important discussions of the group, see Gerald Horne, *The Deepest South: The United States, Brazil, and the African Slave Trade* (New York: New York University Press, 2007), 136; the group was also well connected to Wall Street businesses; Machado served on the board of a Wall Street insurance company. See the advertisement for the Commonwealth Fire Insurance Company in *New York Evening Post* (October 4, 1855), 4. Several men also were involved in other trade; Machado engaged in the opium trade. See the notes in *Massachusetts Spy* (July 15, 1857), 1; and "The Case of the Schooner George E. Townsend," *New York Daily Herald* (January 6, 1855), 10. On Wenberg and Weeks, see "The Panchita Slave Case," *New York Times* (October 23, 1856), 8.

7. On the *Julia Moulton*'s iteration prior to becoming a slaver, see "Arrived at Wilmington," *Wilmington Journal* (March 1, 1850), 3; and *New York Daily Herald* (July 31, 1850), 4, and (June 25, 1851), 4.

8. Benjamin Upton to John A. Machado, August 11, 1854; Robert H. Redmond & Co. to Machado, April 20, 1857; and Dunlife, Moncrief & Co. to Machado, July 1, 1856. Machado later admitted that three of his vessels were seized in 1857 alone. Machado especially had a well-earned reputation as a slave trader who used New York City as his base of operations. "Vence" to John Fenno, June 10, 1856. "Vence" to John Fenno, June 10, 1859. All of the above materials can be found in the Jacob Morris Papers, New-York Historical Society. Regarding Machado's legal entanglements, see Julius Deppermann vs. John A. Machado, October 15, 1857, Court of Common Pleas, Municipal Archives, New York; Christian S. Sloane vs. John A. Machado, October 17, 1857, Superior Court, Municipal Archives, New York; John Harper vs. John A. Machado, November 27, 1857, Superior Court, Municipal Archives, New York; William Pennell vs. John A. Machado, June 18, 1858, Court of Common Pleas, Municipal Archives, New York; Joseph Brummell vs. John A. Machado, August 4, 1859, New York Superior Court, Municipal Archives, New York.

9. Howard, *American Slavers*, 128; Vinson, "The Law as Lawbreaker," n. 13.

10. "Trial for Being Engaged in the Slave Trade," *Brooklyn Daily Eagle* (November 7, 1854), 2; "The Slave Trade," *Barre Gazette* (January 9, 1857), 2; "Our New York Correspondence," *Washington Union* (September 22, 1854), 3; "Alleged Traffic in Slaves," *The Liberator* (September 29, 1854), 3; "Trial for Being Engaged in the Slave Trade," *New York Tribune* (November 7, 1854), 7.

11. Charles Daly, "Charles O'Conor," *Magazine of American History* XIII (June 1885), 525. See also John Bigelow, "The New York Bar—Charles O'Conor," *National Quarterly Review* (June 1865), 73–96.

12. "In Memory of Charles O'Conor," unpublished volume in the Charles O'Conor Papers, New York Law Institute, 39.

13. "The Slave Trade: An Important Trial," *New York Times* (November 10, 1854), 4; "The Slave-Trade," *New York Tribune* (November 11, 1854), 4; "Slavers in New York," *Richmond Dispatch* (November 28, 1854), 2; "Queer Relations at the North," *Fayetteville Weekly Observer* [NC] (November 20, 1854), 2.

14. Howard, *American Slavers*, 51. Howard and Trent in "The Law as Lawbreaker" persuasively argue that Betts should be judged harshly for his unnecessarily narrow and rigid interpretation of the law against slave trading. For a different view, see John D. Gordon III, *This Practice Against Law: Cuban Slave Trade Cases in the Southern District of New York, 1839–1841* (New York: Law Book Exchange, 2016). Betts apparently did sometimes rule in favor of guilt, as he did in the case of the bark *Laurens* in 1849. See "Condemned as a Slaver," *New Orleans Times-Picayune* (July 17, 1849), 2.

15. "Belmont and Buchanan," *Schenectady Cabinet* (June 17, 1856), 2; "The Friends of Wise at Tammany Hall," *New York Evening Post* (June 1, 1855), 1.

16. "Another Slaver Seized in New-York Harbor," *Schenectady Cabinet* (May 5, 1857), 2. Another slaver was seized at about the same time under the authority of Rynders. "The Alleged Slave Ship Merchant," *New York Herald* (May 9, 1857), 10. See also "An Important Verdict," *Trenton State Gazette* (October 6, 1858), 2; and "The Slave Trade," *New York Herald* (December 11, 1859), 5.

17. Howard, *American Slavers*, 155–156; Mutz, "The Portuguese Company," 48–49; "Alleged Slave Piracy," *National Anti-Slavery Standard* (May 12, 1855), 3; "Slave-Ships in New York Harbor," *The Liberator* (January 5, 1855), 1.

18. "Charge of Fitting Out a Slave Ship," *New York Herald* (May 16, 1856), 8. See also "The Slave Trade," *New York Herald* (September 11, 1856), 1; and "The Slave Trade," *Salem* [MA] *Register* (December 1, 1856), 2.

19. Howard, *American Slavers*, 52–55, 157–159, 224–228, 249; Vinson, "The Law as Lawbreaker," 35–41; Mutz, "The Portuguese Company," 53; "Capture of a Slaver in New York Bay," *National Anti-Slavery Standard* (March 22, 1856), 3. Betts was involved in several other cases involving slavers in the 1850s. For example, see "United States District Court," *New York Herald* (July 11, 1856), 5; "The Slave Trade in New York," *New York Herald* (September 24, 1856), 10; "United States District Court," *New York Times* (November 28, 1856), 3. For a historical perspective on the city's legal system, see Mike McConville and Chester Mirsky, "The Rise of Guilty Pleas: New York, 1800–1865," *Journal of Law and Society* 22 (December

1995), 443–474; and Harold E. Hammond, "The New York City Court of Common Pleas," *New York History* 32 (July 1951), 275–295.

20. Driscoll quoted in Howard, *American Slavers*, 176–177.

21. "The Alleged Slaver Panchita," *New York Daily Tribune* (July 10, 1857), 7. For more on the *Panchita* cases, see "The Panchita Seized in the Coast as a Slaver," *New York Daily Tribune* (July 8, 1857), 3; "Panchita," *New York Daily Tribune* (January 9, 1858), 4; "The Case of the Bark *Panchita*," *New York Daily Tribune* (June 23, 1858), 7.

22. On Wenberg and Weeks, see "The Slave Trade in New York," *New York Daily Tribune* (December 26, 1856), 6. Wenberg and Weeks appear frequently in the maritime trade news in city newspapers from 1855 onward. Interestingly, Benjamin and Louis Wenberg died just hours apart in 1885. See "Died Together," *St. Joseph Gazette-Herald* (June 19, 1885), 8.

23. Thanks to a detailed and heartbreaking internet-based exhibition sponsored by the College of Charleston, we know a great deal about the tragic voyage of the slaver *Echo*. Crafted by the Lowcountry Digital History Initiative (LDHI), the online exhibit presents fascinating images and a well-crafted narrative that offers important details about the case of the *Echo*. See "The Voyage of the Echo," http://ldhi.library.cofc.edu/exhibits/show/voyage-of-the-echo-the-trials/the -echo-trials. On the ubiquity of slave trading in New York City in the period between 1857 and 1860, see Farrow, Lang, and Frank, *Complicity*, 122–133; Ernest Obadele-Starks, *Freebooters and Smugglers: The Foreign Slave Trade in the United States After 1808* (Fayetteville: University of Arkansas Press, 2007), 175–181; and Sharla M. Fett, *Recaptured Africans: Surviving Slave Ships, Detention, and Dislocation in the Final Years of the Slave Trade* (Chapel Hill: University of North Carolina Press, 2017).

24. These details are derived from two important sources: the Lowcountry Digital History Initiative and the official transcript of the trials. See "Report of the Trials in the Echo Cases" (Columbia, SC, 1859). Just how lightly the federal government took the international slave trade can be seen in Robert Ralph Davis Jr., "James Buchanan and the Suppression of the Slave Trade," *Pennsylvania History* 33 (October 1966), 446–459.

25. LDHI, College of Charleston online exhibit "The Voyage of the Echo."

26. "Report of the Trials in the Echo Case," 8.

27. Charles O'Conor, "Negro Slavery not Unjust" (New York, 1860), 4.

28. O'Conor, "Negro Slavery Not Unjust," 6, 8, 9.

29. O'Conor, "Negro Slavery Not Unjust," 10, 11, 13.

30. "The Slave Traffic," *Journal of Commerce* editorial reprinted in *The Liberator* (July 25, 1856), 1.

31. Constitution of the Democratic League of the City & County of New York, 1853–1854, New-York Historical Society.

32. For an attack on Wood by a partisan accusing the mayor of corruption, see Abijah Ingraham, "A History of the Mercantile, Political, and Official Career of our 'Model Mayor'" (New York, 1856).

33. "Resignation of Mayor Wood," *New York Herald* (April 5, 1857), 4; Harriet Morse to Richard Cary Morse Jr., October 26, 1857, Box 3, Richard Cary Morse Papers, Clements Library, University of Michigan.

34. Richardson, *The New York Police*, 69–70; Wilbur R. Miller, *Cops and Bobbies: Police Authority in New York and London, 1830–1870* (Chicago, 1973), 151–152.

35. Richardson, *The New York Police*, 70.

36. Richardson, *The New York Police*, 72; see also Stephen H. Branch, *The Life of Stephen H. Branch* (New York, 1857).

37. Richardson, *The New York Police*, 105–106. For more detailed information on the police in the 1850s, see Chadwick, *Law & Disorder*, Chapters 14–16. Wood was indicted for violating the city charter. See Court of Oyer and Terminer Minutes, Box 1 (1796–1859), November 31, 1858, Municipal Archives, New York.

38. "Another Slave Freed," *Journal of Commerce* (October 14, 1859), 3.

39. "Interesting Slavery Case," *National Anti-Slavery Standard* (December 12, 1857), 3.

40. "An Interesting Fugitive Slave Case," *The Liberator* 27 (December 11, 1857), 199.

41. Gay aided more than two hundred fugitives in 1855 and 1856. See Foner, *Gateway to Freedom*, 195.

42. See notice in *Buffalo Weekly Republic* (December 1, 1857), 3; "The Brooklyn Fugitive Slave Case," *The Liberator* (January 15, 1858), 3; "The Recent Kidnapping Affair," *New York Tribune* (January 26, 1858), 8; "The Kidnapping Policemen Discharged," *National Anti-Slavery Standard* (December 19, 1857), 2; "Fugitive Case in Brooklyn," *Brooklyn Daily Eagle* (December 2, 1857), 3; "The Kidnapping Case," *Brooklyn Daily Eagle* (January 25, 1858), 3. By the following spring, in 1858, New York abolitionists would be following a new case of kidnapping. George Anderson had been arrested upstate in Geneva and had been sold as a slave in Richmond. See "Another Case of Kidnapping," *National Anti-Slavery Standard* (February 6, 1858), 3; and "Kidnappers Convicted," *National Anti-Slavery Standard* (April 17, 1858), 3. Particularly important is that unlike Recorder Richard Riker in the 1830s, the new recorder, George C. Barnard, was the one who oversaw the conviction. See "A Kidnapper to Be Punished," *National Anti-Slavery Standard* (May 29, 1858), 3.

CHAPTER ELEVEN: NEW YORK AND SECESSION

1. "Insurrection at Harper's Ferry," *Journal of Commerce* (October 18, 1859), 5. The headlines of the next issue of the paper made clear who was to blame for the raid: "The Abolition Insurrection at Harper's Ferry," *Journal of Commerce* (October 19, 1859), 5; "Who Is Responsible?" *Journal of Commerce* (October 20, 1859), 3; "Correspondence," *Journal of Commerce* (October 21, 1859), 5; "The Lesson," *Journal of Commerce* (October 22, 1859), 3.

2. *New York Herald* quoted in Foner, *Business and Slavery*, 156.

3. J. D. B. De Bow, "A Southern Confederacy: Its Prospects, Resources, and Destiny," *De Bow's Review* 26 (May 1859), 578.

4. Dodson, *Black New Yorkers*, 82. Northern firm of Cameron, Edwards, and Company quoted in Foner, *Business and Slavery*, 161.

5. Lists of "abolition" and "constitutional" firms appeared in "The Commercial Crisis," *New York Times* (February 22, 1860), 3. See also Foner, *Business and Slavery*, 160–161.

6. Editorial, *New York Herald* (October 10, 1857), quoted in Foner, *Business and Slavery*, 140–141; editorial, *Charleston Mercury* (October 14, 1857), quoted in Foner, *Business and Slavery*, 147; "The Insurrection at Harper's Ferry," *Journal of Commerce* (October 19, 1859), 3. On the consequences of secession, see "State of Feeling in Virginia," *Journal of Commerce* (December 1, 1859), 3; and "One of the Consequences of Disunion," *Journal of Commerce* (December 2, 1859), 1.

7. "The Metropolitan Police and the Fugitive Slave Law," *New York Evening Post* (January 14, 1860), 2.

8. "Kidnapping in New York," *National Anti-Slavery Standard* (December 1, 1860), 3.

9. "The Slave Trade," *Weekly Anglo-African* (April 27, 1861); Foner, *Business and Slavery*, 164–167.

10. On Mary Jane Watson, see Obituaries, *New York Daily Herald* (February 8, 1850), 8. Information on slavers in late 1859 and early 1860 can be found in Howard, *American Slavers*, Appendix I. See also Ted Maris-Wolf, "'Of Blood and Treasure': Recaptive Africans and the Politics of Slave Trade Suppression," *Journal of the Civil War Era* 4 (March 2014), 61; and Vinson, "The Law as Lawbreaker," 35–45.

11. "The Alleged Slave Schooner Mariquita," *New York Herald* (June 21, 1860), 1.

12. "The News," *New York Herald* (October 28, 1860), 4; "The Three Negroes and Marshal Rynders," *New York Evening Post* (October 26, 1860), 3; "Special Correspondence of the Evening Post," *New York Evening Post* (October 31, 1860), 2. Rynders was arrested for assault and battery against William Barney but the charges were later dismissed. "City Intelligence," *Commercial Advertiser* (October 29, 1860), 3.

13. Seward quoted in Foner, *Business and Slavery*, 167–168. See Betts's decision regarding the bark *Kate* in "Release of the Alleged Slaver Kate," *New York Herald* (August 31, 1860), 8; and "The Case of Another Alleged Slaver," *New York Times* (February 23, 1861). See also Erik Calonius, *The Wanderer: The Last American Slave Ship and the Conspiracy That Set Its Sails* (New York: St. Martin's, 2006), 73–74.

14. "More Slave-hunting in New York," *Weekly Anglo-African* (May 5, 1860).

15. On the importance of the speech for Lincoln's ascension to the presidency, see Harold Holzer, *Lincoln at Cooper Union: The Speech That Made Abraham Lincoln President* (New York: Simon & Schuster, 2006).

16. Horace Greeley, editorial, *New York Tribune* (February 28, 1860); Foner, *Business and Slavery*, 178–180.

17. Hallock, *Life of Gerard Hallock*, 74–75.

18. Foner, *Business and Slavery*, 182–191, 198–199.

19. "The Attempt to Rescue Capt. Anderson's Slave," *Nashville Union and American* (July 29, 1860), 2; and "Departure of the Savannah Blues," *New York Times* (July 26, 1860), 8.

20. "The Funeral Services in Tammany," *New York Herald* (November 7, 1860), 3.

21. See the city election results printed in *New York Herald* (November 7, 1860), 1.

22. James McCune Smith, "Address of the New York City Suffrage Committee to the Colored People of New York" (New York, 1860). See also James McCune Smith to Stephen A. Myers, September 21, 1860, and Smith to Gerrit Smith, October 20, 1860, in Ripley, ed., *Black Abolitionist Papers*, vol. 5, 84–87.

23. "Results," *New York Herald* (November 7, 1860), 2.

24. Hallock, *Life of Gerard Hallock*, 79, 95, 107.

25. Robert Toombs, "Invasion of the States: Speech Delivered in the Senate" (Washington, 1860), 2, 7. For more on this point, see Wells, *Blind No More*, Chapter 5.

26. Foner, *Business and Slavery*, 227–228. "The Funeral Services in Tammany," *New York Herald* (November 7, 1860), 3. For a refutation of O'Conor's defense of slavery, see George W. Clark, "Refutation of Mr. Charles O'Connor's [*sic*] Defence [*sic*] of Slavery" (Rochester, 1860).

27. Foner, *Business and Slavery*, 230–231.

28. For other perspectives, see Tyler G. Anbinder, "Fernando Wood and New York City's Secession from the Union: A Political Reappraisal," *New York History* 68 (January 1987), 66–92; and Burrows and Wallace, *Gotham*, 831–851.

29. "Anticipated Attack on the Brooklyn Navy Yard," *New York Herald* (January 22, 1861), 1.

30. Foner, *Business and Slavery*, 293–295.

31. Foner, *Business and Slavery*, 248–249.

32. Spencer and Teague to New York City firm, November 14, 1861, Teague Family Papers, South Carolina Historical Society.

33. Foner, *Business and Slavery*, 251–252, 259.

34. Foner, *Business and Slavery*, 272–273, 299.

CHAPTER TWELVE: CIVIL WAR

1. New Yorkers were particularly angry with South Carolinians. See James K. Taylor to "Harriette," April 23, 1861, James K. Taylor Letter, South Carolina Historical Society.

2. Foner, *Business and Slavery*, 236–237, 259–260, 313.

3. Foner, *Business and Slavery*, 313. Richard Cary Morse Jr. to Richard Cary Morse, February 19, 1861, Box 5, Richard Cary Morse Papers, Clements Library, University of Michigan.

4. Samuel Raisbeck to Joseph Young, February 11, 1861, Samuel Raisbeck Papers, Clements Library, University of Michigan.

5. Samuel Raisbeck to Joseph Young, April 22, 1861; Raisbeck to Rankin Walkup, April 13, 1861, Samuel Raisbeck Papers, Clements Library, University of Michigan.

6. Hallock, *Life of Gerard Hallock*, 160–161.

7. Dodson, *Black New Yorkers*, 83; Theodore Winthrop, "New York Seventh Regiment," *Atlantic Monthly* 7 (June 1861), 744–745.

8. "The Slave Trade," *Brooklyn Daily Eagle* (November 3, 1860), 3.

9. "Slave-Trade," *New York Times* (June 19, 1861), 3; "Law Reports," *New York Times* (June 20, 1861), 2; "The Slaver Erie," *New York Times* (June 22, 1861), 3.

10. "The Slaver Erie," *New York Times* (November 8, 1861), 3; notice in *Buffalo Courier* (November 11, 1861), 1.

11. "The Latest News," *Brooklyn Times Union* (December 2, 1861), 2; "Application to Commute Gordon's Punishment," *The Buffalo Commercial* (January 29, 1862), 2.

12. "Execution of Captain Gordon," *Brooklyn Daily Eagle* (February 21, 1862), 2.

13. "The Case of Gordon," *Brooklyn Evening Star* (February 6, 1862), 2.

14. "The Case of Captain Gordon," *New York Daily Herald* (February 7, 1862), 8.

15. "The Execution Tomorrow," *New York Times* (February 20, 1861), 4.

16. "The Execution of Nathaniel Gordon," *New York Times* (February 22, 1862), 4.

17. Article in *The Atlantic* quoted in *The Elevator* 4 (January 1, 1869), 1.

18. October 3, 1861, and November 13, 1861, Minutes of the New York Chamber of Commerce, Chamber Papers, Columbia University.

19. On Boudinot, see notice in *Evening Star* (Washington, DC) (April 20, 1864), 3. On Beebe, Dean, and Donohue, see for example, "Slave Trade," *African Repository* 38 (November 1862), 349. Beebe was killed in a railroad accident in New Jersey in 1884, while Dean became a member of the state assembly in 1863 and died in 1870. For information on Pettis, see his ad for waterproof clothing in the *Washington Globe* (February 7, 1843), 1.

20. "The Society for the Prevention of Cruelty to Animals," *New York Herald* (May 3, 1867), 8; "Resignation of Marshal Rynders," *New York Herald* (March 27, 1861), 5; "City Politics," *New York Herald* (June 4, 1868), 5. In late 1862, several members of the Customs House were arrested for malfeasance and concealing evidence. See "Latest Telegraphic News," *Pacific Appeal* 1 (November 22, 1862), 4.

21. "Death of a Female Slave Trader," *Pacific Appeal* 1 (May 17, 1862), 4; "America," *London Standard* (April 17, 1862), 5.

22. On Figaniere, see the notice in *Buffalo Morning Express* (March 9, 1861), 2; *Weekly Journal of Commerce* (July 7, 1870), 1; and "The Late Consul De Figaniere Solemn Requiem Mass at St. Peter's Catholic Church," *New York Herald* (June 18, 1871), 4. Machado appears to have been arrested in 1861, 1862, and 1863 for slave trading. He traded in a wide variety of items, including cigars and oranges, through Havana. See shipping receipts for 1861 and 1863 in Jacob Morris Papers, New-York Historical Society. Regarding his imprisonment at Fort Lafayette, see A. Cohen to Machado, November 22, 1862, Jacob Morris Papers, New-York Historical Society. On Machado, see "Items of Local Interest," *New-York Atlas* (September 1, 1861), 1; "The Slave Trade—Arrest of Mr. Machado," *New York Daily Transcript* (September 22, 1862), 2; "Indictments," *New York Daily Transcript* (February 2, 1863), 3; and notice in *New York Daily Transcript* (February 23, 1863), 2. Machado was arrested by the Spanish government in Cuba in 1870

on unspecified charges. See "The Outrages Against American Citizens in Cuba," *New York Evening Post* (July 11, 1870), 3. The following year he was arrested in New York for taking tobacco from Havana without paying an import tax. "City Intelligence," *New York Evening Post* (May 16, 1871), 2; and (May 17, 1871), 3. Machado's son apparently followed closely in his father's dubious footsteps. See "The Machado Perjury Case—A Father and Son in Custody," *New York Commercial Advertiser* (May 19, 1876), 3. Regarding Francisco da Cunha e Silva, see his letter to Machado, May 20, 1864, in Jacob Morris Papers, New-York Historical Society.

23. Philip A. Bell, "Southern Rebuke to Fernando Wood's and John Van Buren's Peace Party of the North," *Pacific Appeal* 1 (December 27, 1862), 2. Wood, "Speech of Hon. Fernando Wood Delivered in the House of Representatives, March 19, 1868" (Washington, 1868).

24. See John McKeon's speech "Peace and Union; War and Disunion," Anti-Abolition Tracts No. 1 (New York, 1863).

25. "Public Reception of Robert Small," *Pacific Appeal* 1 (November 1, 1862), 3; "A Colored Female Lawyer," *The Elevator* 8 (May 11, 1872), 1.

26. Jacob Francis to J. R. Starkey, reprinted in *The Elevator* 1 (December 22, 1865), 3.

EPILOGUE: THE HIDDEN PAST AND REPARATIONS DUE

1. Cheryl D. Hicks, *Talk with You Like a Woman: African American Women, Justice, and Reform in New York, 1890–1935* (Chapel Hill: University of North Carolina Press, 2010); Khalil Gibran Muhammad, *The Condemnation of Blackness: Race, Crime, and the Making of Modern Urban America* (Cambridge: Harvard University Press, 2010); Kali N. Gross, *Colored Amazons: Crime, Violence, and Black Women in the City of Brotherly Love, 1880–1910* (Durham: Duke University Press, 2006). On mass incarceration, see Elizabeth Hinton, *From the War on Poverty to the War on Crime: The Making of Mass Incarceration in America* (Cambridge: Harvard University Press, 2016); Michelle Alexander, *The New Jim Crow: Mass Incarceration in the Age of Colorblindness* (New York: The New Press, 2010); and Heather Ann Thompson, "Why Mass Incarceration Matters: Rethinking Crisis, Decline, and Transformation in Postwar American History," *Journal of American History* 97 (December 2010), 703–734.

INDEX

JONATHAN DANIEL WELLS is a social, cultural, and intellectual historian and a professor of history in the departments of Afroamerican and African Studies at the University of Michigan. He is currently a Visiting Scholar at Gonville & Caius College at the University of Cambridge. His published works include *The Origins of the Southern Middle Class*, *Women Writers and Journalists in the Nineteenth-Century South*, and *A House Divided: The Civil War and Nineteenth-Century America.* He lives in Detroit, Michigan.

Photograph by Rudy Thomas, University of Michigan